Seventy years among savages

Henry Stephens Salt

SEVENTY   YEARS
AMONG SAVAGES

SEVENTY YEARS
AMONG SAVAGES

BY

HENRY S. SALT

LONDON: GEORGE ALLEN & UNWIN LTD.
RUSKIN HOUSE, 40 MUSEUM STREET, W.C. 1

First published in 1921

CONTENTS

Seventy Years Among Savages

I

THE ARGUMENT

A strange lot this, to be dropped down in a world of barbarians—
Men who see clearly enough the barbarity of all ages except
their own '—ERNEST CROSBY.

THE tales of travellers, from Herodotus to Marco Polo,
and from Marco Polo to the modern " globe-trotter,"
have in all ages been subject, justly or unjustly, to a
good deal of suspicion, on the ground that those who
go in quest of curious information among outlandish
tribes are likely in the first instance to be imposed on
themselves, and in the sequel to impose on their readers.
No such doubt, however, can attach to the following
record, for I am myself a native of the land whose
customs are described by me. I cannot think that my
story, true as it is, and admitting of corroboration by
the similar witness of others, is any the less adventurous
on that account ; for, like previous writers who have
recorded certain startling discoveries, I, too, have to
speak of solitudes and remotenesses, vast deserts and
rare oases, inextricable forests and dividing gulfs ;
and such experiences are none the less noteworthy
because they are not of the body but of the mind. At
any rate, the tale which I have to tell deals with inci-
dents which have had a very real significance for
myself—quite as real as any of those related by the
most venturesome of voyagers.

The seventy years spent by me among savages form the subject of this story, but not, be it noted, seventy years of *consciousness* that my life was so cast, for during the first part of my residence in the strange land where I was born, the dreadful reality of my surroundings was hardly suspected by me, except now and then, perhaps, in a passing glimmer of apprehension. Then, by slow degrees, incident after incident brought a gradual awakening, until at last there dawned on my mind the conviction which alone could explain and reconcile for me the many contradictions of our society —that we were not " civilized " but " savages "—that the " dark ages," far from being part of a remote past, were very literally present.

And here, in explanation of my long blindness to an unwelcome truth, it must be remarked that there is a fixed and almost insuperable superstition among my savage fellow-islanders—and, indeed, among all the surrounding nations—that they are a cultured and highly civilized race, living in an age which has wholly emerged from the barbarism of their forefathers, the " good old times " to which some of them even affect to look back with feelings of pious regretfulness. It was this delusion, to which I was at first fully subject, that made it so difficult for me to see things in their true light, and still makes it wellnigh impossible to communicate the truth to others, except to those whose suspicions have in like measure been aroused. In reality, it will be seen, the difference between the earlier " barbarism " and the later so-called " civilization " is, in the main, a mere matter of the absence or presence of certain intellectual refinements and mechanical sciences, which, while largely altering and complicating the outward conditions of life, leave its essentially savage spirit almost entirely untouched.

It was not till I was over thirty years of age that I felt any serious concern as to the manners and customs with which I was familiar, and which I had unquestion-

ingly accepted from childhood as part of the natural
order. I had heard and read of "savages," but felt
the more satisfaction to know that I was a native of
a land which had for centuries enjoyed the blessings of
civilization and of religion, which it was anxious to
disseminate as widely as possible throughout the earth
Why the diet of my countrymen should have been the
first thing to set me pondering, I am unable to say,
for as my later discoveries convinced me, the dietetic
habits of these people are not more astonishing than
many kindred practices which I still regarded without
mistrust But it was so ; and I then found myself
realizing, with an amazement which time has not
diminished, that the "meat" which formed the staple
of our diet, and which I was accustomed to regard—
like bread, or fruit, or vegetables—as a mere commodity
of the table, was in truth dead flesh—the actual flesh
and blood—of oxen. sheep, swine, and other animals
that were slaughtered in vast numbers under conditions
so horrible that even to mention the subject at our
dinner-tables would have been an unpardonable offence

Now, when I began to put questions to my friends
and acquaintances about this apparently glaring incon-
sistency in our "civilization," I could not help observing,
novice though I was in such discussion, that the answers
by which they sought to parry my awkward impor-
tunities were extremely evasive and sophistical—
reminding me of the quibbling explanations which
travellers have received from cannibals when they
inquired too closely into certain dietetic observances ;
and from this I could not but suspect that, as far as
diet was concerned, we differed in degree only from the
savages whom we deemed so debased.

It must be understood, however, that here, and in
other references to "savages," I use that term in its
natural and inoffensive meaning, as implying simply
a lack of the higher civilization and not any personal
cruelty or bloodthirstiness. What I write is just a

friendly account of friendly savages (by one of them) ; and I would emphasize the fact that the kindliness and good nature of my fellow-countrymen are in one direction quite as marked features of their character as their savagery is in another. In their own families, to their own kith and kin, to their personal friends— to all those whom fortune has placed within, instead of without the charmed circle of relationship—their conduct, in the great majority of cases, is exemplary ; it is only where custom or prejudice has dug a gulf of division between their fellow-creatures and themselves that they indulge in the barbarous practices to which I refer.

It may be convenient if I here speak briefly of their other customs under two heads   first, those that relate to human beings ; and, secondly, those that relate to the so-called lower animals   In few ways, perhaps, is the barbarism of these islanders more apparent than in their wars and in their preparation for wars.   For what they call " peace " is, in fact, only an armed truce—an interval between two outbreaks of hostility —during which, so far from being at genuine peace with their neighbours, they are occupied in speculating where the next attack shall be delivered, or, rather (for they love to depict themselves as always standing on pious self-defence against the wanton aggressiveness of others), how they shall repel the next attack from abroad.   It is their custom always to have, for the time being, some bugbear among neighbouring tribes, whose supposed machinations against the richer portions of their empire give them constant cause for unrest, and prompt them to cement undying, but equally transitory, alliances with other nations, so that their very friendships are based less on the spirit of amity than on that of distrust   Under pretence of believing in an unbelievable and, indeed, wholly ridiculous maxim—*Si vis pacem, para bellum* (" If you wish for peace, prepare for war ")—they keep their minds for ever set on wars and rumours of wars, with the result

that, in spite of all their profession of benevolence and
brotherhood, the trade of *killing* is that which is above
all others respected by them. Is money required for
purposes of national welfare, such as education or the
relief of the poor ? Every difficulty is at once put in
the way of such expenditure for such ends. But let
there be the least suspicion, however irrational, of
some foreign slight to " the flag," and there is scarce
a savage in the island who is not willing that the public
treasury should be depleted in pursuance of a childish
revenge. To remonstrate against such folly is to incur
the charge of being " unpatriotic."

But comical as their foreign policy is, their social
system is still more so, for under the guise of " charity "
and " philanthropy " there exists, in fact, a civil war,
in which each individual, or group of individuals, plays
a remorseless game of " Beggar my neighbour " and
" Devil take the hindmost " in mad scramble for wealth ;
whence results, of course, a state of gross and glaring
inequality, under which certain favoured persons wallow
in the good things of life, while others pass their years
in the pinch of extremest poverty. Thus, in due course,
and by an unerring process, is manufactured what they
call " the criminal class "—that is, the host of those
who are driven by social injustice to outlawry and
violence. And herein, perhaps, more than in any other
of their customs, is shown the inherent savagery of their
natures, for, instead of attempting to eradicate the
cause of these evils by the institution of fairer and
juster modes of living, my fellow-islanders are almost
to a man in favour of " punishing " (that is the
expression) these victims of their own foolish laws by
the infliction of barbarous sentences of imprisonment,
or the lash, or, in extreme cases, the gallows. To
inculcate habits of honesty they shut a man in prison,
and render him more than ever incapable of earning
an honest livelihood. As a warning against robbery
with violence, they give a lesson in official violence by

flogging the criminal; and, by way of teaching the sanctity of human life, they judicially murder the murderer. Many a grotesque absurdity is solemnly and deliberately enacted in their so-called "courts of law"; and any one who ventures to suggest that this is the case is regarded as a fool and reprobate for his pains.

But it is when we turn to their treatment of the non-human races that we find the surest evidences of barbarism, yet their savagery, even here, is not wholly "naked and unashamed," for, strange to say, these curious people delight to mask their rudeness in a cloak of fallacies and sophisms, and to represent themselves as "lovers" of those very creatures whom they habitually torture for "sport," "science," and the "table." They actually have a law for the prevention of cruelty to animals, under which certain privileged species, classed as "domestic," are protected from some specified wrongs, though all the time they may, under certain conditions, be subjected with impunity to other and worse injuries at the hands of the slaughterman or the vivisector; while the wild species, though presumably not less sensitive to pain, are regarded as almost entirely outside the pale of protection, and as legitimate subjects for those brutalities of "fashion" and "sport" which are characteristic of the savage mind. Their women go furred and feathered with the skins of beasts and birds; and so murderous is their millinery that whole species are sacrificed to this reckless habit. Nothing can exceed the ferocity of the national pastimes, in which, under the plea of affording healthful exercise to their tormentors, park-bred deer, that have been kept in paddocks for the purpose, are turned out before a mob of men and dogs to be baited and worried; foxes, otters, and hares are hunted and "broken up"; bagged rabbits are "coursed" in small enclosures by yelling savages on the eve of the weekly religious festival; pheasants

and other " preserved " birds are mown down in thousands in an organized butchery euphemistically known
as the *battue* ; pigeons are released from traps in order
to be shot by gangs of ruffians who gamble over the
result of their skill ; and almost every conceivable
form of cowardly slaughter is practised as " sportsman-
like " and commended as " manly."   All this, moreover,
is done before the eyes and for the example of mere
youths and children, who are thus from their tenderest
years instructed in the habit of being pitiless and cruel.
Nay, in some cases they are even encouraged to take
part in such doings, and on the first occasion when
they are " in at the death " are initiated by being
" blooded "—that is, baptized with the blood of the
slaughtered victim of their sport.

Nor are these things perhaps so strange as they
might at first appear, for, in spite of their boasted
progress in sciences and arts, my countrymen are still
practically ignorant of the real kinship which exists
between mankind and the other races, and of the duties
which this kinship implies. They are still the victims
of that old anthropocentric superstition which pictures
Man as the centre of the universe, and separated from
the inferior animals—mere playthings made for his
august pleasure and amusement—by a deep inter-
vening gulf ; and it is probable enough that if any one
of these unthinking savages who " break up " a hare,
or baptize their children in the blood of a butchered
fox, were reminded that he himself is in very truth an
" animal," he would resent such statement of an established fact as a slight on his religious convictions and
on his personal self-respect. For, as the author of
Hudibras discovered :

> There's nothing so absurd, or vain,
> Or barbarous, or inhumane,
> But if it lay the least pretence
> To piety and godliness,
> And zeal for gospel truths profess,
> Does sacred instantly commence.

The very scientists themselves, who have in theory renounced the old-fashioned idea of a universe created for mankind, are inclined in practice to belie their own biological faith, for they claim the moral right to devote large numbers of the lower animals, without scruple or remorse, to the tortures of " research," just as if the fact of a close kinship between the vivisector who wields the scalpel and the dog who lies in the trough were a notion of which Science is unaware !

Is it surprising that, to those of us who have gradually realized that we are dwelling in a wild land among savages such as these, the consciousness of the discovery should at times bring with it a sense of unutterable loneliness and desolation—that we should feel cut off, as it were, by interminable leagues of misunderstanding from all human intercourse, and from all possibility of expressing ourselves ? What appeal *can* be made to people whose first instinct, on seeing a beautiful animal, full of joyousness and vitality, is to hunt or eat it ? One can only marvel how such sheer, untempered barbarism has come down to us from the past.

But the facts, though so terrible in their first impression, are capable of being more hopefully regarded ; there is a consolatory, as well as a discomforting, way of interpreting them. For if these countrymen of ours are indeed savages (as who can doubt ?), have we not at least reason to rejoice that, being savages, they in many ways conduct themselves so discreetly, and that, as far as their sense of relationship extends, they are so civil, so kindly, so law-abiding ? Instead, therefore, of too loudly upbraiding them for hunting or eating their little brethren, the animals, ought we not, perhaps, to feel and express some gratitude to them that they do not hunt each other—that they have not eaten *us*? Their self-restraint in many directions is, perhaps, quite as remarkable as their self-abandonment in others ; and the mere fact of one's having *lived* for many years

among savages is in itself a testimony to their good
nature. Looked at in this light, the trouble is not so
much that they are in reality savage, as that they
suppose themselves to be civilized ; for it is from the
false garb of civilization that the misapprehension has
sprung.

But, however that may be, they are, when the worst
is said of them, a quaint and interesting people, and
it is my earnest wish that, by the publication of this
story, I may be the means of drawing to the habits of
my fellow-islanders the closer attention of anthro-
pologists. Surely, in an age when many wild tribes
have been the subject of learned discourse and of
missionary enterprise, it is desirable that a race which
has carried into the twentieth century the primitive
customs which I have described should be critically and
exhaustively studied. If such should indeed be the
result of this book, I shall be more than compensated
for whatever pain I may have felt in the writing of these
strange but faithfully recorded experiences.

II

WHERE IGNORANCE WAS BLISS

Thought would destroy their paradise !
No more : where ignorance is bliss
'Tis folly to be wise.
Gray's Ode on a Distant Prospect of Eton College.

IF it be true, as scientists tell us, that the period of
boyhood corresponds, in human development, with an
early phase of savagery, and that the individual boy
is himself an epitome of the uncivilized tribe, it may
be said with still greater confidence that an English
public school, or " boy-farm," where life is mostly so
ordered as to foster the more primitive habits of mind,
is essentially a nursery of barbarism—a microcosm of
that predatory class whose members, like the hunters
of old, toil not, neither do they spin, but ever seek their
ideal in the twofold cult of sport and soldiership.
Certainly the Eton of the 'sixties and 'seventies, whatever superficial show it might make of learning and
refinement, was at heart a stronghold of savagery—a
most graceful, easy-going savagery, be it granted ;
for savages, as we know, are often a very pleasant
people.

In some reminiscences, *Eton under Hornby*, published in
1910, I gave a description of the public-school education
of fifty years ago, a system probably not much worse
than that of to-day ; and the conclusion reached was
that as Eton never really changes, it is best to regard
her, as she regards other institutions, in a mood of good-
natured unconcern, and as a subject less for argument

than for anecdote. Eton has been pre-eminently the
school " where ignorance is bliss," and in a much wider
sense than that intended by the poet Gray in his famous
ode " On a Distant Prospect of Eton College." For, if
it be true of schoolboys that " thought would destroy
their paradise "—that is, the thought merely of the
personal ailments of mature age—how much more
disturbing would be the contemplation of the vast
social wrongs that fill the world with suffering ! Of
such sombre thought Eton knew nothing, but basked
content in the warmth of her own supreme self-satisfaction ; and the Eton life was probably the most
enjoyable of all hitherto invented forms of heedless
existence. It is, then, of the pleasures of Eton that
I would speak, and of some of the more distinguished
of her sons with whom it was my privilege to be
acquainted.

Long before I was admitted to Eton as a King's
Scholar, I had a personal link with the school in the
fact that John Moultrie, the friend of Praed, and
contributor to that most noteworthy of school magazines, the *Etonian*—himself a Colleger at Eton from
1811 to 1819—was my great-uncle. At Eton and
Cambridge, Moultrie's career had been a brilliant one ;
he was the " Gerard Montgomery " of the *Etonian*—
in Praed's words " the humorous Moultrie, and the
pathetic Moultrie, the Moultrie of ' Godiva,' and the
Moultrie of ' My Brother's Grave,' "—but his later
career did not fulfil the promise of his youth. The
vivid and extravagant fancy of his early poems was
succeeded by a more homely and sober style, and the
pastor-poet in his " Dream of Life " even referred
apologetically to the levities of his youthful muse.[1]
Yet he still retained in some measure the poet's vision ;
and when Rector of Rugby he was famous for the
powerful interpretation which he gave to Shakespeare

[1] In an article published in *Macmillan's Magazine*, December
1887, I dealt with the subject of Moultrie's Poems.

in his reading of the Plays. Him I remember at his
rectory in the early 'sixties, a dignified, kindly old man,
with a quaint mixture of humour and pathos, of
ruggedness and gentleness, in his manner. Many
stories were current in Rugby of his eccentricities and
absent-mindedness ; on one occasion when he had
brought a lengthy sermon to an end, he is said to have
startled his congregation by substituting for the usual
formula the equally familiar post-prandial one : " For
what we have received, the Lord make us truly thankful."

It was from this Etonian worthy that I first heard
of Eton ; and though I little foresaw that nearly twenty
years of my life would be spent there as boy and master,
it thus came about that in the summer of 1866 I found
myself being " coached " for an Eton scholarship by
the Rev. C. Kegan Paul, formerly " Conduct " (Chaplain) at Eton, who held the Eton living of Sturminster
Marshall in Dorsetshire.

Mr. Paul, afterwards founder of a well-known publishing firm, was then a radical parson of very " broad "
views, a friend of Frederick Denison Maurice, Charles
Kingsley, and many other Liberals. A man of fine
taste, he also possessed a large fund of vivacity and
spirits, which, with his unvarying kindness, made him
very popular among his pupils ; indeed, only at Eton
itself could there have been a more delightful life,
regarded from the boyish point of view, than that which
we led in those summer months, fishing, bathing,
bird's-nesting. The one cloud on our horizon was the
impending rite of Confirmation, which some of us had
to undergo at Blandford, and for which Mr. Paul
prepared us. I have always felt grateful to him for
the simplicity of his method, which was free from the
morbid inquiries then common in schools. I think he
asked me only one question : " Is it wrong to doubt ? "
This was a problem in which I felt no sort of concern ;
making a bold shot, I replied " No," and was gratified
to find that I had answered correctly.

At Eton my tutor was Mr. Francis Warre Cornish, one of the gentlest and most accomplished of men, the very antithesis of the bullying, blustering schoolmaster of the good old type which even then was not wholly superseded. Much loved by those of his pupils who learnt to know him intimately, Mr. Cornish was a good deal hampered in his dealings with boys by his shyness and diffidence ; he lacked that gift of geniality which is essential to a successful teacher. This I discovered at an early date, when, in the course of the entrance examination, I was told to show him the rough copy of my Latin verses. It was to these, as it turned out, that I mainly owed my election ; but it somewhat depressed me when my prospective tutor, after reading the lines with a sad and forlorn expression, handed them back to me with no more cheering remark than . " Too many spondees." Years afterwards, when Mr. Cornish, competing for a headmastership, was described in a testimonial as " trembling on the brink of poetic creation " (an odd certificate for such a post), I remembered his criticism of my youthful verses, and could not help thinking that his own poetic genius would also have benefited by a larger infusion of the sprightly or dactylic element. His nature was decidedly spondaic ; but he was a kind and courteous gentleman, in the best sense of the word, and in a less rough environment than that of a public school his great abilities would have found ampler scope.

Much the same must be said of Dr. J. J. Hornby, who succeeded the rigid Dr. Balston in the headmastership of Eton in 1868. It was a marvel that a man who loved leisure and quietude as he did, and who seemed always to desire to doff rather than to don the formalities of high office, should have deliberately sought preferment in a profession which could not have been very congenial to him Not that he lacked the reputed qualities of a ruler · he had a stately presence, a most courteous manner, a charming sense of humour, and the rare power of interesting an audience in any subject of which he spoke. But, behind these external capabilities, he had a fatal weakness—slackness, perhaps, is the proper term—which loosened the reins of authority, and made his headmastership a period of which Eton had no reason to be proud. "Idleness holds sway everywhere," wrote an Eton boy at that time, "and *such* idleness! As a man who has never had dealings with the Chinese can have but a faint idea of what swindling is, so a man who has never been at Eton has but a poor conception of what idleness is."[1] What wonder, when the headmaster was himself as unpunctual as a fourth-form boy?

Hornby was too retiring, too sensitive, to govern a great school. I was in his Division for two years, almost at the beginning of his headmastership; and I can see him still as he sat at his oak table in the middle of the sixth-form room, toying with a pencil, and looking at us somewhat askance, as if to avoid either scrutinizing or being scrutinized, for he was not of the drill-master kind, who challenge their class and stare them down. We liked him the better for it, but divined that he was not quite at ease; and it occurred to one of us that he was aptly described in that terse phrase which Tacitus applied to a Roman emperor: *Capax imperii nisi imperasset* ("Every inch a ruler—if only he had not ruled"). There was a certain maladroitness, too, about him which at times set us wondering; until some one suggested that we should look up the cricket records, and see how he had acquitted himself in that supreme criterion of greatness, the Eton and Harrow match. We did so, and found that he had hit his own wicket. Thus all was explained, our worst misgivings confirmed.

The want of discipline in some of the classrooms was appalling. My first term was spent in the "lag"

[1] Article on "Eton as it is," in the *Adventurer*, No. 23, by "E. G. R." (G. C. Macaulay).

Division of Fifth Form, a very rowdy one, then taken
by a most accomplished classical scholar known as
" Swage," or " Swog," and a more unpleasant introduction for a new boy could hardly have been devised.
So great was the uproar, and so frenzied the attempts of
the unfortunate " Swage " to suppress it, that it was
as dangerous to be a member of the class as it is for a
well-disposed citizen to be mixed up in a street-riot ;
for among so many tormentors there was no security
against being mistaken for a ringleader. " Swage's "
schoolroom was on the ground floor and close to the
road ; and one of the first scenes I witnessed was a
determined attempt on the part of some of the bigger
boys to drive a stray cow into the room ; they got her
to the doorway, but there she was met and headed
back by " Swage " himself, shouting at the top of his
voice and flourishing his large door-key That was
the sort of game that went on almost daily. It was
currently reported, and I believe with truth, that
" Swage " once set a punishment to a bird. To sing
and to whistle were common practices in his Division ,
and when a bird perched near the window and chirruped
in an interval of the din, he rounded on it blindly with
a cry of " A hundred lines."

There was a story, too, that a letter which he once
wrote to the headmaster, complaining of one of his
private pupils who persisted in knocking loudly on
his study door, bore a brief after-cry more eloquent
than many words . " *P.S.* He is knocking still "

To fall into the hands of boys, as this ill-fated master
had done—and his lot was shared by several others—
was to be a captive among savages they did not kill
and eat him, it is true, but that was the extent of their
tender mercies, and every day he was brought out
afresh to be baited and worried

Such was the state of affairs when Hornby was made
headmaster ; and it became worse rather than better
under his lax and listless regime. Yet no one who has

any knowledge of the history of corporal punishment
will be surprised to hear that he was a frequent wielder
of the rod.   Seldom did a day pass without a visit
from the Sixth Form Præpostor to one or more of the
Divisions, to bid some culprit " stay after school " ;
and on those occasions the conduct of the class was a
good indication of the light in which the punishment
was regarded.   As the fatal hour approached, the eyes
of all would be riveted on the offender, who maintained
a dauntless demeanour to the last , pantomimic gestures
would indicate the nature of the penalty which he was
shortly to undergo , watches would be held up to
emphasize the dreadful fact that, as in the case of
Dr Faustus, time was on the wing ; and there would be
audible surmises as to " how many " he would get.
The victim's friends, indeed, were hardly so considerate
and sympathetic as the circumstances might have been
expected to demand

Flogging is an old institution which has found mention
in every book written about the school, and which could
never be omitted from any discourse upon Eton.   It
used to be the custom, in the holidays, for parties of
Windsor trippers to be shown over the school buildings
under the leadership of a woman—the wife, presumably,
of one of the College servants—who gave an oral
explanation of the " sights "   When the headmaster's
room was reached, the guide of course drew attention
to that awful emblem of authority, the " block " ;
and after pointing out the part which it played in the
correction of offenders, she would add, in a croaking
voice befitting the solemnity of the subject   " They
receive the punishment upon their seats."   That was
a true, but rather inadequate description of a practice
which only a very barbarous society could tolerate.
A flogging was a disgusting sight even to the two
" lower boys " who then had to act as " holders-down " ;
still more so to the Sixth Form Præpostor whose duty
it was to be present , most of all, one would suppose,

to the headmaster. It has been described as " an operation performed on the naked back by the head-master himself, who is always a gentleman, and some-times a high dignitary of the Church." [1]

The Lower Master, at the time of which I am speaking, was the Rev. F. E. Durnford, nicknamed " Judy," described in *Eton under Hornby* as " a strange, laughable, yet almost pathetic figure, with whimsical puckered visage and generally weather-beaten aspect, like a sort of Ancient Mariner in academic garb." He, too, used the birch freely in his domain of Lower School, but his castigations were of a more paternal kind, and between the strokes of the rod he would interject moral reproofs in his queer nasal voice, such as : " You nahty, nahty boy ! " It was said that during the punishment he would even enter into conversation with the offender, especially when he knew his " people " personally, and that on one occasion he was overheard to inquire of a boy on the block : " Have you seen your uncle lately ? " a question which, in the circumstances, would at first sight seem irrelevant, but was probably intended to awaken repentance in the criminal by directing his thoughts to some pious and respected relative. To the upper boys, " Judy " Durnford was a never-failing amusement ; his every gesture was noted by them ; as when, in correcting exercises, if some word or phrase eluded his memory, he would sit scratching his temples vigorously, and exclaiming . " It runs in me head "

Among Dr. Hornby's assistant masters were several others whose eccentricities have been a fruitful subject of anecdote and legend. Russell Day, a quiet and insignificant-looking little man, had a mordant wit and gift of ready epigram, which caused him to be dreaded alike by master and boys. " Friend, thou hast learned this lesson with a crib : a crib is a thing in

---

[1] Dr. Lyttelton, when Headmaster of Eton, substituted the cane for the birch in the Upper School.

which thou liest," was his remark in the course of a
Theocritus lesson to a member of his Division, from
whom I heard the story full forty years later.   There
were two boys of the name of Bankes, one known
afterwards as a distinguished K C., the other a lazy
youth who never knew his lessons and was wont to
mumble the Greek or Latin very slowly in order to
postpone the moment of discovery.   On one of these
occasions Day leaned back in his chair and said in his
drawling tones . " Bankes, Bankes, you remind me of
the banks where the bees suck and with their murmuring
make me sleep."   I remember how a friend and schoolfellow of mine named Swan, who was a pupil of Day's,
showed me a copy of his Latin verses which had drawn
the following annotation : " *Olor !* You *cycnus.*"   Not
less characteristic was Day's curt dismissal of a youth
named Cole (report says it was the future director of
the Bank of England) . " Then, Cole, you may scuttle "
Nor did he hesitate to turn his wit against his colleagues
or himself   He called his pony " Lucifer," because,
as he said, " When you see him coming, it announces
the approach of Day."

A still more remarkable teacher was William Johnson,
author of " Ionica," who afterwards took the name of
Cory, a man of real genius, whose enforced departure
from Eton (for he did not leave, as was currently supposed, from some sudden whim of his own) was the
tragedy of his lifetime, a " strange wounding," as he
calls it in one of his published letters.   Of " Billy
Johnson " many descriptions have been written.   Here
is a passage from one of them ·

" In appearance, as in everything else, he was unlike the
typical schoolmaster : his thoughtful, handsome, somewhat
sensuous features were altogether out of the common , and
owing to his short sight he had a dreamy, mystic, inquiring
way of looking at you which was sometimes a little disquieting
to the schoolboy mind   There were occasions, too, when we
dreaded his tart sayings (the very school books written by him
bristled with epigrams), and listened with some anxiety to

his sharp, staccato utterances, or watched him during those
' accusing silences ' by which, hardly less than by his barbed
speeches, he could awe the most unruly class   His blindness
led to a prevalent story (apocryphal, I believe, as it was told
also of other persons at different times) that he had been seen
pursuing a hen down Windsor Hill, and making futile grabs
at her, under the belief that she was his hat , but it is certain
that he was sometimes seen standing stock-still in School Yard,
or some open space, apparently unconscious of all observers
or passers-by, and wrapt in a profound daydream. Singular
he undoubtedly was, to a degree that was inconvenient to a
schoolmaster , and there were queer anecdotes of certain too
generous suppers that he gave to his favourites among the boys,
when he began by politely overlooking that they were getting
drunk, and ended by unceremoniously kicking them downstairs.''[1]

" Formerly wise men used to grow beards. Now
other persons do so " This sentence in *Nuces*, an
exercise-book of William Johnson's compilation, was
supposed by us to be aimed at another assistant
master, a bearded clergyman, bluff, honest, mannerless,
and universally disliked, who went by the name of
" Stiggins " He had a detestable habit of standing at
right angles to any one with whom he was conversing,
while he looked straight away in front of him, his long
red beard streaming down to his waist, and when he
spoke, he jerked his words at you, as it were, from
round the corner   His rudeness was a by-word ; and
the attempt sometimes made to excuse it, on the ground
that it " was not intended," did not appeal very strongly
I think, either to masters or to boys · and justly, for
surely the only sort of rudeness which can be pardoned
is that which *is* intended. There are occasions, rare,
but real, when it is necessary and wholesome to be
rude ; but to be rude without knowing it is the very
acme of ill manners, and that was precisely the kind of
discourtesy in which " Stiggins " was unequalled.

The story of how " Stiggins " was once nearly thrown
into Barnes Pool, a by-water of the Thames, by a

[1] From the chapter on " The Author of Ionica," in *Eton
under Hornby.*

riotous troop of boys, has been told in more than one of the books about Eton ; it was a curious coincidence that he should have almost shared the fate of his reverend predecessor in *Pickwick*, who was dipped in a horse-trough by the infuriated Mr. Weller   This incident was, perhaps, the greatest of the many scandals that occurred at Eton during Dr. Hornby's headmastership

It has often struck me as strange that I should owe to such a plain and unadorned barbarian as '' Stiggins '' my first introduction to Keats's poems . he gave me, as a prize, Moxon's edition of the works.   He also '' sent me up for good '' (for Latin verses), an honour of which I was rather unpleasantly reminded, some twenty or more years afterwards, when he had retired from Eton to a country parsonage , for in order to raise funds for a proposed '' restoration '' of his church, he conceived the idea of soliciting '' for the glory of God,'' as he expressed it, a subscription from every Old Etonian who in bygone days had been '' sent up for good '' in his Division.   There was a naive effrontery about this proposal which was quite characteristic of its author.

The writing of Latin verse, so highly regarded at Eton, was a curious accomplishment.   It was said by Coleridge in his *Table Talk* that Etonians acquired the art '' by conning Ovid and Tibullus '' · my recollection is that we read Ovid but rarely, and Tibullus not at all   Some of us certainly became proficient in making Latin verses of a kind ; but our models were the renderings of English poems in such collections as the *Arundines Cami* or the *Sabrinæ Corolla*, rather than any Latin originals ; and though we could turn out '' longs and shorts '' with facility, and even with neatness, I hardly think our productions would have passed muster in the Augustan age.   Still, the versifier's art, such as it was, brought us a certain gratification ; and in the summer, when, as we all felt, the time of the

leading cricketers was of inestimable value to the
school, we were glad to turn our skill to good account
by composing for them their weekly copy of verses,
and so releasing them, as it were, from a frivolous for
a serious task. On "verse days" members of the
Eleven would often come up into College, where each
would find for himself a poet ; and thus valuable time
would be saved for practice at the nets   It was but
little we could do in so great a cause, but we did it with
willingness ; and I remember the honest pride which
I felt when dictating to the Captain of the Eleven a
copy of verses, made up largely of old tags and stock
phrases, which he copied down with much satisfaction
and without the least understanding.   His ignorance of
the meaning of what purported to be his own composition would lead to no trouble , for tutors and division-
masters alike were aware that they must not press a
good cricketer too hard.   A blue cap covered a multitude
of sins.

But that we were savages, who, looking back on those
bygone times, can doubt ? *Non angeli, sed Angli*   " It
was an era," as Mr Ralph Nevill has well remarked in
his *Floreat Etona*, " when the sickening cant of
humanitarianism, born of luxury and weakness, had
not yet arisen, to emasculate and enfeeble the British
race " The hunting and breaking up of hares then,
as now, was one of the recognized pastimes ; indeed,
even as late as the headmastership of Dr Balston
(1857-68), it had been permitted to the boys, as a
variation from the hare-hunt, to pursue with beagles
a mutilated fox deprived of one of his pads [1] In the
hundreds of sermons which I have heard preached in
Eton College Chapel, never was a word spoken on the
subject of cruelty. And no wonder ; for Eton had
always been a home of cruel sports.

There was the less excuse for these miserable practices, because an abundance and superabundance of

[1] See Brinsley Richards's *Seven Years at Eton.*

the nobler sports was within reach of the Eton boy :
nowhere else could river and playing-field offer such
attractions.   Thrilling beyond all else, and crowning
the glories of the summer school-time, was the great
annual cricket match between Eton and Harrow at
" Lord's," a drama of such excitement as nothing in
mature life could ever equal.   Who, for example, that
witnessed the match of 1869—C. J Ottaway's year,
when Eton broke a long series of defeats by a single-
innings victory—can have forgotten the delirious scene
at the close ?   I can still see Dr Goodford, the venerable
Provost of Eton, dancing ecstatically, hat in hand,
before the pavilion, and looking very much as " Spy "
once pictured him in a famous cartoon in *Vanity Fair*.

Athletics, of course, took precedence of all intellectual
pursuits.   The *Etonian*, in our time, was but a dim
legend of the past, and the genius of Praed and Moultrie
had left no direct line of succession ;   nevertheless
among the upper boys there was not an entire dearth of
literary aspiration, and we had a school magazine,
the *Adventurer*, which existed from the later 'sixties for
about five years   One of its editors, a Colleger named
C C Thornton, was the author of some extremely good
verse ;   and among other contributors, towards the
latter part of the *Adventurer's* career, were Arthur A
Tilley, now a Fellow of King's College, Cambridge ;
E C Selwyn, afterwards headmaster of Uppingham
School , J E C Welldon, the popular Dean of Durham ,
Herbert W. Paul ; George Campbell Macaulay ; J. C.
Tarver ;   and Sir Melville Macnaghten, who wrote as
M² , also, if I mistake not, the *nom de plume* of " Tom "
covered some early poems of Mr F. B. Money-Coutts,
now known as Baron Latymer.   One of the best essays
in the *Adventurer* was that on " Arbitration as a Substitute for War,"[1] by Mr. Herbert Paul.   Another
noteworthy contribution, which has some historical
interest for Etonians of that period, was a poem by

[1] The article, unsigned, appeared in No. 23.

Bishop Welldon, entitled "Adventurer Loquitur "[1] in which the Magazine was represented as giving some description of the several members of its "staff," whether in recognition of their services or in reproof of their remissness. Among those clearly indicated, though unnamed, were A. A. Tilley, R. C. Radcliffe, G. R Murray, Bernard Coleridge (now Lord Coleridge), H. G Wintle, G. C. Macaulay, C C. Lacaita, J. E. C. Welldon, E C Selwyn, and the writer of these reminiscences. The cause of the *Adventurer's* decease was that it ran counter to Etonian sentiment, in acting on the perilous principle that "it is only those who truly love Eton that dare to show her her faults."[2]

Apart from the *Adventurer*, the literary ambition of some of the Collegers sought irregular expression, in those far-off days, by supplying the Windsor press, when opportunity occurred, with exaggerated and absurdly inflated accounts of any exciting incident such as the outbreak of a fire. Nor was it only the local papers that allured us, for I remember how G. C. Macaulay and I once had a daring wager as to which of us should more egregiously hoax the *Field* with some story of a rare bird He tried a too highly coloured anecdote of a bee-eater, and failed to win credence, while I, with a modest narrative of a supposed stork in Windsor Park ("can it have been a stork ? I shall indeed feel myself lucky if my supposition be correct "), not only saw my letter inserted, but drew the gratifying editorial comment · " Most probably it was a stork." Thus we made natural history and beguiled the idle hours.

To look upon a group photograph of the Collegers of fifty years ago brings many memories to the mind. E. C. Selwyn, before we met at Eton, had been my schoolfellow at Blackheath Proprietary School, of which his father was headmaster, and our friendly

[1] The *Adventurer*, No 20.
[2] See the concluding article, " Valete Etonenses," No. 29.

relations were renewed from time to time till his death
in 1919   As I once reminded him, we had but two
quarrels—the first when we were freshmen at Cambridge,
about Moses, in whom I had been rash enough to say
that I " did not believe " ; and the second, at a later
period, because I *did* believe in Mr. H. M. Hyndman,
of whose socialist doctrines Selwyn as vehemently
disapproved   Long years afterwards I made what I
thought was a fair proposal to him—that if he would
give up Moses, I would give up the other patriarch, and
so our two small disagreements would be mutually
adjusted , but his answer was that, though Moses
need no longer delay a settlement, he could not agree
to Mr. Hyndman being given up, because his patriotic
conduct during the Great War had shown him in a new
light.

We used to call Selwyn " bishop " in those days,
either because of a distant relationship to Dr. G. A.
Selwyn, the well-known Bishop of Lichfield, or because
we thought him almost certainly destined to attain
to episcopal rank   his scholarship, not to mention his
defence of Moses, seemed to warrant no less.   J. E. C.
Welldon, who *did* become a bishop, was another most
genial schoolfellow, famous in the football field no
less than in the examination room.   I remember
running second to him in a handicap quarter-mile race,
in which he was allowed a good many yards' start,
and with that advantage just managed to keep the
rest of us in the rear   Herbert Paul, unlike Welldon
or Selwyn, was by no means designated for a bishopric.
I recall him, a sceptic even in boyhood, standing in
Upper Passage, where Collegers often held informal
discussion, as, with thumbs in waistcoat pockets, he
would hold forth, already a fearless disputant, on matters
human and divine

Among other figures in the group are Dr. Ryle,
Dean of Westminster , Sir Richmond Ritchie ; Mr.
George Campbell Macaulay ; Mr C. Lowry, head of

Tonbridge School ; Dr. Burrows, Bishop of Chichester, Dr. Harmer, Bishop of Rochester ; Sir E. Ruggles-Brise, Chairman of the Prison Commission ; Mr. E. C. Tennyson-d'Eyncourt, Rev. J. H. J. Ellison, late Vicar of Windsor ; Sir Lionel Carden, of Mexican fame ; and others who in various ways have become distinguished.

Very provocative of reminiscence, too, are the illustrations, printed in books about Eton, of the College servants, the College buildings, and many well-remembered faces and scenes Take, for example, a picture of " Old College Servants " in Mr Ralph Nevill's *Floreat Etona.*

There stands the old College porter, Harry Atkins, whom, to our disgrace, we used to bombard on dark winter nights in his little lodge at the gateway into School Yard, hurling missiles at his door from behind the pillars of the cloisters under Upper School, and trusting to our superior fleetness of foot when he was goaded into a desperate charge. There, too, are Culliford, the butler, and Westbrook, the cook, who were treated by us with far greater respect than the equally respectable Atkins, as presiding over departments in which our own personal comforts were more closely concerned, and from whose hands, on the occasion of banquets in the College Hall, the smaller Collegers would try to beg or snatch dainties as they carried them up from the kitchen Among the least prominent members of the group is one Wagstaffe, designated " scullion " ; yet, humble though he was in appearance, his name had become a household word among the boys, for the somewhat unappetizing dough which formed the base of the puddings served to the Collegers was then known as " the Wagstaffe," on the supposition, presumably, that the under part of the pudding was the creation of the under-cook I do not think I could eat that pudding now, but looking on the worthy Wagstaffe's image again, I feel that we wronged him

in identifying him, as we did, with an unsavoury composition for which he, a mere subordinate, was not
personally to blame.

To the College Hall there came daily, for the rem-
nants of bread and other victuals, a number of poor
old alms-women ; and if any further proof be needed
of the exceeding thinness of the veneer by which our
youthful savagery was overlaid, it will be found in our
treatment of those humble folk, who were of much
more use in the world than ourselves. We named them
" the hags " ; and one of our amusements was to
construct for them what was called a " hag-trap."
A large square piece of bread was hollowed out in the
centre through a hole bored in the side, and when the
cavity had been filled up with mustard, pepper, salt,
etc., the opening was plugged, and the bread left lying
on the table as a bait for some unwary victim who should
carry it to her home. Whether the Eton Mission in
Hackney Wick has so ameliorated the hearts of later
generations of Etonians that a " hag-trap " would now
be an impossibility, I do not know; but in those days
we certainly had not the smallest atom of sympathy
with the working classes, except perhaps with those
College servants who were known to us personally,
and who ministered to our wants.

We did not pretend to regard the working man as a
brother. Once, when I was travelling with some Eton
friends, a sweep who was standing on the platform
tried to enter our carriage just as the train was about to
start. Instantly we seized the door, and held it closed
from the inside ; and after a short struggle (the black
man's anxious eyes still haunt me), the victory remained with us, for the train began to move, and the
sweep was left behind   That was our idea of Fraternity.
Was it Waterloo that was won in the Eton Playing
Fields ? I have sometimes thought it must have been
Peterloo

But let me turn from the recollection of childish deeds

done by those who were but " scugs," or " lower boys,"
to that of the immense self-importance of which we
were conscious when we had reached the eminence of
sixth form.   Surely nowhere on earth is there such a
tremendous personage as a sixth-form Eton boy ;
he acts continually with that " full sense of responsi-
bility " so dear to the occupants of the Parliamentary
front-bench.   No visitor to Eton College Chapel can
have failed to be impressed by the pompous entry of
those twenty immaculately attired young men as they
precede the Headmaster and the Provost in a sort of
triumphal procession, thinking of anything rather than
the religious service to which their arrival is the prelude.
On speech-days, too, when, arrayed in dress-coat and
knee-breeches, we declaimed passages from the great
writers of antiquity or of modern times, we felt to the
full the colossal seriousness of our position—serious also
it was in another sense, for our self-satisfaction was
then sobered by the possibility of breaking down.   To
keep order in the passages at night , to say the Latin
grace in Hall ; to note the names at " Absence " in
the school-yard, standing by the headmaster's side—
even to read prayers in the Houses on occasions—these
were but a few of the many duties and dignities of
sixth form.   No young feathered " bloods " in red
Indian tribe could have had greater reason to be proud.

Even in the holidays our grave responsibilities did
not wholly cease , for it was a custom for sixth-form
youths to be sent as tutors to lower boys who needed
" coaching " at their homes.   On two occasions it fell
to my lot to perform that service for a lively but very
backward boy at Evans's House, Charley Selwyn,
nephew of the Bishop of Lichfield , and the awe which
I felt at sojourning in a bishop's palace helped to fix
more firmly in my memory some of the impressions
which I got there.

Dr. George Augustus Selwyn was the most stalwart
champion of " muscular Christianity." His face was

somewhat grim and stern, as was to be expected in so
redoubtable a preacher of the gospel of hard work ;
but there was a humorous twinkle in his eyes which
betokened a very kind heart ; and to any one connected
with Eton, present Etonian or Old Etonian, he extended
the warmest of welcomes. In fact, New Zealand, the
scene of his missionary labours, and Eton, where he had
been a successful scholar and athlete, were the standing
subjects of conversation at his table : he and Mrs.
Selwyn used often to converse together in the Maori
tongue ; and had there been an Etonian language
(other than slang) it would assuredly have been spoken
by them. The world was, for the bishop, divided into
Etonian and non-Etonian. I once heard him pressing
upon an old schoolfellow, who was about to leave the
Palace, some table-delicacies of rare excellence, and
quoting the Horatian line :

> Ut libet , hæc porcis hodie comedenda relinques
> (" As you like ! The pigs will eat them up, if left.")

He explained that some other guests who were coming
to Lichfield that day were—non-Etonians

But in spite of the large and lion-like geniality of the
bishop, there were anxious moments when the sight of
some indolent or slovenly action caused his quick
temper to give way, and then one knew not whether
to tremble or be inwardly amused at the forms which
his anger would take   Once, on a dull Sunday afternoon (the Sundays *were* dull at the Palace), he overheard his nephew yawning wearily and saying he did
not know what to do. " What ! " cried the bishop.
" A Christian boy not know what to do on a Sunday
afternoon ! " Then, in terrible tones : " Go and fetch
your Greek Testament." Forthwith, while I made haste
to escape from that scene of wrath, the wretched boy
had to undergo a long lesson from his uncle.

On another occasion it was my pupil's sister, a very
beautiful child of ten or twelve, who caused an eruption

of the volcano. She had left, in the course of luncheon,
"a wasteful plate"—that is, she had put the gristle
of the meat at the side, cleverly hidden, as she thought,
under knife and fork—and the bishop, observing this,
lectured her sharply on the sinfulness of such a habit.
Then, to our consternation, his anger rising higher,
he ended by seizing the girl's plate, and then and there
himself devoured the disgusting stuff as a practical
lesson in frugality. "The bishop's in a very bad
temper, to-day, sir," the butler gravely remarked to
me afterwards.[1]

Eton, then, was the school where ignorance was
bliss, but the bliss was very dear while it lasted, and it
would have been dearer still if we had more fully
realized the nature of the change that was to follow—
the difference between University and School. As the
end of the last summer term drew near, we felt more
and more the pang of the parting that was to come;
and when it was time to write our *Vale*—that last copy
of the weekly verses, in which we were allowed, for
once, to substitute English for Latin—we naturally
likened ourselves to some prophetic dreamer of sad
dreams, or to some despairing convict who sees his
approaching fate.

> So I, who write, feel ever on my heart
>   Such dim presentiment, such dull despair:
> Me, too, a doom awaits, I, too, must part,
>   And change a careless life for toil and care

Doubtless many such elegies periodically found their
way, as mine did, into Dr. Hornby's waste-paper
basket.

[1] The incident is a good example of the way in which the
real ethics of diet are often overlooked, while stress is laid upon
some quite minor and subordinate aspect of it.

III

LITERÆ INHUMANIORES

Next Camus, reverend sire, went footing slow
                                MILTON.

CERTAINLY, after the liveliness of Thames, old Camus
seemed to foot it very slowly. Heavy was the fall
from the exaltation of the sixth form to the lowliness
of the freshman. A needed experience it may have
been, as correcting the natural priggishness of boyhood, but it was a change that we little relished while
we underwent it.

King's College, Cambridge, in the early 'seventies,
was in a phase of transition from the old-fashioned
system, under which it was a mere appanage of Eton,
to a new order of things which was gradually throwing
its gates open to all comers; much, however, of the
ancient pettiness of spirit still remained; the College
was small in numbers and small in tone, dominated by
a code of unwritten yet vexatious ordinances, which it
was waste of time to observe, yet "bad form" to
neglect "King's always had a tyrant," was a remark
made to me by F W. Cornish, himself a Kingsman.

The Provost was Dr. Okes, a short, rather crabbed-
looking old man, whose enormous self-complacency was
the theme of many tales Once, when he was walking
through the court, his pompous gait caused some ill-
mannered undergraduates, who were watching him
from a window, to give vent to audible laughter; whereupon he sent for them and explained that such merriment

30

must not be indulged in while *he* was passing by. That he himself could have been the cause of the merriment was a possibility which had not entered his mind.

Next in authority was the dean, a wan and withered-looking clergyman named Churton, who always seemed unhappy himself and infected every one who entered his rooms with a sense of discomfort. He used to invite undergraduates to breakfast with him, a melancholy function in which he often had the aid of Fred Whitting (the name was pronounced Whiting), a bluff and more genial don whose conversation just saved the guests from utter despair ; and at these entertainments poor Churton's one remark, as he helped the fish, was to say with a sour smile of ineffable wretchedness. " Whitting, will you be a cannibal ? "

Very different from this chilly dean, and much more interesting, as being genuine relics of the brave old days when Kingsmen had no need to study or to exert themselves, inasmuch as their University career was assured them from the first, were two portly and inseparable bachelors, Messrs. Law and Brocklebank, whose sole employment it seemed to be to reap to the full the emoluments of their life-fellowship, which they had held for a goodly number of years. " Brock " and " Applehead " were their nicknames ; both were stout and bulky, but there was a rotundity about Mr. Law's cranial development which gave him a more imposing appearance. As they ambled side by side about the courts and lawns, it amused us to fancy them a pair of strange survivals from a rude prehistoric age, we ourselves, of course, playing the part of the moderns and intellectuals. When " Applehead " died, we were enjoined in a poetical epitaph, by some anonymous admirer, to deck his grave with pumpkins, gourds, melons, cucumbers and other emblematic fruits.

The literary element was not strong in King's ; but in Henry Bradshaw, one of the senior Fellows, the College could boast a University Librarian of much

distinction. He was a kind, but most whimsical and
eccentric man, whose friendship was open to any undergraduate who sought it, only it must be sought, and
under the conditions imposed by Bradshaw himself,
for it was never in any circumstances offered. If you
presented yourself uninvited at his rooms—rather an
ordeal for a nervous freshman—you were welcomed,
perhaps taken to his heart. If you did not present
yourself, he never asked you to come ; on the contrary,
however often he met you on the stairs or elsewhere,
he passed with a look of blank and stony indifference
on his large and somewhat inexpressive visage. I
knew a scholar of King's who lived on Bradshaw's
staircase, and who for more than a year was thus passed
by as non-existent : then, one evening, moved by a
sudden impulse, he knocked at the great man's door,
entered, and was immediately admitted to the cheery
circle of his acquaintance. It was useless to resent
such waywardness on Bradshaw's part , there was no
" ought " in his vocabulary ; you had to take him on
his own terms, or " go without " ; and the great number
of University men who came on pilgrimage to his rooms
was in itself a proof of his mastery.   I recall the following
lines from an epigram which some rebellious undergraduate wrote on him ·

> Throned in supreme indifference, he sees
> The growing ardour of his devotees :
> He cares not if they come, yet more and more
> They throng subservient to the sacred door :
> He cares not if they go, yet none the less
> His " harvests ripen and his herds increase."

It was so ; and Bradshaw, having a gift of very pungent
speech, was well able to keep his " herds " in order when
they were assembled : he would at times say a sharp
and wholesome word to some conceited or presumptuous
visitor. Even his nearest friends could take no liberties
with him. It was said that when Mr. G. W. Prothero,

then a Fellow of King's, took to omitting the " Esquire " in the address of letters, and wrote plain " Henry Bradshaw," the librarian retaliated in his reply by addressing laconically to " Prothero "—nothing more

To attend lectures and chapel services formed the chief duties of undergraduates ; and the lectures were much the less tedious task   It was a chilly business, however, on a cold winter morning, to hear the great Greek scholar, R Shilleto, hold forth for an hour on his beloved Thucydides ; for he was an elderly man with a chronic cough, and his enthusiasm for a Greek idiom hardly compensated his audience for the physical difficulties with which he laboured.   He would begin cheerily on a difficult passage, and, overtaken by a bout of coughing, lose the place for a while , then, with a drawling " yes," catch up the thread of his discourse, till another spasm overwhelmed him ; while we, desiring our breakfasts much more than the privilege of listening to a second Porson, fumed and fidgeted, and took notes, or neglected to take notes, till the stroke of the clock released us.   Much more popular were some of the lectures which we attended, in other Colleges, given by such skilled exponents of the Classics as Henry Jackson and R. C. Jebb.   Jebb was always the same—self-composed, neat and eloquent ; Jackson, on the contrary, though not at all less competent, used to work himself into a fever of fretfulness when he could not find the exact word he sought for ; and then, to our amusement, he would upbraid himself as " dolt " and " idiot," even while he was giving a most suggestive address.

The compulsory " chapels " were a great trial to some of us ; and each King's scholar was further liable, in turn, to the function of reading the Lessons for a week. I do not know why this should have seemed more formidable than " speeches " at Eton, but it was an office which we would very thankfully have escaped. It needed some courage to step down from a stall in that spacious chapel—most of all when, as on a Sunday afternoon, there was a large concourse of visitors—and then to mount, by what cragsmen would call an " exposed ridge," the steps that led up to the big lectern in the middle of the nave   The sensation was one of extreme solitariness and detachment, with little but the lectern itself to give support and protection , so that we could almost sympathize with the plight of that disreputable undergraduate who, according to a current story (which, be it hoped, was fictitious), had essayed to read the Lessons, in some college chapel, when he was not so sober as he should have been   Throwing his arms round the eagle—for his lectern was fashioned in the shape of that pagan bird—he appalled the congregation, it was said, by exclaiming, in a pensive voice · " If it wasn't for this [something] duck, I'd be down."

But practice makes all things easier ; and after a time one or two of us so far overcame our nervousness as to utilize our position at the lectern for the benefit, as we thought, of the congregation at large—certainly for our own personal comfort ; for we ventured to dock and shorten the Lessons as we felt inclined. " Here endeth the Lesson," we would cry, when we had read, perhaps, no more than a dozen verses out of twice or thrice that number ; and immediately the great organ would sound, and the pompous choral service continued on its course. We had private information that this irregularity did not pass unobserved by some of the dons , but as nothing was said we concluded that they blessed us for it in secret

The relations between dons and undergraduates were for the most part very friendly ; but the blandness of the dons was somewhat measured and condescending— not without reason, perhaps, for undergraduates, like schoolboys, were apt to take undue advantage of any excess of affability   Once, when I was walking along King's Parade with a friend, we saw the great Dr. Lightfoot coming from the opposite direction. " Now

just look," said my companion, " how polite Lightfoot
will be. See how I'll make him smile as he passes "
And sure enough, the learned divine, in response to an
audacious salute from one who had no sort of claim
to his acquaintance, was instantly wreathed in smiles
and benignity, as if he were meeting the son of his
dearest friend, instead of being impudently imposed on
by a stranger.

We rather dreaded the invitations that sometimes
reached us to a formal breakfast, or worse still, a *soirée*
(familiarly known as a " stand-up "), at the residence
of some high authority. I have spoken of the Churton
breakfasts in King's ; still more serious an affair was
it to be one of a dozen undergraduates summoned *en
bloc* to breakfast at Trinity Lodge, for Dr. Thompson,
the Master of Trinity, was a great University magnate,
widely famed and feared for his sententious sayings
and biting sarcasms, many of which were reported
from mouth to mouth. We had heard of that deadly
verdict of his on a University sermon preached by
Dean Howson, joint author of Conybeare and Howson's
Life of St Paul: " I was thinking what a very clever
man Mr Conybeare must have been " As a member
once or twice of such a breakfast-party, I recollect
how awkwardly we stood herded together when we had
entered the sage's presence, and how, as we passed into
the breakfast-room, we almost jostled each other in our
anxiety to get a seat as far as possible away from that
end of the long table where the Master in his majesty
sat. As for the *soirées* at Trinity Lodge and elsewhere,
they demanded some strength of limb , for the number
of visitors exceeded the number of seats, and to stand
for two hours in a corner, and look as if one liked it,
was irksome even for youth. At these ceremonials,
when the Provost of King's was the host, he used to
invite undergraduates with immense condescension to
" be seated " , and when he added with emphasis .
" You may sit down *here*," he was understood to be

reflecting on the superior comfort of a Provost's entertainment as compared with that of Trinity Lodge.

One thing that rather galled the feelings of undergraduates was that none but Provost and Fellows
might set foot on the extensive lawns at King's—a
selfish privilege of the few, as it appeared, maintained to
the exclusion of the many.   However that may have
been, there came a night when a small party of Kingsmen
committed the sacrilegious act of releasing a mole in
front of the Provost's Lodge, and dauntlessly awaited
the result, thus anticipating Lord Milner's policy of
" damning the consequences."   There were no serious
consequences, except to the most innocent of all the
persons concerned—the mole.   We watched him with
admiration as he sank into that soft green turf, like a
seal into water , and the next morning we were thrilled
to see a small line of earthen hillocks on the sacred
sward.   Then followed a great to-do of gardeners and
mole-catchers ; and on the third day, to our regret
and remorse, the poor mole paid the penalty for the
trespasses of others.   We put a London newspaper on
the track of this incident, and the editor published
some humorous speculations, for the benefit of readers
interested in natural history, as to how the mole could
have found his way to that cloistered spot.

The *Cambridge Undergraduates' Journal* (I am now
speaking of the year 1873 and thereabouts) was a
fortnightly paper—edited at one time by G. C Macaulay,
at another by Hallam (now Lord) Tennyson—in which
some of us used to try our hands at the higher journalism,
and write satirical essays on the various anomalies of
Cambridge life   Compulsory chapels ; compulsory Latin
and Greek ; " cribbing " in examinations ; antiquated
college customs , the exactions of college servants ;
the social functions known as " stand-ups "—these were
but a few of the topics on which we held forth with all
the confidence of youth   It was the *Adventurer* over
again, but on a more comprehensive scale ; for the

undergraduate could express his feelings more openly than the schoolboy, else the writer of an article on compulsory chapels could hardly have inveighed, as he did, against the ordinance of full choral service, where " the man without an ear " was doomed, for two long hours, " to sit, stand, and kneel in wearisome succession."

The annual competition for the English Prize Poem afforded another opportunity for nascent ambition. The subject one year was the recovery of the Prince of Wales (afterwards King Edward) from a serious illness ; and it was this rather snobbish theme that drew from one of the competitors a couplet which went the round of a delighted University.

> Flashed o'er the land the electric message came :
> " He is not better, but he's much the same " [1]

Then there were the " Sir William Browne's Medals," offered annually for Greek and Latin odes and epigrams These prizes were usually the perquisite of a few select scholars (my friend E C. Selwyn had a way of carrying them off) ; but as the poems were sent in anonymously, the envelope containing the competitor's name not being opened except when he won the medal, it was a safe and rather good sport to try one's luck in the contest. One of the surprises of my life was when old Shilleto (the coughing grammarian) walked into my room one evening, and told me that the examiners had awarded me the medal for Greek epigram. There being a defect in one of the lines, he sat down and corrected it, there and then, by an emendation which was doubtless better Greek and certainly worse poetry.

Another high Cambridge authority, at that time, was Dr Benjamin Kennedy, famed as former headmaster of

---

[1] I was not aware of these lines having appeared in print, until they were quoted by Sir Edward Cook in his *More Literary Recreations*, 1919 My version of them is slightly different from his ; but I think my recollection is trustworthy.

Shrewsbury School, and as author of a Latin Grammar familiar to many generations of schoolboys   I had been told to call on him at his house, for my father had been under him at Shrewsbury, and there was an old friend-ship between the families ; and when I did so with some trepidation—perhaps because a recent experience at Trinity Lodge had made me fearful of " receptions "—I found him a most benign old gentleman, quite free from the awful stateliness of a Provost or a Master ; indeed, when he asked undergraduates to dinner he relaxed to an extent which could not but restore con-fidence in the most timid   After dinner he would give us " words " to decipher, in ivory letters, according to that rather inane Victorian pastime ; or he would recite odd verses to us in his quaint sing-song voice, something between a whisper and a wheeze   Who could have feared even the most learned of Professors, when he stooped to conquer by rehearsing for us such an example of an English pentameter as the following, presumably of his own composition

Strawberry jam jam jam , strawberry, strawberry jam.

But even the genial Dr Kennedy could not wholly release himself from the rigidness of Cambridge eti-quette · it was impossible, so he had stated when he desired me to call on him, for *him* to call on an under-graduate. No such difficulty existed for the greatest yet least assuming of the distinguished men then living in Cambridge, Frederick Denison Maurice. Having heard of me as a pupil of Mr. Kegan Paul's, he came, though he was an old man, to my room on the top story in King's, and talked so quietly and naturally that I felt quite at ease with him.   On a later occasion I breakfasted at his house, alone with him, a privilege which I much valued , for even then I was aware of his real greatness, unlike as he was to the pompous University magnates who figured so largely in public.

If only the heads of Colleges and Universities could know—but, of course, they rarely know—how much more powerful is the influence of simple unaffected kindness than of the affability which betrays a touch of patronage and condescension !

St. Edward's Church, of which Maurice was the incumbent, was close to the gates of King's—and some of us undergraduates used to go there on Sunday evenings, notwithstanding our weariness of our own chapel services, in order to hear him preach, for we were drawn to him by the obvious impression which he gave of quiet sympathy and strength   At a time when the revolting doctrine of eternal punishment was still widely held, his humanizing influence must have been very valuable within the Church. Matthew Arnold's clever gibe, that he beat about the bush, but without starting the hare, left a good deal unsaid ; for if he did not start the hare he helped to silence the hell-cat.

Not very long before the time of which I am speaking, Maurice's curate at St. Edward's had been a namesake of that saint's, Edward Carpenter, who, as is related in his autobiography,[1] resigned his Orders, together with his Fellowship at Trinity Hall, in 1871. Some thirteen years later I made his acquaintance in London ; and I have often regretted that I went to Cambridge too late to hear him preach, for I have never been able quite to picture the author of *Towards Democracy* in the pulpit, arrayed canonically in surplice or gown

The goal of a Kingsman's career at Cambridge was the Classical Tripos, and for three years he would read steadily, and with increasing intentness, keeping that end in view   It was generally thought advisable to have a " coach ", but experience led me to doubt whether, for those who knew how to direct their own reading, and had the necessary perseverance, it was not

[1] *My Days and Dreams*, by Edward Carpenter, 1916.

a waste of time to invoke such assistance ; a good
" crib " was a far speedier and more effective instructor.
Some " coaches," moreover, were apt to be rather lazy
at times, and to put off their pupils' attendance on the
plea, perhaps, that they had to go to London for the
day, or were called off by some equally important
engagement ; and now, by a curious reversal, we, who
at Eton should have been only too delighted if our
tutors had perennially shirked their duties, had become
in turn the studious ones, and having ourselves paid
for the tuition were annoyed if we did not get it !   One
contemporary of mine at King's was so upset by his
" coach's " remissness that he wrote him a letter of
remonstrance, more in sadness than anger, and roused
him to fury by quoting some words from Thucydides
(οἱ δὲ προλαβόντες τὸ ἀργύριον), in open allusion to
those who first get their fee and then neglect to
earn it.

Young men often fail to realize the sensitiveness of
their elders, and thus say and do things which cause
more hurt than was intended.   We used to be resentful,
in those too fastidious pre-war days, of the considerable
amount of shale, schist, and rubble which was sold to
us with our coal ; and a fellow Kingsman once asked
me to accompany him to the coal-merchant's, to whom
he proposed to return a basketful of the refuse in
question.   Foreseeing sport, I went ; but the scene
that ensued was sorrowful rather than amusing, for
the head of the firm, a venerable-looking old man with
white hair, happened to be in the office, and when the
coal-substitutes were handed to him over the counter
his wrath was so great that his hand positively shook
with passion.   Savages though we were, we came away
rather penitent.

There was, however, one Kingsman at that time, an
undergraduate senior to myself, who was unpleasantly
famed for the remorseless devilry with which he scored
off any unfortunate person whom chance placed in his

power. His tailor, it was said, having by mistake
sent him in a bill that had already been paid, was
ordered to set the matter right, on pain of being dismissed He did so, and then the offended customer
said to him : " And now I dismiss you just the same."
On another occasion it was a broken-down clergyman
who had the ill-luck to appeal to this young gentleman
for pecuniary aid · so rare an opportunity could not
be allowed to slip " You trust in God, I suppose,"
said the undergraduate It was not possible for a
clergyman to gainsay it. " Then I will toss up," said
the other ; "and if you cry rightly, I shall know you
deserve assistance"; and forthwith he spun the coin,
and the clergyman cried—" heads " or " tails " as
might be But unluckily for the poor pilgrim, the
Kingsman was a skilled manipulator of the coin in
hazards of this sort, and the result was never in doubt.
The mendicant was proved, on the highest authority,
to be undeserving.

But to return to the Classical Tripos. Coached or
uncoached, we came at last to that great final examination, a sort of Judgment Day in miniature, which, for
some of us, would have an important bearing on our
later lives. The examination system is in various ways
open to criticism, and critics have by no means been
lacking, but it need not be denied that intellectual
benefit in many cases may result from the sustained
effort to prepare oneself for a very searching test,
necessitating a thorough study of the chief Classical
writers. But the weightiest charge against the University education is the one which least often finds
expression—that a learning which would strengthen the
intellect only, and does not feed the heart, is in the
main but barren and unprofitable, a culture of the
literæ inhumaniores. Except from F D. Maurice, I
never heard, during my four years at Cambridge—from
preacher or professor, from lecturer, dean, or don—the
least mention of the higher social ethics, without

which there can be no real culture and no true
civilization.

I remember, with shame, that I was once so moved
by the florid rhetoric of Dean Farrar, in a missionary
sermon preached before the University, that I made a
contribution to the offertory which I could ill afford.
A day or two afterwards, with the return of sanity, I felt
the force of the adage that " fools and their money are
soon parted," and I saw that it was worse than folly
to send missions to other countries, when we ourselves
were little better than pagans at home. The mischief
of this spurious religionism was that it lessened the
chance of any genuine awakening of conscience to the
facts that stared us in the face. We were made to
study Paley's fantastic " Evidences," while the evidence
of nature, of the human heart, and of actual life, was
sedulously hidden away.

In the Tripos of 1875 the Senior Classic was Mr.
Peskett, who belonged properly to the preceding
year, but owing to illness or some other cause had
" degraded " into ours, and thus robbed my friend Mr.
Arthur Tilley of an honour which should rightly have
been his. Dr. J. Gow, Headmaster of Westminster
School, was third ; the fifth place was shared by Mr.
Gerald Balfour and myself.

It was the custom in those days for headmasters of
Eton to draw largely on King's College for their supply
of assistants : thus a King's Scholar of Eton, after
taking his degree at Cambridge, would often return
to the school as a Classical assistant master, and so
complete the academical round. The process might,
perhaps, have been likened to the three stages of
butterfly life, but with the first and the last phase
transposed. We *began* as the gay Eton insects, whose
ignorance was bliss ; and then, after passing through the
chrysalis period by the Cam, reappeared on Thames's
bank, metamorphosed into the caterpillars locally known
as " beaks," and usually content thenceforth to crawl

soberly along on a wingless but well-nourished career. But even a worm, as we know, will turn , and, as the next chapter must relate, some of the grubs would at times be so unconscionable as to take new and un-settling notions into their heads.

IV

THE DISCOVERY

"Why, they are cannibals!" said Toby. "Granted," I replied; "but a more gentlemanly and amiable set of epicures do not exist."—HERMAN MELVILLE.

WHAT are the feelings of the poacher transformed into the gamekeeper? They must, I think, be similar to those of a youth who, after studying for a few years at the University, returns as master to the school which he left as boy *Quantum mutatus ab illo!* The scene itself is the same, but the part which he must play in it is now to a great extent reversed; and the irony of the situation is that though henceforth an upholder of law and order, he still, perhaps, sympathizes at heart with the transgressors whom it is his duty to reprimand.

To be summoned as an assistant by Dr. Hornby, and at a few days' notice (his arrangements were frequently made in desperate haste), was to be thrown very suddenly upon one's own resources; for, an appointment once completed, he showed no further interest in the matter, and did not even trouble himself to provide a school-room in which his latest lieutenant should teach · that the number of Divisions exceeded the number of rooms was a trifle which did not engage his attention. A novice had therefore to consider himself rather lucky when he was able to secure, for his first term or two, even an apartment so ill equipped for educational purposes as a sort of cupboard, situated under the stairs that led to the headmaster's room, and popularly known as "The Dog-Kennel." Here, with a class of about forty boys, a pleasant summer school-time had to be spent.

It was a curious sensation, which I suppose all teachers of large classes must have felt, to be confronted by serried ranks of boys whose faces were entirely strange, though their names were entered on the list which lay, like a map, upon the desk. Some time was required before each name could be correctly fitted to the face; and in this process any abnormality of feature or size in individuals, which might constitute a landmark, was a great help. A red-haired boy, or a fat boy, served to punctuate a row; and that classification of boys (I forget who made it) into the beef-faced and the mealy-faced was a thing to be kept in mind.

Such were the auspices under which an Eton master was in those days started on his career—shut up in the Dog-Kennel with a horde of young barbarians, whom, in the circumstances, it was hardly possible to instruct, and not very easy to control. There were a few masters at Eton, as doubtless at other public schools, who had a real gift for teaching; also a few, like our friend "Swage," who were unable to maintain any semblance of authority. Between these two extremes were those, the great majority of us, who, while courteously and respectfully treated by the boys, and having pleasant relations with them, could not in strict truth flatter themselves that, except in special cases, they had overcome the natural tendency of boyhood to be idle. So much has been written about the defects of the Eton system that it suffices here to say that while a reputation for cleverness was maintained by a few of the boys, mostly King's Scholars, the bulk of the school was inflexibly bent upon other activities than those of the mind.

Nor were the masters themselves unaffected by the general tone of the school. There were some fine scholars, it is true, on Dr. Hornby's staff, experts not in Classical literature only, but in various branches of learning, yet in not a few cases these gifted specialists seemed as artless in their outlook on life as they were skilled in their particular department. "A d——d fool, with a taste for the Classics," was the too unceremonious description given of one of them by a sarcastic acquaintance, and the epigram, however reprehensible in expression, hit the mark. Knowledge is not wisdom; and this academical learning often went together with a narrow and pedantic spirit which blindly upheld the old order of things and resented every sign of change. For example, there was one learned master who used to assert, in those years of peace, that what England most needed was a war—a grim, hard-fought war; and this was the sort of reckless talk often indulged in by the mildest-mannered of men, who themselves were in no danger whatever of exchanging the gown for the sword.

New ideas were under a ban at Eton; notwithstanding the specious invitations given to some distinguished men to lecture before the school. Gladstone, Arnold, Ruskin, Morris and Lowell were among those who addressed the boys in the School Library; and it was instructive to note the reception which they severally obtained. Lowell was the most popular; his cheery contention that this world of ours is, after all, "not a bad world to live in," being delightedly received by an audience which had good personal reasons for concurring in such a sentiment: William Morris, on the other hand, having ventured on the then dangerous ground of Socialism, was hissed. Gladstone discreetly kept to the unimpeachable subject of Homer; and Matthew Arnold's staid appearance, with his "mutton-chop" whiskers and mechanical bowing of the head in accord with the slow rhythm of his sentences, was sufficient to lull to sleep any insidious doubts of his respectability As a speaker, Ruskin was by far superior to the rest; his lucid train of thought and clear, musical voice could hold enchanted an audience, even of Eton boys, for the full space of an hour.

Science lectures formed another branch of the intellectual treats that were provided for the school ; but Science was still rather under a cloud at that date. I recollect the title of but one discussion, and that only because I happened to be able to throw some light on the geological problem with which it dealt; I was living in a small house (once famous as " Drury's "), which had a much higher one on either side ; and as it was the practice for the boys in neighbouring houses to bombard each other with any missiles or minerals that might be handy, my garden became a sort of " no-man's-land " between the two rival fortresses, and its surface was enriched with a very varied deposit. When, therefore, a lecture was announced on the question, " Will coal be found in the Thames valley ? " I was able to solve the problem affirmatively by the production from my own premises of some remarkably fine samples

It would doubtless have shocked Dr. Hornby if any one had suggested that there was a lack of religious instruction in that most conservative of schools. Chapel services there were in plenty ; and a Greek Testament lesson on Monday morning ; and " Sunday Questions " to be answered in writing , and " Sunday Private " to be attended in the Tutor's pupil-room , and Prayers every evening in each House. Yet the general tone of Eton was far from being religious, even in the conventional meaning of the term ; for the many superficial observances did not affect the deep underlying worldliness of the place. It was Vanity Fair on Sundays and week-days alike There was an Eton story of a servant in a private family who, when the bell was rung for evening devotions, was overheard to cry in a weary voice : " Oh, dear ! *Why* do gentry have prayers ? " The reference to " gentry " shows the light in which such ceremonies are regarded downstairs.

In the same way, the religious teaching in schools is looked upon by the boys as imposed on them for purposes of discipline.

It was not the boys only who found the Chapel services very tedious ; for most of the masters were laymen, many of them unorthodox, and for these it was no agreeable duty to be victimized both on Sundays and on Saints' Days for the sake of keeping up appearances before the school. Calculations are sometimes made of the number of years spent in prison by some hardened criminal or " gaol-bird." Why does no one tell us how many hours, amounting to how many years, some zealous church-goer, or pew-bird, has spent on such devotions ? Without claiming that distinction, I calculate that during some twenty years spent in connection with public school and University I passed several thousands of hours in church and chapel.

Human nature could not but chafe under the fearful dulness and length of the sermons in Eton College Chapel. Dr. Goodford, the Provost, was a sort of personified Doom ; when once he mounted the pulpit he was in the saddle, so to speak, and rode his congregation well-nigh to despair with his merciless homilies, all uttered in that droning voice, with its ceaseless *burr* and inevitable cadence, which became to generations of Etonians as familiar as the Chapel bell itself. Scarcely less fearsome were some of the elder Fellows, retired masters, such as Bishop Chapman and the Rev. John Wilder, who were often let loose on us on Sunday mornings and blithely seized the opportunity : it was their field-day, and they were out to enjoy themselves, quite unconscious that what was pious sport to them was death to their unwilling audience. Small wonder that some assistant masters used to dread the weeks when they were on duty (" in desk " it was called) ; but providentially there were others who, disliking still more the labour of correcting Latin verses, were willing to barter " verses " for " desks " ; that is, they would take so many of a colleague's desks, while he in return would look over a stipulated number of exercises. Thus did the Muse come to the aid of her devotees:

Sic me servavit Apollo.

Perhaps the strangest form that religion took at Eton was that of missionary zeal , we used to have sermons periodically about carrying the gospel to " the heathen "; though if ever there was a benighted spot on earth, it was that pleasant school by the Thames.   Some of the boys were at times infected by the passion for making proselytes : on one occasion an extremely dull and idle youth, who had lately left Eton, wrote to tell me, as his former tutor, that he had decided to become a missionary " to the poor perishing heathen "—in his case, the Chinese, a people much less ignorant and barbarous than many of their self-appointed rescuers.

" Divinity " was one of the studies most encouraged and fostered at Eton ; one would have thought the place was a training-school for theologians, from the prominence that was given in examinations to this particular branch of learning   The result, as might have been expected, was the same as in the writing of Latin verses : a few boys became adepts in the Bible Dictionary, while the bulk of the school scarcely advanced beyond that stage of biblical knowledge exhibited by a certain Etonian who, when invited to write an account of St. James the Elder and St. James the Less, was able to give a brief description of the Elder, but was reduced, in the case of the Lesser saint, to the rather inadequate, though so far correct, statement that : " The other was another."

We were perhaps somewhat overdone with the Saints at Eton : the masters who had to set the Sunday Questions were nearly as tired of asking about St. Peter and St. Paul as the boys of answering ; and in the Chapel sermons we suffered, year after year, under the whole Hagiology, until some of us, it must be confessed, sighed in secret for the time :

> When Reason's rays, illuming all,
>   Shall put the Saints to rout,
> And Peter's holiness shall pall,
>   And Paul's shall peter out.

But if Christianity was the nominal religion at Eton, the real creed was Respectability. To do the " proper thing ", not to offend against any of the conventional canons , to dress, walk, speak, eat and live in the manner prescribed by " good form "—this was the ever-present obligation which neither boy nor master could disregard. Any slip in matters of etiquette was regarded as deadly There was a dark rumour about one of the masters, a good and worthy man, but very short-sighted, that by a tragic error in the High Street he had taken off his hat to his cook : it was only less dread-ful than if he had failed to perform that act of courtesy in some case where it was required

As is usual in barbarous societies, the number of things that were " taboo " was considerable. In the early 'eighties the bicycle and tricycle were frowned upon, not for boys only but for masters ; and a lady living in Eton once received from Mrs. Hornby, who of course, was at the head of the Fashions, a message that to ride a tricycle was " not a nice thing to do " Yet for the boys it *was* considered a nice thing to hunt and " break up " hares. I once witnessed the virtuous indignation of one of the masters, a clergyman, and a follower of the Eton hounds, when some rather " shady " incident of the hunt was reported to the headmaster , but Dr. Hornby soon set matters right by explaining that, as *all* hunting was cruel, he obviously could not take notice of any particular malpractice That was the sort of reasoning with which any attempts to humanize Eton customs were parried and thwarted.

Yet new ideas could not be wholly excluded, even

from that stronghold of the antique ; there were, in fact, several members of Hornby's staff who held views too advanced to be avowed in such surroundings. One of the least prejudiced men at Eton was the French Master, M Roublot, who was a close personal friend of his German colleague, Herr Griebel ; and it is pleasant to recall the fact that during the horrors of the Franco-German War, some ten years earlier than the period of which I am speaking, these two " enemies " had kept their friendship unbroken, and might be seen daily taking their walk together, just as if their countrymen were not insanely engaged in cutting each other's throats.

Among the Classical tutors, two of the most enlightened spirits, men of great personal charm, were Mr. E. S. Shuckburgh, afterwards lecturer at Emmanuel College, Cambridge, and the Rev. Duncan Tovey, who a few years later took the Eton living of Worplesdon. Shuckburgh, though himself most impatient of the old traditions, and sympathizing largely with the newer thought, was of a very critical habit of mind, and used to delight, for argumentative purposes, in dwelling on the difficulties and shortcomings of the reforms which some of us advocated. Tovey was a literary man (his works on Gray and Thomson are well known), out of his element in such a place as Eton, but in his happier moods a most delightful talker and companion. Mrs. Tovey, too, had a lambent wit which could play lightly round the anomalies of Eton life. She once wrote a charming list of some imaginary books of fiction, the authorship of which she assigned to various local celebrities : one of the works, the supposed creation of an Eton upholsterer notorious for his big bills, had a title which might make the fortune of a modern philosophical novelist . " Man's Time ; a Mystery."

Some of the junior masters played a useful part in challenging the old superstitions Mr J. D. Bourchier, afterwards a famous correspondent of *The Times* in south-east Europe, was the first rider of the bicycle at Eton, and incurred much obloquy through his persistence in a practice which no Eton master could then countenance with safety. My brother-in-law, J L Joynes, jun., was a still worse offender. He had been impressed by Henry George's *Progress and Poverty*, and in the summer holidays of 1882 travelled with George in Ireland. By a ridiculous blunder of the Irish Constabulary, the two were arrested and locked up as dangerous conspirators ; and, though they were quickly discharged when the magistrates discovered the error, the whole Press of the country rang with amused comments. The Government had to apologize to Henry George as an American citizen ; and an account of the fiasco, written by Joynes, and published in *The Times*, caused great scandal in Etonian circles, where publicity was regarded, not without good reason, as the thing of all things to be deprecated. Great, then, was the horror of the Eton authorities when, a few weeks later, an advertisement announced Joynes's forthcoming volume, *Adventures of a Tourist in Ireland*. In hot haste he was informed by the headmaster that he must choose between his mastership and his book · he chose the latter, and resigned his post. That was the result, as a patriotic colleague and friend pointed out to me, of giving heed to " a mouldy American." Thus fallen from the high estate of an Eton mastership, Joynes became a leading spirit in the Social Democratic Federation ; and by him I was introduced to many well-known socialists whose names will be mentioned later on.

During the sixteen years of his headmastership Dr. Hornby dismissed no fewer than four assistants, and was himself involved at times in serious conflicts with the Governing Body A weak man, he was obstinate to the last degree when once engaged in controversy ; as was shown by his determination to get rid of Mr. Oscar Browning, who, whatever the merits

of their quarrel, was worth much more to Eton than
Hornby himself.   It was not generally known that three
other assistant masters proffered their resignations as a
protest against Mr. Browning's dismissal ; a most ill-
judged step, because matters had then reached a point
where either Hornby or Browning had to go   The
resignations were accepted, and the three mutineers
had to ask leave to withdraw them, which they did
with as good a grace as they could muster.   Thus the
headmaster triumphed ; but it was a victory that
brought him little credit, and it was a lucky day for
Eton when, on the death of Dr Goodford, he was
appointed to the Provostship in 1884.

   Dr. Warre, succeeding Dr. Hornby, was like King Stork
following King Log · it was as if the school, after a long
period of " go as you like," had been suddenly placed
under a military dictatorship.   Warre had nearly been
appointed headmaster in 1868 ; and though, during
Hornby's reign, he continued to serve loyally as an
assistant, it was evident that it galled him to watch the
nervelessness and vacillation with which the government of the school was conducted   I have heard him
at a " masters' meeting " appeal to Dr. Hornby in
terms which, however respectful in form, conveyed a
reproach which could hardly have been unnoticed :
" Will the headmaster insist upon his rule being kept ?
Will you pull us up, sir, if we neglect it ? "   We listened
in amusement, knowing full well that Hornby would
himself be the first to break his own rule, if it was one
that demanded either punctuality or perseverance

   One of Dr Warre's earliest innovations was to visit
the different Divisions in person while a lesson was
going on ; a very right and proper course to take, but
one which came rather as a shock to the assistant
masters of that time, who had been accustomed to
consider their class-rooms, like the proverbial English-
man's house, as their " castles."   We each wondered,
not without anxiety, when his own turn would come.

When mine came, I was spared a lengthy inspection owing to an incident which was as amusing as it was unforeseen. The next room happened to be occupied that day by a colleague who was entirely unable to keep order ; and as neither the unfortunate man, nor his rowdy Division, was aware that the headmaster was so near them, I had hardly begun my lesson when there rose a terrific din from next door—shrieks, cat-calls, peals of laughter, stamping of feet, all the noises of a madhouse. With a wave of his hand to me, the headmaster slipped swiftly from the room ; and a moment later I knew what had happened, not by hearing, but by the instant *cessation* of sound, for that wild uproar stopped as suddenly as if it had been cleft with an axe, and was succeeded by a deep silence more eloquent than words.

A few days later, Dr. Hornby, the new-made Provost, came up to a small group of masters who were standing near the school-yard, and smilingly asked us if we had been " inspected " yet. " I'm glad," he added, with a sigh of relief, " that they didn't inspect *me*."

Dr. Warre was in every way a contrast to Dr. Hornby. Far less sensitive and refined, he had much more real sympathy, if not with the masters, at any rate with the boys, and under a rough exterior showed on many occasions a practical kindness which was quite want-ing in his predecessor. For example, the setting of " Georgics " (i.e. the writing of 500 lines of Virgil), one of the most senseless punishments in vogue at that time, was always encouraged by Hornby. When Warre heard an assistant master remark that he was " looking out for an opportunity " to set a " Georgic " to a troublesome boy, he interrupted him with : " You should look out *not* to set him a ' Georgic.' " He had that kindly understanding of boyhood which is of great value to a teacher ; and from the point of view of those who believe that Eton is an ideal school, and the " hub " of the universe, it is difficult to see how a

better headmaster than Dr Warre could have been
found ; but he was a Tory of the strictest type, and
his appointment meant the indefinite postponement of
reform.

Enough has now been said to show why a ten-years'
sojourn as a master at Eton was likely to bring disillusionment, even if outside influences had not quickened
the process. Socialism was even then " in the air " ;
and to have become personally acquainted with Bernard
Shaw, Edward Carpenter, H. M. Hyndman, Henry
George, William Morris, John Burns, H. H. Champion,
Belfort Bax, and other apostles of what was then
termed " revolution," was not calculated to strengthen
a waverer in the pure Etonian faith. Still earlier, in
the winter holidays of 1878–79, I had met at Coniston,
in the Lake District, an ardent disciple of Ruskin,
Mr. William Harrison Riley, who held communistic
views ; and in the course of some long walks with him
on the mountains, in which I acted as his guide, he
more than repaid the obligation by opening my eyes to
certain facts which I had previously overlooked. He
brought me a message from another world

This Riley, with all his fiery zeal, was a man of
touching simplicity. He was then working some land
of Ruskin's, at St. George's farm, near Sheffield, and
he had come to Coniston to visit the Master, for whom
he felt and expressed an almost childlike veneration.
By Mr. Ruskin's invitation I accompanied Riley to
luncheon at Brantwood, and was greatly struck by the
meeting between the two—the devotion of the follower,
and the geniality of the sage. Early in the morning
Riley, who was much surprised by the luxuriance of the
verdure at Coniston, as compared with the grey desolation of the Sheffield hills, confided to me his intention
of taking as a present to Ruskin a clump of moss from
a wall-top near the hotel ; but as there was hardly a
wall in the district that was not similarly covered, I
suggested to him, as delicately as I could, that it

might be a case of carrying "coals to Newcastle."
Disregarding such hints, he arrived at Ruskin's door
with a big parcel of the moss, and gravely presented
it as soon as the first salutations were complete.   The
delightful charm of Ruskin's manner was seen in this
little incident ˙ he laughed—for who could have helped
laughing ?—yet took the gift—and turned the subject
—with a graciousness that could leave no hurt.   A few
years later Riley migrated to Massachusetts, but took
with him his quenchless ardour for " the cause "   The
last letter I received from him concluded with the
words   " My feeble hand still holds aloft the banner
of the ideal."

I remember that one of the subjects on which Ruskin
discoursed was the poetry of Tennyson, who was still
regarded by most people, certainly by the *literati* of
Eton, as a thinker of extraordinary power.   He was
an instance, said Ruskin, " of one who, with proper
guidance, *might* have done something great " ; as it
was, he had written nothing of real value, except,
perhaps, *In Memoriam*   *Maud* and *The Princess* were
" useless," *Enoch Arden* " disgusting " ;   the hero of
Maud " an ass and a fool," and the war-spirit in the
poem " downright mischievous."   Thus, again, was
sapped the simple faith of an Eton master, who knew
by heart a large portion of Tennyson's poetry, including
the whole of *Maud*

In addition to such dangerous doctrines, Vegetarianism
was now beginning to be heard of in Eton ;   and this
was in one respect a worse heresy than Socialism,
because it had to be practised as well as preached, and
the abstinence from flesh-foods could not fail to attract
unfavourable attention.   There was a distinguished
scientist among the Eton masters at that time, Dr. P. H.
Carpenter, a son of Dr. W. B. Carpenter ;   and when he
expressed a wish to speak with me on the subject of
the new diet which he heard I had adopted, I felt that
a critical moment had arrived, and as a novice in

vegetarian practice I awaited the scientific pronouncement with some awe. When it came, spoken with friendly earnestness, it was this: "Don't you think that animals were *sent* us as food?" I have since heard the same pathetic question asked many scores of times. What can one say in reply to it, except that the invoice has not yet been received?

A book of rare merit, filled with a multifarious store of facts about the food question in relation to the humaner thought, is Mr. Howard Williams's *Ethics of Diet*, which was then appearing by instalments in the magazine of the Vegetarian Society. I had the good fortune to make Mr. Williams's personal acquaintance, which was the beginning of a valued friendship; I also had helpful correspondence with Professor F. W. Newman, then President of the Vegetarian Society, and with Professor J. E. B. Mayor, who afterwards succeeded to that post. Thus equipped, I was not greatly impressed by the proofs which friendly colleagues offered me of the "impossibility" of the humaner diet; nor was I troubled when, of the two medical men with whom I was acquainted at Eton, the one said to me: "Well, I will give you two years," [1] and the other, a rather foolish person whom the boys used to call "Mary," inquired with a look of puzzled despair at such incredible madness: "Do vegetarians eat meat *by night*?" A vegetarian was of course regarded as a sheer lunatic in the Eton of those days. Twenty-five years later Eton had a vegetarian headmaster in Dr. Edward Lyttelton, who was an assistant there in the 'eighties. "Little did I think," he wrote to me, "when we used to chaff you about cabbages, that it would come to this!"

It happened, in one of those years, that it fell to my lot to set the subject for "Declamations," a Latin theme on some debatable point, which had to be com-

[1] The two years allowed for vegetarianism have now become forty, and all of them years of hard work.

posed and " spouted " annually by two of the sixth-
form boys, who took opposite sides in the discussion ;
and I chose for subject, rather to Dr. Hornby's disgust,
the question of vegetarianism (*An Pythagorei qui carne
abstinent laudandi sint*). Another channel for vegetarian propaganda was afforded by the Ascham Society,
a learned and select body organized by some of the
masters, who met periodically to read and discuss
papers on ethical and literary subjects. It happened that
the members were hospitably invited to a dinner by
one of their colleagues, who specially announced a dish
of roast veal as an attraction : thus provoked, I could
not but decline that treat in the accredited Eton manner,
a set of Latin verses, of which the conclusion was
obvious : Spare the calf, or let *me* be excused :

Si non vis vitulo parcere, parce mihi.

Thus gradually the conviction had been forced on me
that we Eton masters, however irreproachable our
surroundings, were but cannibals in cap and gown—
almost literally cannibals, as devouring the flesh and
blood of the higher non-human animals so closely akin
to us, and indirectly cannibals, as living by the sweat
and toil of the classes who do the hard work of the
world.[1] To speak of this, with any fulness, in such
a society as that of Eton, except to the two or three
friends who held a similar belief, would have been an
absurdity ; and I do not think I exaggerated, in the
first chapter of this book, when I described the discovery as bringing with it a sense of being cut off from
one's neighbours by interminable leagues of misunderstanding. I was living *in partibus infidelium*. It
became a necessity to leave a place where there could

[1] " Our competitive system of industry is a vestigial institution. It is a survival from the militant ages of the past.
. . . It is a system of cannibalism. Instead of instilling the
feeling of brotherhood, it compels us to eat each other."—
Savage Survivals, by J. Howard Moore, 1916.

be no sympathetic exchange of thought upon matters which were felt to be of vastly more importance than the accepted religion and routine.

I treasure the recollection of the interview in which I took farewell of Dr. Warre. Most kindly he expressed his regret that I had lost faith in that public school system to which he himself, as all Etonians are aware, devoted a lifetime of unsparing service. " It's the Vegetarianism," he gravely remarked, and I understood him to mean that it was the abandonment of the orthodox diet that had led, by inevitable weakening of the *mens sana in corpore sano*, to my apostasy in regard to Education. When I told him that Socialism must take its share of blame, as having been at least an auxiliary cause, he was really shocked. " Socialism ! " he cried, in his hearty tones. " Then blow us up, blow us up ! There's nothing left for it but that "

It is strange to reflect that between thirty and forty years ago the mere mention of Socialism should have suggested desperate acts of violence the term was then the bugbear, for the time being, of the respectable classes, who always keep on hand some convenient scare-word, for the purpose of making an alarm. " Anarchism " has since served its turn ; " Bolshevism " is the latest. Something to fear, something to hate, seems to be an indispensable requirement ; hence the periodical outbreak of war-cries and flogging-crazes. it matters little what the bogey is, so long as there is a vendetta of some kind, even if it be only, for a diversion, a campaign against the sparrow or the rat. There is no surer token of the barbaric mind than this capricious state of panic, described by George Meredith as " all stormy nightcap and fingers starving for the bell-rope."

My one irreparable loss in leaving Eton was not that of culture or scholarship or social position, but of the game of Fives ; for I used to think that the evolution of the Eton fives-court, the original of which was a flagged space between two buttresses of the Chapel ("Tax not the royal Saint with vain expense "), was the most valuable contribution ever made by the school to the well-being of mankind.   Fives is a great game ; and to have played it with such master-hands as A. C. Ainger, E. C. Austen-Leigh, Edward Lyttelton, or C. T. Studd, was a privilege neither to be forgotten nor to be replaced.   I used afterwards to dream at times that I was again engaged in the game—" serving," perhaps, or taking the service, or enjoying a duel of long sweeping strokes on the outer court, or mixed up in one of those close-fought rallies that centred round the " pepper-box " ; until a perfect shot from one side or the other had sent the ball to its resting-place in " dead man's hole."

My parting gift to the school was an article entitled " Confessions of an Eton Master," which appeared in the *Nineteenth Century* in January, 1885, and led to a good deal of discussion on the Eton system of education.

V

CANNIBAL'S CONSCIENCE

If any one should be educated from his infancy in a dark cave till he were of full age, and then should of a sudden be brought into broad daylight . . . no doubt but many strange and absurd fancies would arise in his mind.—From BACON'S *Advancement of Learning.*

" Do you think me a cannibal ? " is the remark often made by a cheery flesh-eater, when enjoying his roast beef in the presence of a vegetarian ; and it may not be denied that such is the thought which commonly suggests itself, for the more highly developed non-human animals are very closely akin to man " We do not eat negroes," says Mr. W. H. Hudson, " although their pigmented skin, flat feet and woolly heads proclaim them a different species—even monkey's flesh is abhorrent to us, merely because we fancy that that creature, in its ugliness, resembles some old men and some women and children that we know. But the gentle, large-brained social cow . . . we slaughter and feed on her flesh—monsters and cannibals that we are." No apology, then, shall be made for the heading of this chapter. There is a very real likeness, not only between anthropophagy and other forms of flesh-eating, but between the excuses offered by cannibals and those offered by flesh-eaters.

Forty years ago, the possibility of living healthily on a non-flesh diet was by no means so generally admitted as it is now ; and consequently very naïve and artless objections used to be advanced against abstinence from

butcher's-meat. Mr. Kegan Paul told me that he had
once heard a lady say to F. W. Newman: " But,
Professor, don't you feel very weak ? " to which the
Professor sturdily replied : " Madam, feel my calves."
" What on earth do you live on ? " used to be a frequent
question at Eton in those days, the implication being
that there is no " variety " in the vegetarian diet ;
an amusing complaint, in view of what Richard Jefferies
has described as " the ceaseless round of mutton and
beef to which the dead level of civilization [sic] reduces
us." So obvious is this monotony in the orthodox
repasts that the *Spectator*, a good many years ago,
published an article headed, " Wanted, a New Meat,"
in which it was explained that what is needed is some
new and large animal, something which " shall combine
the game flavour with the substantial solidity of a leg
of mutton." The *Spectator's* choice ultimately fell upon
the eland, but not before the claims of various other
" neglected animals," among them the wart-hog, had
been conscientiously debated.

That the cannibal conscience is somewhat guilty and
ill at ease seems evident from the nature of the arguments
put forward by the apologists of flesh-eating ; else why
did Dr. P. H. Carpenter suggest that the lower animals
were " sent " to us for food, when, as a scientist, he knew
well the absurdity of that remark ? Why not say
frankly what Nathaniel Hawthorne wrote in his *English
Notebook* that " the best thing a man born in this island
can do is to eat his beef and mutton, and drink his
porter, and take things as they are, and think thoughts
that shall be so beefish, muttonish, and porterish, that
they shall be matters rather material than intellectual " ?
The reckless hardihood of a simple and barbarous people
is essentially *un*conscious, just as the action of a hawk
or weasel is unconscious when it seizes its prey ; but
when consciousness is once awakened, and a doubt
arises as to the morality of the action, the habit begins
of giving sophistical reasons for practices that cannot

be justified. Herman Melville tells us in his *Typee* that the Polynesians, being aware of the horror which Europeans feel for anthropophagy, "invariably deny its existence, and, with the craft peculiar to savages, endeavour to conceal every trace of it." The existence of flesh-eating cannot be denied ; but do we not see a savage's craft in the shifty and far-fetched reasons alleged for its continuance ?

It is only fair to "the noble savage" to draw this distinction between the natural barbarism and the sophisticated, between the real necessity for killing for food and the pretended necessity. Commander Peary, the Arctic explorer, once wrote in the *Windsor Magazine*, under the title of " Hunting Musk Oxen near the Pole," a story of the genuine hunger, and expressed a doubt whether a single one of his readers knew what hunger was. He was actually in a famishing state when a herd of Musk Oxen came in view . " The big black animals," he said, " were not game, but meat, and every nerve and fibre in my gaunt body was vibrating with a savage lust for that meat, meat that should be soft and warm, meat into which the teeth could sink and tear and rend." Here was a savagery that can at least be understood and respected, that did not need to postulate the " sending " of the oxen for its sub- sistence ; yet, strange to say, Peary's story would be voted disgusting in many a respectable household which orders its " home-killed meat " from the family butcher and employs a cook to disguise it. Certainly, if there is a " noble savage," we must recognize also the ignoble variety that has developed the " conscience " of which I speak.

To this " cannibal's conscience " we owe those delight- ful excuses, those flowers of sophistry, which strew the path of the flesh-eater and lend humour to an otherwise very gruesome subject. By far the most entertaining of them is what may be called the academical fallacy, inasmuch as it seems to have a special attraction for learned men—the argument that it is a kindness to the animals themselves to kill and eat them, because otherwise they would not be bred at all, and so would miss the pleasures of existence. This "Canonization of the Ogre," as it has been named, was propounded by Professor D. G. Ritchie, Sir Leslie Stephen, Sir Henry Thompson, Dr. Stanton Coit, and other distinguished publicists,[1] every one of whom, with the single exception of Dr. Coit, prudently evaded discussion of the question when the flaw in his reasoning was pointed out, viz. that existence cannot be compared with non-existence. Of existence it is possible to predicate certain qualities— good or bad, happiness or unhappiness—but of non-existence we can predicate nothing at all; we must first have the actual ground of existence to argue from, and he who bases his reasoning on the non-existent is building upon the treacherous sands.

"The Pig has a stronger interest than any one in the demand for bacon," wrote Sir Leslie Stephen in his *Social Rights and Duties*. Sir Leslie was repeatedly invited to make some answer to the criticisms which this dictum called forth; but courageous champion of intellectual freedom though he was, he preferred in this instance to take refuge in silence. To no one but Dr. Stanton Coit has philosophy been indebted for a full exposition of a comfortable theory which may be expressed (with the alteration of one word) in Coleridge's famous lines :

> He prayeth best who *eateth* best
> All things both great and small.

"If the motive that might produce the greatest number of happiest cattle," said Dr. Coit, "would be the eating of beef, then beef-eating, so far, must be commended.

---

[1] Since the above was written, Dean Inge has added his name to the illustrious list. Is it not time, by the way, that some one collected the Gloomy Dean's golden sayings in a volume— under the title of *Ingots*, perhaps ?

And while heretofore the motive has not been for the sake of cattle, it is conceivable that, if vegetarian convictions should spread much further, love for cattle would (if it be not psychologically incompatible) blend with the love of beef, in the minds of the opponents of vegetarianism." [1] According to this ethical dictum, it will be seen, mankind will continue to eat cows, sheep, pigs, and other animals for conscience sake—we must be, not conscientious objectors to butchery, but conscientious *promoters* of it So far, Dr Coit only set forth in greater detail the argument stated by Professor Ritchie, Sir Leslie Stephen, and the other casuists in cannibalism ; but now we come to that " psychological incompatibility " to which in a parenthesis he referred.

" But we frankly admit," he continued, " that it is a question whether the love of cattle, intensified to the imaginative point of individual affection for each separate beast, would not destroy the pleasure of eating beef, and render this time-honoured custom psychologically impossible. We surmise that bereaved affection at the death of a dear creature would destroy the flavour "

Nothing in controversy ever gave me keener satisfaction than to have drawn this " surmise," this pearl of great price, from Dr. Stanton Coit in the very serious columns of the *Ethical World*. It shows clearly, I think, why his co-adjutors in the metaphysic of the larder were wise in their avoidance of discussion.

It seems to be a benign provision of Nature that those who allege altruistic reasons for selfish actions invariably make themselves ridiculous. " What would become of the Esquimaux ? " was one of the questions often put to advocates of vegetarianism ; probably it is the only instance on record of any solicitude for the welfare of that remote people. Then, again, we were frequently asked : " What would become of the animals ? " the implication being that under a vegetarian regime there

[1] Article on " The Bringing of Sentient Beings into Existence," the *Ethical World*, May 7, 1898.

would be large numbers of uneaten and neglected quadrupeds left straying about the earth. An artist friend of mine once drew an amusing picture to illustrate this " Flesh-Eaters' Dilemma." A gentleman and lady, sitting at a well-ordered dinner-table, are terribly inconvenienced by an invasion, through the conservatory door, of a number of such superfluous animals : a cow is putting her head through the window ; a sheep is snatching at the bread ; a pig is playing with a rabbit on the floor ; and in the distance a forlorn ox is seen lying in desperation against the garden gate.

Such are some of the sophisms of which cannibal's conscience is prolific. They belong to that class of subterfuge which Bacon designated *eidola specus*, " idols of the cave," as lurking in the inmost and darkest recesses of the human mind. " Fallacies of the Cave-Dweller " might perhaps be a fitting name for them ; for they seem to be characteristic of the more primitive and uncivilized intelligence.

VI

GLIMPSES OF CIVILIZATION

Wealth is acquired by overreaching our neighbours, and is spent in insulting them.—WILLIAM GODWIN.

IN the 'eighties there were two movements especially attractive to one who was breaking away from the old academical traditions, to wit, Socialism, the more equitable distribution of wealth ; and Simplification, the saner method of living   William Godwin, in many ways a true prophet, had foreshadowed the need of both these reforms in that pungent sentence of his *Political Justice*

Simplification of life has in all ages had its advocates, but it was not till the time of Rousseau and the revolutionary epoch that it acquired its full significance, when the connection between simple living and a juster social state became obvious and unmistakable, and it was seen that luxury on the part of one man must involve drudgery on the part of another.   Thoreau's *Walden*, published in America in 1854, was beginning to be known in England some thirty years later ; and Edward Carpenter's essays, afterwards collected in his *England's Ideal* (1887), were pointing the way to a wiser and healthier mode of life.   I read some of those essays while still at Eton ; and amid such surroundings they had a peculiarly vivid interest, as revealing, what was there quite overlooked, that it was possible to dispense with the greater part of the trappings with which we were encumbered, and to live far more simply and cheaply than was dreamed of in polite society.

The removal from a public school to a cottage among the Surrey hills was something more than a change of residence   it was an emigration, a romance, a strange new life in some remote antipodes, where the emblems of the old servitude, such as cap and gown, found new and better uses, like swords beaten into ploughshares. My gown was cut into strips for fastening creepers to walls . my top-hat, the last time I remember seeing it, was shading a young vegetable-marrow. Servants there were none , and with the loss of them we learnt two things : first that servants do a great deal more than their employers give them credit for ; secondly, that much of what they do may be lessened or rendered needless by a little judicious forethought in the arrangement of a house.

One ungrateful office that servants perform is that of protecting their employers from personal interviews with beggars and tramps ; they act as plenipotentiaries in the business of saying No. In country districts this certainly saves a good deal of a householder's time, but whether it is altogether a benefit to him may be doubted, for tramps are sometimes an amusing folk, and by no means devoid of humour in their mode of levying taxes upon the well-to-do. One old mendicant, I remember, who called at my back door to solicit a small sum for a very special purpose, and told his tale so skilfully that from admiration, not conviction, I relieved him, as he himself expressed it, of his immediate difficulty   Two minutes later there was a gentle knock at my *front* door, and behold the same old rascal commencing the same old tale ! He had made the mistake of supposing that a single cottage was two semi-detached ones, and when the door was opened by his late benefactor, I saw him shaken by a momentary spasm of laughter, so human as to disarm wrath.

Then there were the " tramps " in the metaphorical sense, the friends and bidden or unbidden guests whose visits were welcomed in that secluded region of bare

heaths and hills. Edward Carpenter, as the writer of
the books which had shown such life to be possible,
was, of course, the tutelary deity of the place . Bernard
Shaw, on the other hand, was the *advocatus diaboli*,
whose professed hatred of the country gave an additional
zest to his appearances there, and culminated in a
characteristic article, " A Sunday on the Surrey Hills,"
in which he described a wet walk on Hindhead and the
extremity of his sufferings until he was restored to
London by " the blessed rescuing train " [1] But it is
dangerous to jest on such subjects ; and I regret to
say that a local paper, some years afterwards, in re-
printing " G B.S.'s " jeremiad, added some scathing
editorial comments, which showed a resentment unmitigated by time, on " a cockney gentleman possessing
a very fine liver, but no soul above his stomach." [2]
In the simplification of household life, Shaw easily
held his own ; he was most conscientious and exemplary
in " washing up," and to see the methodical precision
with which he made his bed was itself a lesson in
domestic orderliness. Thus was realized the truth of
what Clough had written in his *Bothic* ·

How even churning and washing, the dairy, the scullery duties,
Wait but a touch to redeem and convert them to charms and
          attractions ;
Scrubbing requires for true grace but frank and artistical hand-
          ling,
And the removal of slops to be ornamentally treated.

In dealing with tramps, however, even Shaw could
be at fault. We once had a visit from a very undesirable vagrant who held forth at great length about a
fearful wound which he bore on his person ; and when
his lecture was ended, Shaw, in the approved Fabian
fashion, proceeded to ask a Question or two. But in
such company to question is to suspect ; and the tramp,

[1] *Pall Mall Gazette*, April 28, 1888
[2] *Farnham Herald*, September 16, 1899.

deeply hurt at any reflection on his veracity, at once commenced to divest himself of his clothing, so as to offer ocular proof. " A sight to dream of, not to tell." We were just saved from it by an earnest disavowal of any fragment of unbelief.

Among the most welcome of our visitors was " the Wayfarer," Mr. W. J. Jupp, author in after years of one of the wisest and most gracious of books, a real spiritual autobiography, a true story of the heart.[1] Himself a devoted nature-lover, he brought us tidings of the greatest of poet-naturalists, Henry David Thoreau, and thus laid me under the first of the many obligations which I owe to a friendship of old date.

But refreshing though it was thus to throw off the signs and symbols of Respectability, it is not so easy to drop " the gentleman " as one could wish, for the tattoo-marks of gentility are almost as ineffaceable as those of the barbarous ritual in which the islanders of the Pacific delight. Once a gentleman, always a gentleman · the imputation, like that of criminality, is hard to live down. I once met the author of *Towards Democracy* walking and talking with a very ragged tramp whom he had overtaken on the high road. The tramp accosted me, as if wishing to explain matters : " This gentleman——" he began, indicating Mr. Carpenter. " I'm *not* a gentleman," sharply interjected the philosopher ; whereupon the tatterdemalion, with a puzzled look, and a shake of the head that showed entire bewilderment, forsook us and went shambling on his way.

As an organized movement, Simplification has not been so successful as the importance of the subject might have warranted The Fellowship of the New Life, a society established in 1883, had the services of many thoughtful men, among them Mr. Maurice Adams, Mr W. J. Jupp, Mr Herbert Rix, Mr. J. Ramsay

[1] *Wayfarings* : a Record of Adventure and Liberation in the Life of the Spirit, 1918.

Macdonald, and Mr. Percival Chubb ; but though its protagonist, Mr. Adams, brought to the cause an exceptional knowledge and ability, the Fellowship, after lasting a good many years, gradually flagged and expired. This was the more to be regretted, because simplification of life is peculiarly liable to misunderstanding and cheap ridicule, and therefore needed to be set permanently before the public in a rational form ; whereas now it is largely associated in people's minds with Pastor Wagner's book, *The Simple Life*, and similar banalities. For it is stupid, nothing less, to represent Simplification as merely a personal matter, and as amounting to little more than moderation and sincerity in the various departments of life : there is a *social* aspect of the question which cannot thus be ignored As Thoreau says : " If I devote myself to other pursuits and contemplations, I must first see, at least, that I do not pursue them sitting upon another man's shoulders." Simplicity is not only " a state of mind " : it implies action as well as taste.

It is not very surprising, perhaps, that this doctrine has been ridiculed by critics, in view of the unwise manner in which some of its adherents have preached and practised it.   The attractions of Rousseau's " return to nature " have been too powerful for the weaker enthusiasts, who, in their desire to be " natural," have missed the qualities in which true naturalness consists. I remember the case of a clever young man, fresh from the University, who, bitten by the creed of simplicity, rented a large tract in a sandy wilderness where crops could hardly be made to grow, and induced an experienced labourer, of the old school, to bring his family to reside upon this model farm in the hope of there realizing the ideal. He would be " natural " ; that was his constant cry. A Hardy would have been needed to portray the agricultural tragedies that ensued. In the fierce heat of a fiery summer the crops withered one by one, until the heart of the old husbandman was

sick within him with a savage despair. I recall a
Sunday stroll, with the party from the farm, to a hill
which overlooked that Sahara where their hopes were
buried, and the deep fervour of the veteran's ejaculations
as he gazed across the desolate scene. "Well, I *am*
——" was his repeated remark; and the language was
quite unfitted for the mixed company at his side.

Against fiascos of this sort stood the fact that the
writings of the true exponents of Simplicity were
increasingly read and pondered. In Thoreau's genius
there was a magnetism which could influence not only
those who knew him, but a later generation of readers,
among whom a common love for the " poet-naturalist "
of Concord has often been a link of friendship (as I
have reason to remember with gratitude) between lives
that were otherwise far apart. A first reading of
Walden was in my own case an epoch, a revelation;
and I know that in this respect my experience was not
a singular one; nor has the impression which I then
formed of Thoreau's greatness been in any way lessened,
but on the contrary much strengthened, by my
correspondence or personal intercourse with those who
were numbered among his friends.

One of the most remarkable chapters in *Walden* is
that on " Higher Laws," in which the ideal of humaneness is insisted on as an essential part of Simplification.
How often, from the lack of such principle, in the
efforts to lead the simple life, has simplicity itself
become little more than sentimentality! Who but
a savage, for example, would include the keeping and
killing of pigs as a feature of a model homestead?
Yet in that establishment of which I have spoken,
where the avowed aim was to be " natural," the pig-
killing was a festive event. " Father sticks 'em, brother
cleans 'em," was the description vouchsafed by a
charming young " land-girl " (to use a later-invented
term), who dwelt with delight upon these unsavoury
divisions of labour in her Blithedale Romance. Well

might Tolstoy use this pig-killing process in illustration of his argument that, in any advance toward civilization, a disuse of butchery must be " the first step."

Socialism was at that time in its early and romantic stage, when the menace of the Social Democratic Federation was becoming a terror to the well-to-do, and when many a dignitary of Church and State shared Dr. Warre's belief that to " blow us up " was the diabolical desire of the incendiaries who denounced Capitalism. Doubtless it was the novelty of the attack that made it seem so terrible ; for Chartism had been largely forgotten, and Secularism had been filling up the interval as the national bogey. Certainly in that period of the 'eighties the leading socialist figures seemed more ominous and sinister than do any in the Labour movement of to-day. To William Morris, indeed, as being a poet of wide renown, a sort of licence was accorded to speak as bluntly as he chose ; but Hyndman, Burns, Bax and H. H. Champion were names of dark import to the " bourgeois " of that date. Mr. Hyndman's repeated prophecies of a Revolution were none the less disturbing because they were always unfulfilled ; Mr Burns was dreaded as a demagogue who had been imprisoned owing to his defiance of law and order, Mr Champion, as a retired army officer, who might possibly turn his military knowledge to deadly account. To one who knew those reformers personally, and their fearless labours in an unpopular cause, it is strange to recall the storm of obloquy which they then had to face ; to them and others of like mettle is due in large measure such progress as has since been made in the betterment of the conditions of Labour. Their weakness was that they could not agree among themselves (reformers seldom can) ; hence the internal ruptures that wrecked the influence of the S.D.F. Round Champion in particular the discord raged, until he was ostracized by his former colleagues ; yet no juster word was ever said of him than a remark

made to me, years afterwards, by Mr. John Burns—
that if he were ever in a tight place at a tiger-hunt
there was no one whom he would so gladly have at
his side as H. H. C.

With William Morris it was impossible, even for a
" comrade," to have any quarrel, his utter sincerity
and great-heartedness forbad it. But broad as his
geniality was, he used to seem rather nonplussed by
such new ideas as vegetarianism in conjunction with
teetotalism. " I'd like to ask you to have a drink,"
he would say, after a meeting or lecture ; and then
would add, as in despair. " But you *won't* drink."

One of the memories of those years is the great
meeting held in February, 1888, to welcome John Burns
and Cunninghame Graham on their release from prison.
Apart from my admiration for the heroes of the
evening, I had some cause to remember the occasion,
because, like many others who were present, I lost a
valuable watch. This placed us in an embarrassing
position ; for having assembled to protest against the
conduct of the police in the Square, we could not with
dignity invoke their aid against the pickpockets.

Quite the strangest personality among the socialists
of that time was Dr. Edward Aveling. It is easy to
set him down as a scoundrel, but in truth he was an
odd mixture of fine qualities and bad ; a double-dealer,
yet his duplicities were the result less of a calculated
dishonesty than of a nature in which there was an
excess of the emotional and artistic element, with an
almost complete lack of the moral. The character of
Dubedat in Mr. Bernard Shaw's play, *The Doctor's
Dilemma*, in some ways recalls that of Aveling, for
nearly every one who had dealings with him, even those
who were on the friendliest of terms, found themselves
victimized, sooner or later, by his fraudulence in money
matters   One's feelings towards him might, perhaps,
have been summed up in the remark made by one
of the characters in *The Doctor's Dilemma :* " I can't

help rather liking you, Dubedat. But you certainly are a thorough-going specimen."

Yet Aveling's services to the socialist cause were perfectly sincere; and so, too, was his love of good literature, though it sometimes manifested itself in rather too sentimental a strain. He was a skilled reciter of poetry, and on one occasion when, with Eleanor Marx, he visited our Surrey cottage, he undertook to read aloud the last Act of Shelley's *Prometheus Unbound*. As he gave effect to chorus and semi-chorus, and to the wonderful succession of spirit voices in that greatest of lyrical dramas, he trembled and shook in his passionate excitement, and when he had delivered himself of the solemn words of Demogorgon with which the poem concludes, he burst into a storm of sobs and tears. I used to regret that I had never heard his recitation, said to be his most effective performance, of Poe's " The Bells ", for there was something rather uncanny and impish in his nature which doubtless made him a good interpreter of the weird.

There was real tragedy, however, in Aveling's alliance with Karl Marx's daughter; for Eleanor Marx was a splendid woman, strong both in brain and in heart, and true as steel to the man who was greatly her inferior in both, and who treated her at the end with a treachery and ingratitude which led directly to her death.

As a corrective of the romantic socialism of the S.D.F arose the sober doctrine of Fabianism, a name derived, we are told, from the celebrated Fabius, who won his victories on the principle of " more haste, less speed "; else one would have been disposed to trace it to a derivative of the Latin *fari*, " to talk," as seen in the word " con*fabul*ation." In the early and most interesting days of Fabianism, its chief champions, known as " the four," were Sidney Webb, Bernard Shaw, Sydney Olivier, and Graham Wallas; and assuredly no Roman three ever " kept the bridge so well " as the Fabian four kept the planks of their platform in all the assaults that were made on it. Rarely have better debates been heard than at those fortnightly meetings in Willis's Rooms. The trouble indeed with Fabianism was that it became almost *too* brainy ; it used to remind me of Sydney Smith's remark about some one who was all mind—that " his intellect was indecently exposed." Humaneness found little place in the Fabian philosophy. Once, when visiting a suburban villa that had just been occupied by a refined Fabian family, I learned that the ladies of the household, highly intellectual and accomplished women, had themselves been staining the floors of their new and charming residence with bullock's blood brought in a bucket from the shambles.

Shaw was, of course, the outstanding figure of Fabianism, as he was bound to be of any movement in which he took permanent part ; but he was a great deal more than Fabian, he was humanitarian as well ; and it gives cause for reflection, as showing how much easier it is to change men's theories than their habits, that, while his influence on social and economic thought has been very marked, his followers in the practice of the Humanities have been few. It has been noticeable, too, how, in the many appreciations that have been written of Shaw, his humanitarianism has been almost entirely ignored, or passed over as an amiable eccentricity of a man of genius. Yet it is clear that if " G.B.S.," who, during the past forty years, has done enough disinterested work to make the reputation of a score of philanthropists, is " not to be taken quite seriously," there is no sense in taking any one seriously. A man is not less in earnest because he has a rich gift of humour or veils his truths in paradoxes. Shaw, in fact, is one of the most serious and painstaking of thinkers : his frivolity is all in the manner, his serious-ness in the intent ; whereas, unhappily, in most persons it is the intent that is so deadly frivolous, and the manner that is so deadly dull.

Perhaps the dulness of our age shows itself most

clearly in its humour ; the professional jester of the dinner-table or comic journal is of all men the most saddening. It is related that when Emerson took his little boy to see a circus clown, the child looked up with troubled eyes and said : " Papa, the funny man makes me want to go home." Many of us must have felt that sensation when we have heard or read some of the banalities that pass for humorous. It is here that " G.B.S. " stands out in refreshing contrast ; his wit is as genuine and spontaneous as that of Sydney Smith ; but whereas Sydney Smith was constrained in his old age to calculate how many cartloads of flesh-meat he consumed in his lifetime, Bernard Shaw has been able to tell the world that his funeral will be followed " not by mourning coaches, but by herds of oxen, sheep, swine, flocks of poultry, and a small travelling aquarium of live fish "—representatives of grateful fellow-beings whom he has *not* eaten.[1]

If socialists had cared for the poetical literature of their cause one half so well as the Chartists did, the names of Francis Adams and John Barlas would have been far more widely known It was Mr. W. M. Rossetti who drew my attention to Adams's fiery volume of verse, the *Songs of the Army of the Night*, first published in Australia in 1887 ; and as I was then preparing an anthology of *Songs of Freedom* I got into communication with the writer, and our acquaintance quickly ripened into friendship. Francis Adams was a poet of Socialism in a much truer sense than William Morris ; for, while Morris was a poet who became a socialist, Adams, like Barlas, was less a convert to Socialism than a scion of Socialism, a veritable *Child of the Age,* to quote the title of his own autobiographical romance, in the storm and stress of his career He had received a classical education at Shrewsbury School (the " Glastonbury " of his novel), and after a brief spell of schoolmastering, had became a journalist and

[1] *The Academy*, October 15, 1898.

wanderer   He was connected for a short time, in
1883 or thereabouts, with the Social Democratic
Federation, and enrolled himself a member under the
Regent's Park trees one Sunday afternoon at a meeting
addressed by his friend, Frank Harris.   In Australia,
for a time, where he took an active part in the Labour
movement, and wrote frequently for the *Sydney Bulletin*
and other journals, he had many friends and admirers ;
but just as a Parliamentary career was opening for him he
was crippled by illness, and returned to England, a con-
sumptive, in 1890, to die three years later by his own hand.

Of Adams's prose works the most remarkable is
A Child of the Age, written when he was only eighteen,
and first printed under the title of *Leicester, an Autobiography*, an extraordinarily fascinating, if somewhat
morbid story, which deserves to be ranked with *Wuthering
Heights* and *The Story of an African Farm*, among
notable works of immature imagination.   He told me
that it was written almost spontaneously :   it just
" came to him " to write it, and he himself felt that it
was an abnormal book   Of the *Songs of the Army of
the Night*, he said that they were intended to do what
had never before been done—to express what might be
the feelings of a member of the working classes as he
found out the hollowness, to him, of our culture and
learning ;   hence the pitiless invective which shows
itself in many of the poems.   As surely as Elliott's
" Corn Law Rhymes " spoke the troubled spirit of
their age, so do these fierce keen lyrics, on fire alike
with love and with hate, express the passionate sympathies and deep resentments of the socialist movement
in its revolt from a sham philanthropy and patriotism.
No rebel poet has ever " arraigned his country and
his day " in more burning words than Adams in his
stanzas " To England "

> I, whom you fed with shame and starved with woe,
>   I wheel above you,
> Your fatal Vulture, for I hate you so,
>   I almost love you.

But the *Songs* are not only denunciatory ; they have a closer and more personal aspect, as in the infinitely compassionate " One among so Many," which endears them to the heart of the reader as only a few choice books are ever endeared. In their strange mixture of sweetness and bitterness, they are very typical of Francis Adams himself : he was at one moment, and in one aspect, the most simple and lovable of beings ; at another, the most aggressively critical and fastidious.[1]

But if Francis Adams has not received his just meed of recognition, what shall be said of John Barlas, whose seven small volumes of richest and most melodious verse were printed (they can hardly be said to have been published) under the *nom de plume* of " Evelyn Douglas," and mostly in places remote from the world of books ? When full allowance is made for such drawbacks, it is strange that literary critics, ever on the look-out for new genius, failed to discover Barlas ; for though the number of modern poets is considerable, the born singers are still as few and far between as before ; yet it was to that small and select class that Barlas unmistakably belonged. His *Poems Lyrical and Dramatic* (1884) contained, with much that was faulty and immature, many exquisitely beautiful lyrics, the expression of a genuine gift of song. A Greek in spirit, he also possessed in a high degree the sense of brotherhood with all that breathes, and was ever aspiring in his poetry not only to the enjoyment of what is best and most beautiful on earth, but to a fairer and happier state of society among mankind Nor was he a dreamer only, intent on some far horizon of the future ; he was an ardent lover of liberty and progress in the present , and this hope, too, found worthy utterance in his verse.

[1] The substance of what is here said about Francis Adams is taken from my editorial note to the revised edition of the *Songs of the Army of the Night*, published by Mr. A. C. Fifield, 1910

It would be difficult to say where Freedom has been
more nobly presented than in his poem to " Le Jeune
Barbaroux " :

> Freedom, her arm outstretched, but lips firm set,
> Freedom, her eyes with tears of pity wet,
>   But her robe splashed with drops of bloody dew,
> Freedom, thy goddess, is our goddess yet,
>   Young Barbaroux.

Of Barlas's *Love Sonnets* (1889) it may be said without
exaggeration that, unknown though they are to the
reading public and to any but a mere handful of students,
they are not undeserving to be classed among the best
sonnet-sequences.   It was Meredith's opinion that
as sonnet-writer Barlas took " high rank among the
poets of his time " ;   and that the concluding sonnet
was " unmatched for nobility of sentiment."   Nobility
was indeed a trait of all Barlas's poetry, and of his
character.   Sprung from the line of the famous Kate
Douglas who won the name of Bar-lass, he was noted
even in his school-days for magnanimity and courage ;
and in no way did those qualities show themselves
more clearly than in the dignity with which he bore
long years of failure and misfortune, darkened at times
by insanity.

The winter of 1891–1892 had brought the one occasion
on which Barlas's name came before the public.   He
was charged with firing a revolver at the House of
Commons, which he did to mark his contempt for
Parliamentary rule ;   but when H. H. Champion and
Oscar Wilde offered themselves as sureties, he was
discharged in the care of his friends.   I first heard
from him, through Champion, soon after that event,
in a letter in which he spoke of his poetry as having
been " three parts of my religion " ;   but it was not till
ten or twelve years later that I became closely acquainted
with him, and then he wrote to me regularly till his
death in 1914.   His letters, written mostly from an

asylum in Scotland, are among the most interesting I have ever received , for in spite of his ill health he was an untiring student, a great classical scholar, and deeply read in many Greek and Latin authors whose works he outside the narrow range of school and University curriculum. But his genius was in his poems ; and it is to be hoped that a selection from these may yet see the light.

Thus it was that these two poets, Adams and Barlas, though true-born children of Socialism, were precluded, owing to the misfortunes which beset their lives, from taking active part in its advocacy. Edward Carpenter, on the other hand, if unattached to any one section of reformers, has been one of the most influential writers and speakers in the socialist cause ; and his name is deservedly honoured not only for his many direct services to the movement, but for the personal friendship which he has extended to fellow-workers, and indeed to all who have sought his aid—giving freely where, in the nature of the case, there could be little or no return. His cottage at Millthorpe had already become, in the 'nineties, a place of pilgrimage, the resort of " comrades " who dropped down on him from the surrounding hills, or swarmed up the valley from Chesterfield like a tidal wave, or " bore," as he aptly described it. His friend George Adams and family were then living with him at Millthorpe ; and those who had the good fortune to be intimate with that delightful household will always remember their visits with pleasure George Adams, the sandal-maker, was as charming a companion as the heart could desire, full of artistic feeling (witness his beautiful water-colours), of quaint humorous fancies, and of unfailing kindliness His memory is very dear to his friends.

One of the strangest things said about Edward Carpenter, and by one of his most admiring critics, is that he has no faculty for organization. I used often to be struck by the great patience and adroitness with

which he marshalled and managed his numerous uninvited guests.   He might fairly have exclaimed, with
Emerson :

> Askest " how long thou shalt stay " ?
> Devastator of the day !

But though the pilgrims often showed but little consideration for their host, in the manner and duration
of their visits, he seemed to be always master of the
emergency, receiving the new-comers, however untimely
their arrival, with imperturbable urbanity, and gently
detaching the limpets with a skill that made them seem
to be taking a voluntary and intended departure.   It
was hospitality brought to a fine art.

For many years there was a quaint division of
Carpenter's writings in the British Museum catalogue,
his earlier works being attributed to one Edward
Carpenter, " Fellow of Trinity Hall, Cambridge," and
the later to another Edward Carpenter, placed on the
lower grade of " Social Reformer."   There was, perhaps, some propriety, as well as unconscious humour
in this dual arrangement ;   for Carpenter, like Morris,
was not a socialist born, but one who, by force of natural
bias, had gravitated from Respectability to Freedom ;
and his writings bore obvious tokens of the change.

Another and more audacious classification was once
propounded to me by Bernard Shaw, viz   that future
commentators would divide Carpenter's works into two
periods ;   first, that of the comparatively trivial books
written   before   he came   in contact with   " G.B.S. " ;
secondly, that of the really important contributions
to literature, where the Shavian influence is dis-
cernible.   I mentioned this scheme to Carpenter ;
and he smilingly suggested that if there were any
indebtedness, the names of the debtor and the
creditor must be reversed.   But it would have
been as reasonable for an elephant to claim to have
influenced a whale, or a whale an elephant, as for

either the thinker or the seer, each moving in quite a different province, to suppose that he had affected the other's course One common influence they felt— the desire to humanize the barbarous age in which they lived—and it is strange that Carpenter, in his book on "Civilization," should have bestowed so fair and unmerited a name on a state of society which, in spite of all its boasted sciences and mechanical inventions, is at heart little else than an ancient Savagery in a more complex and cumbrous form.

VII

THE POET-PIONEER

I know not the internal constitution of other men. . . . I see that in some external attributes they resemble me, but when, misled by that appearance, I have thought to appeal to something in common, and unburthen my inmost soul to them, I have found my language misunderstood, like one in a distant and savage land.—SHELLEY.

THE words quoted above would savour of self-righteousness, if put into the mouth of any one but the poet who wrote them. Coming from Shelley, they do not give that impression; for we feel of him that, as Leigh Hunt used to say, he was " a spirit that had darted out of its orb and found itself in another world . . . he had come from the planet Mercury " Or, rather, he was a prophet and forerunner of a yet distant state of society upon this planet Earth, when the savagery of our past and present shall have been replaced by a civilization that is to be.

During the latter half of the nineteenth century Shelley's influence was very powerful, not only upon the canons of poetry, but upon ideals of various kinds— upon free-thought, socialism, sex-questions, food-reform, and not a few other problems of intellectual and ethical import. The Chartist movement set the example. In a letter which I received from Eleanor Marx in 1892 she spoke of the " enormous influence " exercised by Shelley's writings upon leading Chartists: " I have heard my father and Engels again and again speak of this; and I have heard the same from the many Chartists it has been my good fortune to know—Ernest Jones, Richard Moore, the Watsons, G. J. Harvey, and others." What was true of Chartism held equally good of other movements; as indeed was admitted by Shelley's detractors as well as claimed by his friends: witness Sir Leslie Stephen's complaint that "the devotees of some of Shelley's pet theories" had become "much noisier." In the 'eighties, the interest aroused by the controversies that raged about Shelley, both as poet and as pioneer, was especially strong, as was proved by the renewed output of Shelleyan literature, such as Mr. Forman's and Mr. W. M. Rossetti's editions of the works, the biography of Dr. Dowden, and the numerous publications of the Shelley Society, dating from 1886 to 1892. It was a time when the old abusive view of Shelley, as a fiend incarnate, was giving way to the equally irrational apologetic view—the " poor, poor Shelley" period—of which Dowden was the spokesman; yet a good deal of the old bitterness still remained, and Mr. Cordy Jeaffreson's lurid fiction, entitled " The Real Shelley," was published as late as 1885.

It is difficult for a humble student of such a genius as Shelley to speak frankly of the debt that he owes to him, without seeming to forget his own personal unimportance; but I prefer to risk the misunderstanding than to leave the tribute unsaid. From the day when at a preparatory school I was first introduced to Shelley's lyrics by having some stanzas of " The Cloud " set for translation into Latin, I never doubted that he stood apart from all other poets in the enchantment of his verse; and I soon learnt that there was an equal distinction in the beauty and wisdom of his thoughts; so that he became to me, as to others, what Lucretius found in Epicurus, a guide and solace in all the vicissitudes of life:

> Thou art the father of our faith, and thine
> Our holiest precepts; from thy songs divine,
> As bees sip honey in some flowery dell,
> Cull we the glories of each golden line,
> Golden, and graced with life imperishable. [1]

---

[1] *De Rerum Naturâ*, iii. 9-13, as translated in *Treasures of Lucretius*.

At Eton there was little knowledge of Shelley, and still less understanding. When it was first proposed to place a bust of the poet in the Upper School, Dr. Hornby is said to have replied: " No : he was a bad man," and to have expressed a humorous regret that he had not been educated at Harrow. I once read a paper on Shelley before the Ascham Society, and was amazed at the ignorance that prevailed about him among Eton masters . only one or two of them had any acquaintance with the longer poems ; the rest had read the lines " To a Skylark " ; one told us with a certain amount of pride that he had read " Adonais " ; many thought the poet a libertine ; and though they did not say that he was a disgrace to Eton, it was evident that that was the underlying sentiment. Several years after I had left Eton, William Cory wrote a paper for the Shelley Society on " Shelley's Classics " (viz. his knowledge of Greek and Latin), which, in his absence, I read at one of the Society's meetings ; and I remember being surprised to find that even he regarded Shelley as a verbose and tedious writer.

From Mr. Kegan Paul, who was a friend of Sir Percy and Lady Shelley, I had heard all that was known of the inner history of Shelley's life ; and as, after the publication of Dowden's biography in 1886, the main facts were no longer in dispute, it seemed to me that the best service that could then be rendered to his memory was to show how, far from being a " beautiful and ineffectual angel," he was a beautiful but very efficient prophet of reform. This I did, or tried to do, in various essays published about the time when the Shelley Society was beginning its work ; and I was thus brought into close touch with it during the seven years of its existence. As illustrating how the old animosities still smouldered, more than sixty years after Shelley's death, I am tempted to quote a testimonial received by me from a critic in the *Westminster Review*, where I found myself described as one of the writers who grubbed amongst " the offensive matter " of Shelley's life " with gross minds and grunts of satisfaction," and as having made " an impudent endeavour to gain the notoriety of an iconoclast amongst social heretics with immoral tendencies and depraved desires." There was the old genuine ring about this, and I felt that I must be on the right track as a Shelley student. I knew, too, from letters which I had received from Lady Shelley, the poet's daughter-in-law, whose *Shelley Memorials* was the starting-point of all the later appreciations, that I was not writing without credentials. " For the last thirty-five years," she wrote to me in 1888, speaking for Sir Percy Shelley and herself, " we have suffered so much from what has been written on Shelley by those who had not the capacity of understanding his character, and were utterly ignorant of the circumstances which shaped his life, that I cannot refrain from expressing our heartfelt thanks and gratitude for the comfort and pleasure we have had in reading your paper." And later : " It is a great happiness to me to know, in my old age, that when I am gone there will be some one left to do battle for the truth against those whose nature prevents them from seeing in Shelley's beautiful unselfish love and kindness anything but evil."

The Shelley Society, founded by Dr. F. J. Furnivall in 1886, had the support of a large number of the poet's admirers, among whom were Mr. W. M. Rossetti, Mr. Stopford Brooke, Mr. Buxton Forman, Mr. Hermann Vezin, Dr. John Todhunter, Mr. F. S. Ellis, Mr. Stanley Little, and Mr. Bernard Shaw ; and much useful work was done in the way of meetings and discussions, the publication of essays on Shelley, and facsimile reprints of some of his rarer volumes, thus throwing new light, biographical or bibliographical, on many doubtful questions. I will refer only to one of these, in which I was myself concerned, a study of " Julian and Maddalo," which I read at a meeting in 1888, and which

was subsequently printed in the *Shelley Society's Papers*
and reissued as a pamphlet. Its object was to make
clear what had been overlooked by Dowden, Rossetti,
and the chief authorities, though hinted at by one or
two writers, viz. that the story of " the maniac "
(in " Julian and Maddalo ") was not, as generally
supposed, a mere fanciful interpolation, but a piece of
poetical autobiography, a veiled record of Shelley's
own feelings at the time of his separation from Harriet.
On this point Dr. Furnivall wrote to me (April 16,
1888) : " Robert Browning says he has always held the
main part of your view, from the first publication of
' Julian and Maddalo,' but you must not push it into
detail   I had a long talk with him last night "

The greatest single achievement of the Shelley Society
was the staging of *The Cenci* at the Islington Theatre,
in 1886. The performance was technically a private
one, as the Licenser of Plays had refused his sanction ;
but great public interest was aroused, and the acting
of Mr. Hermann Vezin as Count Cenci, and of Miss Alma
Murray as Beatrice—" the poetic actress without a
rival " was Browning's description of her—made the
event one which no lover of Shelley could forget. If
the Society had done nothing else than this, its existence
would still have been justified.

Every literary association, like every social movement,
is sure to have a humorous aspect as well as a serious
one, and the Shelley Society was very far from being
an exception to this beneficent rule ; indeed, on looking
back over its career, one has to check the impulse to
be absorbed in the laughable features of the proceedings,
to the exclusion of its really valuable work. The
situation was rich in delightful incongruities ; for the
bulk of the Committee, while admiring Shelley's poetical
genius, seemed quite unaware of the conclusions to
which his principles inevitably led, and of the live
questions which any genuine study of Shelley was certain
to awake. Accordingly, when Mr. G. W. Foote, the

President of the National Secular Society, gave an address before a very large audience on Shelley's religion, the Committee, with a few exceptions, marked their disgust for the lecturer's views, which happened also to be Shelley's, by the expedient of staying away. I think it was on an earlier occasion that Bernard Shaw appalled the company by commencing a speech with the words: " I, as a socialist, an atheist, and a vegetarian . . ." I remember how the honorary secretary, speaking to me afterwards, as to a sympathetic colleague, said that he had always understood that if a man avowed himself an atheist it was the proper thing " to go for him "; but when I pointed out that, whatever might be thought of such a course as a general rule, it would be a little difficult to act on it in a Shelley Society, he seemed struck by my suggestion. Anyhow, we did not go for Shaw; perhaps we knew that he had studied the noble art of self-defence.

Then there was sad trouble on the Committee when Dr. Aveling applied for membership, for the majority decided to refuse it—his marriage relations being similar to Shelley's—and it was only by the determined action of the chairman, Mr W. M. Rossetti, who threatened to resign if the resolution were not cancelled, that the difficulty was surmounted. This was by no means the only occasion on which William Rossetti's sound sense rescued the Society from an absurd and impossible position; but sane as were his judgments in all practical matters, he was himself somewhat lacking in humour, as was made evident by a certain lecture which he gave us on " Shelley and Water "; a title, by the way, which might have been applied, not inaptly, to the sentiments of several of our colleagues. There are, as all Shelley students know, some curious references, in the poems, to death by drowning; and we thought that the lecturer intended to comment on these, and on any passages which might illustrate the love which Shelley felt for sailing on river or sea; we were therefore rather taken aback when we found that the lecture, which was divided into two parts, viz. " Shelley and Salt Water " and " Shelley and Fresh Water," consisted of little more than the quotation of a number of passages   We heard the first part (I forget whether it was the salt or the fresh), and then, at Dr. Furnivall's suggestion, the second was withdrawn. There was comedy in this ; but none the less all lovers of Shelley owe gratitude to Mr. W. M. Rossetti, for he was one of the first critics to understand the real greatness of Shelley's genius, and to appreciate not the poetry alone, but the conceptions by which it was inspired. He likewise did good service in introducing to the public some original writers, Walt Whitman among them, whose recognition might otherwise have been delayed.

But the outstanding figure of the Shelley Society was that of its founder, Dr. F. J. Furnivall, the veteran scholar and sculler, a grand old man whose unflagging ardour in his favourite pursuits might have shamed many enthusiasts who were his juniors by half a century. A born fighter, the vehemence of his disputes with certain men of letters (Swinburne, for example), was notorious ; but personally he was kindness itself, and I have most pleasant recollections of the many visits which I paid him in his house near Primrose Hill, where, sitting in a big arm-chair, he would talk eagerly, as he took tea, over the men he had known or the Societies he had founded. His tea-tray used to be placed on a sort of small bridge which rested on the arms of the chair, and in his excitement over a thrilling anecdote, I have seen him forget that he was thus restricted, and springing forward send tray and tea flying together across the room   He once told me that, for hygienic reasons, he had been a vegetarian for twenty years, and had done the hardest work of his life without flesh-food : then, happening to be confined to the house with sprained ankles, he got out of health by neglecting to reduce his daily diet. Just at that moment a friend sent him a turkey, and he said to himself : " Now, why should this fine bird be wasted, owing to a mere whim of mine ? " Thus had he relapsed into cannibalism as lightly as he relinquished it.

There was an innocence and *naïveté* about Furnivall which at times was almost boyish ; his impetuosity and total lack of discretion made him insensible to other persons' feelings, so that he gave direful offence, and trod on the toes of many good people, without being in the least conscious of it   He ruined the Browning Society, of which he was both founder and *con*founder, by an ill-advised speech about Jesus Christ, in a discussion on " Christmas Eve and Easter Day " ; and in like manner, though with less serious results, he startled his Shelleyan friends, when Prometheus was the subject of debate, by asking in tones of impatience : " *Why* did the fellow allow himself to be chained to the rock ? *Why* didn't he show fight, as I should have done ? " And certainly, when one thinks of it, there would have been trouble in the Caucasus, if Dr. Furnivall had been bidden to play the martyr's part.

Knowing of my connection with Eton, Dr. Furnivall once came to me, in high spirits, with the news that in some researches at the British Museum he had by chance unearthed the fact that Nicholas Udall, a headmaster of Eton in the sixteenth century, and one of the recognized " worthies " of the school, had been convicted of a criminal offence—its nature I must leave my readers to surmise. I had heard this before, but I could not spoil the old man's glee by saying so ; I therefore congratulated him warmly, and asked him, in jest, whether he would not write to Dr. Warre and tell him of so interesting a discovery. " I *have* written to him," he cried ; and then, with a shade of real surprise and disappointment on his face : " But he's not answered me ! "

During the latter part of the Shelley Society's career, when its fortunes were dimmed, and many of

7

its fashionable members had dropped off, we still continued to hold our monthly meetings at University College, Gower Street, and very quaint little gatherings some of them were   The audience at times numbered no more than five or six, and the " proceedings " might have altogether failed had it not been for two or three devoted enthusiasts who never slackened in their attendance   One of these was Mrs. Simpson, an old lady who became to the Shelley Society what Miss Flite was to the Court of Chancery in *Bleak House,* an ever-present spectator and ally.   We all liked and respected her—she was humanitarian as well as Shelleyan—but we were a little embarrassed when her filial piety prompted her to give us copies of her father's writings, a bulky volume entitled *The Works of Henry Heavisides.*   It was a sobering experience to become possessed of that book, the title of which conveyed a true indication of the contents.

The Shelley Centenary (August 4, 1892) marked the climax of the cult which had had so great a vogue in the previous decade.   The local meeting held at Horsham in the afternoon, when Sussex squires and literary gentlemen from London united in an attempt to white-wash Shelley's character—those " shining garments " of his, " so little specked with mire," as one speaker expressed it—was a very hollow affair which contrasted sharply with the London celebration held in the evening at the Hall of Science, when Mr. G W. Foote presided, and Mr Bernard Shaw convulsed the audience by his description of the Horsham apologetics.   An account of both these meetings was written by " G.B.S. " in his best vein, and printed in the *Albemarle Review :*   it was in this article that he made the suggestion that Shelley should be represented, at Horsham, on a bas-relief, " in a tall hat, Bible in hand, leading his children on Sunday morning to the church of his native parish."

That piece of sculpture has never been executed ; but it would hardly have been more inappropriate than the two chief monuments that have been erected, the one in Christchurch Priory, Hants, the other at University College, Oxford ; for what could be less in keeping with the impression left by Shelley's ethereal genius than to figure him, as is done in both these works, as a dead body, stretched limp and pitiful like some suicide's corpse at the Morgue ?   Let us rid our thoughts of all such ghastly and funereal notions of Shelley, and think of him as what he is, the poet not of death but of life,[1] that nobler life to which mankind shall yet attain, when they have learnt, in his own words :

> To live as if to love and live were one.

The most human portrait of Shelley, to my thinking, is the one painted by a young American artist, William West, who met him at Byron's villa near Leghorn, in 1822, and being greatly struck by his personality, made a rough sketch which he afterwards finished and took back to America   There it was preserved after West's death, and reproduced for the first time in the *Century Magazine* in October, 1905, with an explanatory article by its present owner, Mrs John Dunn.   By the courtesy of Mrs. Dunn, I was able to use this portrait as a frontispiece to a revised edition of my study of Shelley, published in 1913.   Mr. Buxton Forman told me that he did not believe in the genuineness of the picture ; but readers of *Letters about Shelley* (1917) will see that Dr. Richard Garnett held a contrary opinion, and so, as I know, did Mr. W M. Rossetti. Some account of West's meeting with Shelley, and of his recollections of Byron, may be found in Henry Theodore Tuckerman's *Book of the Artists*.   His portrait of Byron is well known ; and there seems to be no inherent improbability in the account given of the origin and preservation of the other picture, which

---

[1] It is significant that the title of Edward Carpenter's lines to Shelley : " To a Dead Poet," became, in later editions of *Towards Democracry*, " To One who is where the Eternal are."

certainly impresses one as being more in agreement with
the verbal descriptions of Shelley in his later years
than the almost boyish countenance so familiar in
engravings.

Shelley is the greatest of the poet-pioneers of civilization, and his influence is still very far from having
reached its zenith . he is " the poet of the young " in
the sense that future generations will be better and
better able to understand him.

> Thy wisdom lacks not years, thy wisdom grows
> With *our* growth and the growth of time unborn.[1]

---

[1] *Sonnet to Shelley*, by N. Douglas Deuchar.

VIII

VOICES CRYING IN THE WILDERNESS

I suffer mute and lonely, yet another
Uplifts his voice to let me know a brother
Travels the same wild paths though out of sight.

JAMES THOMSON (B V.).

POETS, as Shelley said, are " the hierophants of an unapprehended inspiration, the mirrors of the gigantic shadows which futurity casts upon the present." The surest solace for the conditions in which men's lives are still lived is to be found in the utterances of those impassioned writers, poets or poet-naturalists as we may call them, who are the harbingers of a higher social state, and, as such, have power to cheer their fellow-beings with the charm of their speech, though it is only by the few that the full purport of their message can be understood. It is of some of these lights in the darkness, these voices crying in the wilderness, that I would now speak.

There would seem, at first sight, to be a great gulf fixed between Shelley and James Thomson, between optimist and pessimist, between the poet of *Prometheus Unbound* whose faith in the future was immutable, and him of *The City of Dreadful Night*, who so despaired of progress as to hold that before we can reform the present we must reform the past. Yet it was on Thomson's shoulders that the mantle of Shelley descended, in so far as they were the singers of free-thought ; and he was one of the earliest of all writers of distinction to apprehend the greatness of that " poet of poets and

purest of men " to whom his own *Vane's Story* was
dedicated. Though we do not assent to the pessimistic contention that we are the product of a past which
has foredoomed human effort to failure, we may still
profit by the *mood* of pessimism, the genuine vein of
sadness that is found in all literatures and felt at times
by all thoughtful men ; for in its due place and proportion it is as real as the contrary mood of joy. Why,
then, should the darker mood be sedulously discountenanced, as if it came from the source of all evil ? It
stands for something ; it is part of us, and it is not to
be arbitrarily set aside.

So wonderful a poem as *The City of Dreadful Night*
needs no apology ; its justification is in its own grandeur
and strength · nor ought such literature to be depressing
in its effect on the reader's mind, but rather (in its
right sphere and relation) a means of enlightenment
and help For whatever the subject and moral of a
poem may be, there is nothing saddening in Art, provided
the form and treatment be adequate ; we are not
discouraged but cheered by any revelation of feeling
that is sincerely and nobly expressed. I hold Thomson,
therefore, pessimist though he was, to have been, by
virtue of his indomitable courage and love of truth,
one of the inspired voices of democracy

Over thirty years ago I was requested by Mr.
Bertram Dobell, Thomson's friend and literary executor,
to write a Life of the poet ; and in the preparation
of that work, which involved a good deal of search for
scattered letters and other biographical material, I was
brought into touch not only with many personal friends
of Thomson, such as Mr. Charles Bradlaugh, Mr G. W.
Foote, Mr and Mrs. Theodore Wright, Mrs H.
Bradlaugh Bonner, Mr. J. W. Barrs, Mr. Charles Watts,
and Mr. Percy Holyoake, but also with some well-
known writers, among them Mr. George Meredith,
Mr. Swinburne, Mr. Watts-Dunton, Mr. W. M. Rossetti,
and Mr William Sharp. I was impressed by the

warm regard in which Thomson's memory was held by those who had known him, the single exception being a sour old landlady in a gloomy London street, of whose remarks I took note as an instance of the strangely vague views held in some quarters as to the function of a biographer. She could give me no information about her impecunious lodger, except that he had " passed away " ; but she added that if I wished to write the Life of a good man, a real Christian, and a total abstainer—here she looked at me dubiously, as if questioning my ability to carry out her suggestion—there was her dear departed husband !

In another case an old friend of Thomson's, who told me many interesting facts about his early life, detained me just as I was taking my departure, and said in a meditative way, as if anxious to recall even the veriest trifle · " I think I remember that Jimmy once wrote a poem on some subject or other." What he imagined to be my object in writing a Life of an obscure Army schoolmaster, except that he *had* written a poem, I did not discover ; perhaps the idea was that the biographer goes about, like the lion, seeking whom he may devour.

In literary circles there has always been a strong prejudice against " B.V.," owing, of course, to his atheistical views and the general lack of " respectability " in his life and surroundings. I was told by Mr William Sharp that, just after the *Life of James Thomson* was published, he happened to be travelling to Scotland in company with Mr. Andrew Lang, and having with him a copy of the book, which he was reviewing for the *Academy*, he tried to engage his companion in talk about Thomson, but was met by a marked disinclination to discuss a subject so uncongenial   I was not surprised at hearing this , but I had been puzzled by a refusal which I received from Mr. Swinburne to allow me to publish a letter which he had addressed to Mr. W. M. Rossetti some years before, in high praise of Thomson's

narrative poem " Weddah and Om-el-Bonain," which
he had described as possessing " forthright triumphant
power." That letter, so Mr. Swinburne wrote to me,
had been inspired by " a somewhat extravagant and
uncritical enthusiasm," and he now spoke in rather
severe reprobation of Thomson, as one who might have
left behind him " a respectable and memorable name."
The word " respectable," coming from the author of
Poems and Ballads, deserves to be noted

About two years later, in 1890, the immediate cause
of this change of opinion on Mr. Swinburne's part was
explained to me by no less an authority than Mr. Watts-
Dunton, who had invited me to pay him a visit in
order to have a talk about Thoreau. During a stroll
on Putney Heath, shared by Mr. Bernard Shaw, Mr.
Watts-Dunton told me the story of James Thomson's
overthrow ; and as the similar downfall of Whitman,
and of some of Swinburne's other early favourites, was
probably brought about in the same manner, the process
is worth relating. Mr. Swinburne, as I have said, had
written in rapturous praise of one of " B V.'s " poems.
One day Mr. Watts-Dunton said to him . " I wish you
would re-read that poem of Thomson's, as I cannot see
that it possesses any great merit." A few days later
Swinburne came to him and said : " You are quite
right. I have re-read ' Weddah and Om-el-Bonain,'
and I find that it has very little value." Watts-
Dunton's influence over his friend was so complete
that there are in fact *two* Swinburnes : the earlier,
democratic poet of the *Songs before Sunrise*, who had
not yet been rescued by Mr. Watts-Dunton ; and the
later, respectable Swinburne, whose bent was for the
most part reactionary. A " lost leader " indeed !
Contrary to the proverb, the appeal, in this case, must
be from Philip sober to Philip drunk.

At the luncheon which followed our walk, Mr.
Swinburne was present, and one could not help observing
that in personal matters, as in his literary views, he

seemed to be almost dependent on Mr. Watts-Dunton : he ran to him with a new book like a poetic child with a plaything. His amiability of manner and courtesy were charming ; but his delicate face, quaint chanting voice, and restlessly twitching fingers, gave an impression of weakness He talked, I remember, of Meredith's *Sandra Belloni* and *Diana of the Crossways*, and complained of their obscurity (" Can you construe them ? ") ; then of his reminiscences of Eton, with friendly inquiries about my father-in-law, the Rev. J. L. Joynes, who had been his tutor and house-master ; also about one of the French teachers, Mr. Henry Tarver, with whom he had been on very intimate terms. Here a few words on the poet's adventures at Eton may not be out of place [1]

It is stated in Gosse's Life of Swinburne that there is no truth in the legend that he was bullied at Eton ; it is, however, a fact that his Eton career was not altogether an untroubled one. Mr Joynes used to tell how Swinburne once came to him before school and begged to be allowed to " stay out," because he was afraid to face some bigger boys who were temporarily attached to his Division—" those dreadful boys," he called them. " Oh, sir, they wear tail coats ! Sir, they are men ! " The request was not granted , but his tutor soothed the boy by reading a Psalm with him, and thus fortified he underwent the ordeal.

One very characteristic anecdote has unfortunately been told incorrectly. Lady Jane Swinburne had come to Eton to see her son, who was ill, and she read Shakespeare to him as he lay in bed. When she left him for a time, a maid, whom she had brought with her, was requested to continue the reading, and she did so, with the result that a glass of water which stood on a table by the bedside was presently dashed over her by the invalid. In the version quoted by his biographer

[1] From a letter on " Swinburne at Eton," *Times Literary Supplement*, December 25, 1919.

the glass of water has become "a pot of jam"—
quite wrongly, as I can testify, for I heard Mr Joynes
tell the story more than once.

Swinburne was not allowed to read Byron or Shelley
while he was at Eton. In Mr. Joynes's house there was
a set of volumes of the old English dramatists, and the
young student urgently begged to be permitted to
read these. "Might he read Ford?" To settle so
difficult a question recourse was had to the advice of
Mr. W. G. Cookesley, a master who was reputed "to
know about everything"; and Mr. Cookesley's judgment was that the boy might read all Ford's plays
except one—the one, of course, which has a title calculated to alarm   But this, it transpired, was one that
he had specially wished to read !

Mr Watts-Dunton has been well described by Mr.
Coulson Kernahan as "a hero of friendship"; and his
personal friendliness was shown not to distinguished
writers only, but to any one whom he could encourage
or help, nor did he take the least offence, however
bluntly his own criticisms were criticized. In reviewing
The City of Dreadful Night, on its first appearance in
book form (1880), he had said that Thomson wrote
in his pessimistic style "because now it is the fashion
to be dreadful," a denial of the sincerity of the poet to
which I referred in my *Life of James Thomson* as one
of the strangest of misapprehensions. When I met
Mr. Watts-Dunton, he alluded to this and other matters
concerning Thomson so genially as to make me wonder
how he could at times have written in so unsympathetic
and unworthy a manner of authors whom he disliked.
Admirers of Walt Whitman, in particular, had reason
to resent the really disgusting things that were said of
him , as when he was likened to a savage befouling
the door-step of the civilized man. That Whitman
himself must have been indignant at the jibes levelled
at him from Putney Heath can hardly be doubted :
I was told by a friend of his that he had been heard to

speak of Swinburne—the *second* Swinburne—as "a damned simulacrum"

Very different from Swinburne's ungenerous attitude to Thomson was that of George Meredith, as may be seen from several of his letters to me, published in the *Life of James Thomson*, and reprinted in *Letters of George Meredith*. A proposal was made that Mr. Meredith should himself write an appreciation of " B.V " ; this he could not do, but he gave me permission to make use of any opinions he had expressed by letter to me or in conversation ; I visited him at Box Hill in 1891, and he talked at great length on that and other subjects. Of Thomson he spoke with feelings akin to affection, exclaiming more than once : " Poor dear fellow ! I bitterly reproach myself that I did not help him more, by getting him work on the *Athenæum.*" But he doubted if he could at that date have been reclaimed : earlier in life he might have been saved, he thought, by the companionship of a woman who would have given him sympathy and aid ; praise, too, which had been the ruin of many writers (he instanced George Eliot and Dickens, with some trenchant remarks about both) would have been good for " B V ," who was so brave and honest. He himself, he said, had often felt what it was to lack all recognition, and sometimes, when he had looked up from his writing and seen a distant field in sunlight, he had thought, " it must be well to be in the warmth " What above all he admired in Thomson was his resolute clear courage. There had been no mention of pessimism in their talk, except that when he had been speaking of the brightest and the darkest moods of Nature, Thomson answered · " I see *no* brightest."

Meredith was evidently repelled by this gospel of despair , he said that the writing of *The City of Dreadful Night* had done its author no good, inasmuch as he there embodied his gloomier images in a permanent form which in turn reacted on him and made him more despondent. He considered " Weddah and Om-el-Bonain " to be Thomson's masterpiece, and the finest narrative poem we have " Where can you find its equal ? " I told him of Swinburne's change of opinion about it, and he said instantly: " You know whose doing *that* is." A playful account followed of the way in which his own poems used to be reviewed by Watts-Dunton in the *Athenæum.* " We always receive anything of Mr. Meredith's with respect." " You know," said Meredith, " what that sort of beginning means." Of late he had ceased to send out review copies of his poems, being sickened by the ineptitude of critics. " There are a good many curates about the country," he added, " and the fact that many of them do a little reviewing in their spare hours does not tend to elevate literature."

Of social problems he spoke with freedom ; most strongly of the certain change that is coming, when women get their economic independence. Infinite mischief comes to the race from loveless marriages. But he anticipated it would take six or more generations for women to rid themselves of the intellectual follies they now inherit from their grandmothers.

At dinner Mr. Meredith talked of his distaste for flesh food, and his esteem for simplicity in all forms, and stated emphatically that it was quite a mistake to suppose that his own experiments in vegetarianism had injured his health Yet, if he were to try that diet again, he knew how his friends would explain to him that it is " impossible to live without meat," or (this in dramatically sarcastic tones) that " if it be possible for *some* persons, it is not possible for *me*." [1] I was

[1] The assertion made in Mr. H. M. Hyndman's *Records of an Adventurous Life* (1911) that Meredith's vegetarianism was " almost the death of him," and that he himself " recognized the truth," viz. that flesh food is a necessity for those who work with mind as well as body, is directly at variance with what Meredith himself told me twenty years nearer the date of the experiment in question.

struck by his great kindliness as host ; he was in fact
over-solicitous for the welfare of vegetarian guests.

The formality and punctiliousness of Mr. Meredith's
manner, with his somewhat ceremonious gestures and
pronunciation, perhaps affected a visitor rather un-
favourably at first introduction ; but after a few minutes
this impression wore off, and one felt only the vivacity
and charm of his conversation. It was a continuous
flow of epigrams, as incisive in many cases as those in
his books ; during which I noticed the intense sensitiveness and expressiveness of his mouth, the lips
curling with irony, as he flung out his sarcasms about
critics, and curates, and sentimentalists of every order.
His eyes were remarkably keen and penetrating, and he
watched narrowly the effect of his points ; so that even
to keep up with him as a listener was a considerable
mental strain.   It was in consequence of my mentioning
this to Mr. Bernard Shaw, a few days later, that he
made his sporting offer that, if he were taken down to
Box Hill, he " would start talking the moment he entered
the house, and not let Meredith get a word in edgeways."
In Mr. S. M. Ellis's biography of Meredith, Shaw is
quoted as saying that the proposal emanated from
Mr. Clement Shorter or myself : this, however, is quite
incorrect, for the suggestion was his own, and much
too reckless to have had any other source.   Such
an encounter, had it taken place, would not have
been, as Shaw flattered himself, a monologue, but a
combat so colossal that one shrinks from speculating on
the result : all that seems certain is that it would have
lasted till the talk-out blow was given, and that upon
the tomb of one or other of the colloquists a *hic tacet*
would have had to be inscribed.

I noticed a certain resemblance in Meredith's profile
to that of Edward Carpenter (it may be seen in some of
the photographs) ; and this was the more surprising
because of the unlikeness of the two men in tempera-
ment, Meredith's cry for " More brain, O Lord, more

brain ! " being in contrast with Carpenter's rather slighting references to " the wandering lunatic Mind." Yet Meredith, too, was an apostle of Nature ; his democratic instincts are unmistakable, though the scenes of his novels are mostly laid in aristocratic surroundings, so that his " cry for simplicity" came " from the very camp of the artificial." This was the view of his philosophy taken by me in an article on " Nature-lessons from George Meredith," published in the *Free Review*, in reference to which Mr. Meredith wrote . " It is pleasant to be appreciated, but the chief pleasure for me is in seeing the drift of my work rightly apprehended."

To Mr. Bertram Dobell, the well-known bookseller, whose name is so closely associated with Thomson's and Traherne's, I was indebted for much information about books and writers of books, given in that cosy shop of his in the Charing Cross Road, which was a place of pleasant recollections for so many literary men   I had especial reason to be grateful to him for directing me to the writings of Herman Melville, whose extraordinary genius, shown in such masterpieces as *Typee* and *The Whale*, was so unaccountably ignored or undervalued that his name is still often confused with that of Whyte Melville or of Herman Merivale. Melville was a great admirer of James Thomson ; this he made plain in several letters addressed to English correspondents, in which he described *The City of Dreadful Night* as the " modern Book of Job under an original form, duskily looming with the same aboriginal verities," and wrote of one of the lighter poems that " *Sunday up the River*, contrasting with the *City of Dreadful Night*, is like a Cuban humming-bird, beautiful in fairy tints, flying against the tropic thunderstorm."

Mr. Dobell was a man of very active mind, and he had always in view some further literary projects   One of these, of which he told me not long before his death, was to write a book about his friend, James Thomson , and it is much to be regretted that this could not be accomplished Another plan—surely one of the strangest ever conceived—was to render or re-write Walt Whitman's poems in the Omar Khayyám stanza · a proposal which reminded me of the beneficent scheme of Fourier, or another of the early communists, to turn the waters of the ocean into lemonade. It is difficult to speak of *Leaves of Grass* and the *Rubáiyát* in the same breath ; yet I once heard the Omar Khayyám poem referred to in a still stranger connection by a clergyman who was the "autocrat of the breakfast table" in a hotel where I was staying Suddenly pausing in his table-talk, he did me the honour of consulting me on a small question of authorship. "I am right, am I not," he said, "in supposing that the translator of Omar Khayyám was—Emerson ? "

Mr Dobell's experiences in book-lore had been long and varied, and he could tell some excellent stories, one of which especially struck me as showing that he had a rare fund of shrewd sense as well as of professional knowledge. He once missed from his shop a very scarce and valuable book, in circumstances which made it a matter of certainty to him that it had been abstracted by a keen collector who had been talking to him that very day, though no word concerning the book had been spoken. Dobell was greatly troubled, until he hit upon a plan which was at once the simplest and most tactful that could have been imagined. Without any inquiry or explanation, he sent in a bill for the book, as in course of business, and the account was duly paid.

Through *Songs of Freedom*, an anthology edited by me in 1892, I came into correspondence with many democratic writers, several of whom, especially Mr. Gerald Massey and Mr W J. Linton, showed much interest in the work and gave me valuable assistance. Dr. John Kells Ingram's famous verses, "The Men of 'Ninety-Eight," were included in the book ; and as curiosity has sometimes been expressed as to how far the sentiments of that poem accorded with the later views of its author, it may be worth mentioning that, in giving me permission to reprint the stanzas, he wrote as follows: "You will not suppose that the effusion of the youth exactly represents the convictions of the man. But I have never been ashamed of having written the verses They were the fruit of genuine feeling" A request for Joaquin Miller's spirited lines, "Sophie Perovskaya," brought me a letter from the veteran author of that very beautiful book, *Life amongst the Modocs* (a work of art worthy to be classed with Herman Melville's *Typee*), which was one of the strangest pieces of penmanship 1 ever received, having the appearance of being written with a piece of wood rather than a pen, but more than compensating by its heartiness for the labour needed in deciphering it : " I thank you cordially ; I am abashed at my audacity long ago, in publishing what I did in dear old England. I hope to do something really worth your reading before I die." But *that* he had done long before.

The liberality with which writers of verse allow their poems to be used in anthologies is very gratifying to an editor ; the more so, as such republication is by no means always a benefit to the authors themselves. Mr. John Addington Symonds was an example of a poet who had suffered much, as he told me, from compilers of anthologies, especially in regard to some lines in his oft-quoted stanzas, " A Vista," which in the original ran thus :

> Nation with nation, land with land,
> Inarmed shall live as comrades free.

" Inarmed " signified linked fraternity, but the word being a strange one was changed in some collections to " *un*armed," and in that easier form had quite escaped from Mr. Symonds's control. This error still continues to be repeated and circulated, and has practically taken the place of the authorized text. Truth, as the saying is, may be great, but it does not always prevail.

Mr. J. A. Symonds, like his friend Mr. Roden Noel, at whose house I met him, was one of those writers who, starting from a purely literary standpoint, came over in the end towards the democratic view of life. His appreciation of Whitman is well known ; and he told me that since he wrote his study of Shelley for the " English Men of Letters " series he had changed some of his views in the more advanced Shelleyan direction.

Robert Buchanan was another of Roden Noel's friends with whom I became acquainted and had a good deal of correspondence. His later writings, owing to their democratic tendencies and extreme outspokenness, received much less public attention than the earlier ones ; in *The New Rome*, in particular, there were a number of trenchant poems denouncing the savageries of an aggressive militarism, and pleading the cause of the weak and suffering folk, whether human or sub-human, against the tyrannous and strong. So marked, in his later years, became Buchanan's humanitarian sympathies, that when his biography was written by Miss Harriett Jay, in 1903, I was asked to contribute a chapter on the subject.

An anthologist, as I have said, meets with much courtesy from poets, yet his path is not altogether a rose-strewn one. When I undertook the work, I was warned by Mr. Bernard Shaw that the only certain result would be that I should draw on myself the concentrated resentment of all the authors concerned : this forecast was far from being verified ; but in one or two instances I did become aware of certain irritable symptoms on the part of poetical acquaintances whose own songs of freedom had unluckily escaped my notice. Then the over-anxiety of some authors as to which of their master-pieces should be included, and which withheld, was at times a trial to an editor. One of my contributors, who had moved in high circles, was con-

8

cerned to think that certain royalties of his acquaintance
might feel hurt by his arraignment of tyrants · " but
if the Czar," he wrote, " takes it home to himself,
I shall be only too delighted." Whether any protest
from the Czar or other crowned heads was received
by the publishers of the Canterbury Poets Series, I
never heard

But if poets are the forerunners of a future society,
to " poet-naturalists " also must a like function be
assigned Of Thoreau, to whom that title was first
and most fittingly given, I have already spoken , and
his was the genius which, to me, next to that of Shelley,
was the most astonishing of nineteenth-century por-
tents , a scion of the future, springing up, like some
alien wild-flower, unclassed and uncomprehended ·
like Shelley's, too, his wisdom is still far ahead of our
age, and destined to be increasingly acknowledged

It was with this thought in mind that I wrote a
biography of Thoreau, in which task I received valuable
aid from his surviving friends, Mr. Harrison Blake,
Mr Daniel Ricketson, Mr Frank B. Sanborn, Dr.
Edward Emerson, and others. With Mr. Sanborn, the
last of the Concord group, I corresponded for nearly
thirty years, and I had several long talks with him on
the occasions of his visiting England · he was a man
of great erudition and extraordinary memory, so that
his store of information amassed in a long life was
almost encyclopedic I learnt much from him about
Concord and its celebrities ; and he collaborated with
me in editing a collection of Thoreau's " Poems of
Nature," which was published in 1895. Mr. Daniel
Ricketson, the " Mr D R " of Emerson's edition of
Thoreau's *Letters*, was another friend to whom I was
greatly indebted , his correspondence with me was
printed in a memorial volume, *Daniel Ricketson and his
Friends*, in 1902. By no one was I more helped and
encouraged than by that most ardent of Thoreau-
students, Dr. Samuel A Jones, of Ann Arbor, Michigan,

who, with his fellow-enthusiast, Mr Alfred W Hosmer, of Concord, sent me at various times a large amount of *Thoreauana*, and enabled me to make a number of corrections and amplifications in a later edition of the *Life*. It was through our common love of Thoreau that I first became acquainted with Mr. W. Sloane Kennedy, of Belmont, Massachusetts, a true nature-lover with whom I have had much pleasant and friendly intercourse both personally and by letter.

Richard Jefferies, unlike Shelley or Thoreau, was so far a pessimist as to believe that " lives spent in doing good have been lives nobly wasted " ; but while convinced that " the whole and the worst the worst pessimist could say is far beneath the least particle of the truth, so immense is the misery of man," he could yet feel the hope of future amelioration " Full well aware that all has failed, yet side by side with the sadness of that knowledge, there yet lives on in me an unquenchable belief, thought burning like the sun, that there is yet something to be found, something real, something to give each separate personality sunshine and flowers in its own existence now." If ever there was an inspired work, a real book of prophecy, such a one is Jefferies's *Story of my Heart*, in which, with his gaze fixed on a future society, where the term *pauper* (" inexpressibly wicked word ") shall be unknown, he speaks in scathing condemnation of the present lack of just and equitable distribution, which keeps the bulk of the human race still labouring for bare sustenance and shelter.

In a study of Jefferies's life and ideals, published in 1894, I drew attention to the marked change that came over his views, during his later years, on social and religious questions, a ripening of thought, accompanied by a corresponding growth of literary style, which can be measured by the great superiority of *The Story* over such books as *The Gamekeeper at Home* ; and in connection with this subject I pointed out that the incident recorded by Sir Walter Besant in his

Eulogy of Richard Jefferies of a death-bed return to the
Christian faith, at a time when Jefferies was physically
and intellectually a wreck, could not be accepted as
in any way reversing the authoritative statement of
his religious convictions which he had himself published
in his *Story.* For this I was taken to task in several
papers as having perverted biography in the interest
of my own prejudiced opinions ; but under this censure,
not to mention that my views were shared by those
friends and students of Jefferies with whom I was
brought in touch, I had one unsuspected source of
consolation in the fact that Sir Walter Besant told me
in private correspondence that, from what he had learnt
since the publication of his *Eulogy,* he was convinced
that I was quite right. I did not make this public
until many years later, when a new edition of my book
appeared : there was then some further outcry in a
section of the press ; but this was not repeated when
Mr. Edward Thomas, in the latest and fullest biography
of Jefferies, dismissed the supposed conversion as a
wrong interpretation by " narrow sectarians " who
ignored the work of Jefferies's maturity.

I have thought it worth while to refer to these facts,
not that they are themselves important, but as illustrating a Christianizing process which is often carried on with
boundless effrontery by " religious " writers after the
death of free-thinkers. Another instance may be seen
in the case of Francis W. Newman, where a similar
attempt was made to represent him as having abandoned
his own deliberate convictions.

From Jefferies one's thoughts pass naturally to
Mr. W. H. Hudson   It must be over twenty-five years
since through the hospitality of Mrs. E Phillips, of
Croydon, an ardent bird-lover and humanitarian, I had
the good fortune to be introduced to Mr. Hudson and
to his books. A philosopher and keen observer of all
forms of life, he is far from being an ornithologist only ;
but there are certain sympathies that give rise to a sort

of natural freemasonry among those who feel them ; and of these one of the pleasantest and most human is the love of birds—not of cooked birds, if you please, associated with dining-room memories of " the pleasures of the table," nor of caged birds in drawing-rooms, nor of stuffed birds in museums ; but of real birds, live birds, wild birds, free to exercise their marvellous faculties of flight and song From this love has sprung a corresponding bird-literature ; and of the notable names among the prophets and interpreters of bird life, the latest, and in my opinion the greatest, is that of Mr. Hudson : his books, in not a few chapters and passages, rise above the level of mere natural history, and affect the imagination of the reader as only great literature can. If he is an unequal writer and somewhat desultory, perhaps, in his manner of work, yet at his best he is the greatest living master of English prose. Such books as *The Naturalist in La Plata* and *Nature in Downland* (to name two only) are classics that can never be forgotten. And Mr. Hudson's influence, it should be noted, has been thrown more and more on the side of that humane study of natural history which Thoreau adopted . his verdict is given in no uncertain language against the barbarous habits of game-keeper and bird-catcher, fashionable milliner, and amateur collector of " specimens."

If a single title were to be sought for Mr. Hudson's writings, the name of one of his earlier books, *Birds and Man*, might be the most appropriate ; for there seems almost to be a mingling of the avian with the human in his nature I have sometimes fancied that he must be a descendant of Picus, or of some other prehistoric hero who was changed into a bird There is a passage in Virgil's *Æneid* where Diomede is represented as lamenting, as a " fearful prodigy," such metamorphosis of his companions.

> Lost friends, to birds transfigured, skyward soar,
> Or fill the rocky wold with wailing cries.

But if such a vicissitude were to befall any of Mr Hudson's friends, I feel sure that, far from being dismayed by it, he would be able to continue his acquaintance with them on terms of entire understanding : they would in no sense be " lost " because they were feathered.   To him a much more fearful prodigy is the savage fashion of wearing the skins and feathers of slaughtered birds as ornamental head-gear.

One of the most devoted followers of this new school of natural history, and himself a naturalist of distinction, was Dr Alexander H. Japp, who, under the pen-name of " H. A. Page," wrote the first account of Thoreau published in this country   I have a recollection of many pleasant chats with him, especially of a visit which he paid me with Mr. Walton Ricketson, the sculptor, a son of that intimate friend of Thoreau's of whom I have spoken   Walton Ricketson was a boy at the time when Thoreau used to visit his father at New Bedford ; but he was present on the occasion when the grave hermit of Walden surprised the company by a sudden hilarious impulse, which prompted him to sing " Tom Bowling " and to perform an improvised dance, in which, it is said, he kept time to the music but executed some steps more like those of the Indians than the usual ballroom figures.

Dr Japp was also a biographer of De Quincey, and by his sympathetic understanding did much to correct the disparaging judgments passed on " the English opium-eater " by many critics and press-writers.   As a result of a study of De Quincey which I published in 1904, I made the acquaintance, three years later, of Miss Emily de Quincey (she spelt her name in that manner), his last surviving daughter.   She was a most charming old lady, full of vivacity and humour ; and her letters, of which I received a good many, were written with a sprightliness recalling that of her father in his lighter moods ; some of her reminiscences, too, were very interesting   She remembered the opium decanter and glass standing on the mantelpiece when she was a child, but she said that De Quincey quite left off the use of the drug for years before his death She told me that the grudge against her father, which frequently found expression in "grotesque descriptions" of him, was caused in part by his neglect to answer the letters, many of a very flattering kind, addressed to him by readers of his books ; a remissness which was due, not to any lack of courtesy or gratitude, but to his inveterate procrastination ; he would always be going to write "to-morrow" or "when he had a good pen." On one occasion an admirer wrote to him from Australia, begging him for "some truths" that he might give to his little son (who had been named after De Quincey) when he should be able to understand them. De Quincey said sadly to his daughter . "My dear, truths are very low with me just now. Do you think, if I sent a couple of lies, they would answer the purpose ? " She feared that he never sent either truths or lies Among the unanswered letters which her father received she recollected that there was one from " three brothers," accompanied by a volume of poems by "Currer, Ellis and Acton Bell." It was by the poetry of Ellis that the De Quinceys were most struck, but not till years afterwards did they guess that those " brothers " were the Brontë sisters in disguise.

Were it not a common practice of reviewers, in estimating the work of a great writer, to omit, as far as possible, any mention of humane sympathies shown by him, it would be strange that De Quincey should be represented as a mere "dreamer" and visionary ; for in truth, in spite of the transcendental Toryism of his politics, he was in several respects a pioneer of advanced humanitarian thought, especially in the question of corporal punishment, on which he spoke, a hundred years ago, with a dignity and foresight which might put to shame many purblind "progressives" of to-day. His profound regard for a suffering humanity is one of the noblest features in his writings ; he rejoiced, for instance, at the interference of Parliament to amend the " ruinous social evil " of female labour in mines ; and he spoke of the cruelty of that spirit which could look " lightly and indulgently on the affecting spectacle of female prostitution." " All I have ever had enjoyment of in life," he said, " seems to rise up to reproach me for my happiness, when I see such misery, and think there is so much of it in the world " It is amusing to read animadversions on De Quincey's " lack of moral fibre," written by critics who lag more than a century behind him in some of the matters that afford an unequivocal test of man's advance from barbarism to civilization

IX

A LEAGUE OF HUMANENESS

Hommes, soyez humains. C'est votre premier devoir. Quelle sagesse y a-t-il pour vous, hors de l'humanité.—ROUSSEAU.

FROM the vaticinations of poets and prophets I now return to the actualities of the present state. Thirty years ago there were already in existence a number of societies which aimed at the humanizing of public opinion, in regard not to war only but to various other savage and uncivilized practices. The Vegetarian Society, founded in 1847, advocated a radical amendment; and the cause of zoophily, represented by the Royal Society for the Prevention of Cruelty to Animals, had been strengthened by the establishment of several Anti-Vivisection Societies. In like manner the philanthropic tendencies of the time, with respect to prison management and the punishment or reclamation of offenders, were reflected in the work of the Howard Association.

The purpose of the Humanitarian League, which was formed in 1891, was to proclaim a *general* principle of humaneness, as underlying the various disconnected efforts, and to show that though the several societies were necessarily working on separate lines, they were nevertheless inspired and united by a single bond of fellowship. The promoters of the League saw clearly that barbarous practices can be philosophically condemned on no other ground than that of the broad democratic sentiment of universal sympathy. Humanity and science between them have exploded the time-honoured idea of a hard-and-fast line between white man and black man, rich man and poor man, educated man and uneducated man, good man and bad man : equally impossible to maintain, in the light of newer knowledge, is the idea that there is any difference in kind, and not in degree only, between human and non-human intelligence The emancipation of men from cruelty and injustice will bring with it in due course the emancipation of animals also. The two reforms are inseparably connected, and neither can be fully realized alone.

We were well aware that a movement of this character would meet with no popular support ; on the contrary, that those who took part in it would be regarded as " faddists " and " visionaries " , but we knew also that the direct opposite of this was the truth, and that while we were supposed to be merely building " castles in the air," we were in fact following Thoreau's most practical advice, and *putting the foundations under them*. For what is " the basis of morality," as laid down by so great a thinker as Schopenhauer, except this very doctrine of a comprehensive and reasoned sympathy ?

A year or two before the founding of the League, I had read at a meeting of the Fabian Society a paper on " Humanitarianism," which afterwards formed a starting-point for the League's publications The idea of a humane society, with a wider scope than that of any previously existing body, was suggested by Mr. Howard Williams ; and it was at the house of a very true friend of our cause, Mrs. Lewis (now Mrs. Drakoules), in Park Square, London, that a small group of persons, among whom were Mrs. Lewis, Mr Edward Maitland, Mr Howard Williams, Mr Kenneth Romanes, and the present writer,[1] assembled, early in 1891, to draw up a

[1] Here perhaps I had better say that my own work for the League, though mostly private and anonymous, was continuous during the twenty-nine years of the League's existence ; so

manifesto and to launch the Humanitarian League.
The title " humanitarian " was chosen because, though
fully aware of certain objections to the word, we felt
that it was the only term which sufficiently expressed
our meaning, and that, whether a good name or a bad
name, it must be taken up, like a gauntlet, by those
who intended to fight for the cause which it denotes.

For it was to be a fighting, not a talking Society
that the League was designed, even if it were a forlorn
hope. In an interesting letter, read at the first meeting,
the opinion was expressed by our veteran friend,
Professor Francis W. Newman, that the time was not
ripe for such a venture as the assertion of a humanitarian
ethic ; but we came to the conclusion that however
small a beginning might be made, much good would be
done by a systematic protest against the numerous
barbarisms of the age—the cruelties inflicted by men on
men, and the still more atrocious ill-treatment of the
lower animals

Edward Maitland, who, in spite of his advanced
years, took a good deal of interest in our meetings,
had had rather a remarkable career as traveller, writer,
and mystic ; and his earlier book, *The Pilgrim and the
Shrine,* had been widely read. Those who knew him
only as occultist would have been surprised to see how
extremely critical he was—to the verge of fastidious-
ness—in discussing practical affairs ; there was no one
on that committee more useful in bringing the cold
light of reason to bear on our consultations than the
joint-author of, Dr Anna Kingsford's very strange
revelations. At the time I knew him, he was writing
his *magnum opus*, the Life of Anna Kingsford, and he
would often discourse to me freely, after a committee
meeting, on his spiritual experiences, to the astonish-
ment, perhaps, of our fellow-travellers by rail or tram

that in describing the various aspects of the movement I am
writing of what I know. The opinions expressed are, of course,
only personal, as in the remarks about the war (Chap. XV).

on one occasion he described to me on the top of an omnibus how he had been privileged to be a beholder of the Great White Throne. There was something in these narrations so natural and genuine as to compel the respectful attention of the listener, whatever his personal belief might be as to the reality of the visions described.

Mr. Howard Williams, on the other hand, was as pronounced a rationalist as Maitland was a mystic, and one who by word and by pen, in private and in public, was a quiet but untiring champion of the humanitarian cause. His *Ethics of Diet*, which had the honour, at a later date, of being highly commended by Tolstoy, whose essay entitled "The First Step" was written as a preface to his Russian translation of the book, is a veritable mine of knowledge, which ranges over every period of history and covers not only the subject of humane dietetics but the whole field of man's attitude toward the non-human races · if Ethical Societies were intended to be anything more than places of debate, they would long ago have included this work among their standard text-books. For the writing of such a treatise, Mr. Williams was specially qualified by the fact that with a wide classical knowledge he united in a remarkable degree the newer spirit and enthusiasm of humanity; he was in the truest sense a student and professor of *literæ humaniores*. It is difficult to estimate precisely the result of labours such as his; but that they have had an appreciable influence upon the growth of a more humane public opinion is not to be doubted.

The Committee was gradually strengthened by the inclusion of such experienced workers as the Rev. J. Stratton, Colonel W. Lisle B. Coulson, Mrs. L. T. Mallet, Mr. J. Frederick Green, Miss Elizabeth Martyn, the first secretary of the League, and Mr. Ernest Bell, a member of the well-known publishing firm and now President of the Vegetarian Society, who for over twenty years was a bulwark of strength as chairman and treasurer. A campaign against the Royal Buckhounds had at once commanded respect ; the pamphlets were well noticed in the press—better, perhaps, in those days, when they were still a novelty, than later, when they were taken as a matter of course—some successful meetings were held, and the general interest shown in the League's doings was out of all proportion to its numerical strength.

It was in 1895 that the second phase of the League's career began with the acquirement of an office in Great Queen Street, and the institution of a monthly journal, *Humanity*, so-called at first because its later title, *The Humanitarian*, was at that time appropriated elsewhere. The holding of a National Humanitarian Conference, at St. Martin's Town Hall, in the same year, was the first big public effort that the League had made, and attracted a good deal of attention ; and the scope of the work was considerably extended by the appointment of special departments for dealing with such subjects as Sports, Criminal Law and Prison Reform, Humane Diet and Dress, and the Education of Children ; and by a much wider use of the press as a medium for propaganda, in which sphere the League was now able to avail itself of the services of Mr. Joseph Collinson, whose numerous press letters soon became a distinctive feature of its work. In the summer of 1897 the League shifted its headquarters to Chancery Lane. where it remained till it was brought to an end in 1919.

The League was soon engaged in controversies of various kinds. A little book entitled *Animals' Rights*, which I wrote at the request of my friend, Mr. Ernest Bell, and which was published by his firm in 1892, led to a great deal of discussion, and passed through numerous editions, besides being translated into French, German, Dutch, Swedish, and other languages. Among its earliest critics was Professor D. G. Ritchie, who, in his work on *Natural Rights*, maintained that though

" we may be said to have duties of *kindness towards* the animals, it is incorrect to represent these as strictly *duties towards* the animals themselves, as if they had rights against us." (The italics are Mr. Ritchie's.) There is a puzzle for you, reader. I took it to mean that, in man's duty of kindness, it is the kindness only that has reference to the animals, the duty being a private affair of the man's; the convenience of which arrangement is that the man can shut off the kindness whenever it suits him to do so, the kindness being, as it were, the water, and the duty the tap. For instance, when the question of vivisection arose, Mr. Ritchie at once turned off the water of kindness, though it had been very liberally turned on by him when he gave approval to the humanitarian protests against the barbarities of sport.

To this sophistical hair-splitting, in a matter of much practical importance, we from the first refused to yield, and made it plain that it was no battle of words in which we were engaged but one of ethical conduct, and that while we were quite willing to exchange the term "rights" for a better one, if better could be found, we would not allow the concept either of human "duties" or of animals' "rights" to be manipulated in the manner of which Mr. Ritchie's book gave a conspicuous example. Meanwhile the word "rights" held the field

The old Catholic school was, of course, antagonistic to the recognition of animals' rights, and we had controversies with Monsignor John S. Vaughan, among other sacerdotalist writers, when he laid down the ancient proposition that "beasts exist for the use and benefit of man." It may be doubted whether argument is not a pure waste of time, when there is a fundamental difference of opinion as to data and principles: the sole reason for such debate was to ensure that the humanitarian view of the question was rightly placed before the public, and to show how strange was the alliance between sacerdotalist and vivisector. Evolutionary science has demonstrated beyond question the kinship of all sentient life ; yet the scientist, in order to rake together a moral defence for his doings, condescends to take shelter under the same plea as the theologian, and having got rid of the old anthropocentric fallacy in the realm of science avails himself of that fallacy in the realm of ethics a progressive in one branch of thought, he is still a medievalist in another.

Thus scientist and sacerdotalist between them would perpetuate the experimental tortures of the laboratory. *Laborare est orare* was the old saying ; now it should be expanded by the Catholic school of vivisectionists into *laboratorium est oratorium ·* the house of torture is the house of prayer. It is a beautiful and touching scene of reconciliation, this meeting of priest and professor over the torture-trough of the helpless animal. They might exclaim in Tennyson's words :

> There above the little grave,
> O there above the little grave,
> We kissed again with tears.

More exhilarating was the discussion when Mr. G. K. Chesterton entered the lists as champion of those high prerogatives of Mankind, which he saw threatened by the sinister devices of humanitarians, who, as he has explained in one of his books, " uphold the claims of all creatures against those of humanity." A debate with Mr. Chesterton took place in the Essex Hall ; and for several years afterwards the argument was renewed at times, as, for instance, when reviewing a book of mine on *The Logic of Vegetarianism,* he insisted[1] that " the difference between our moral relation to men and to animals is not a difference of degree in the least · it is a difference of kind." The human race, he held, is a definite society, different from everything else. " The man who breaks a cat's back breaks a cat's back. The

[1] *Daily News,* April 10, 1906.

man who breaks a man's back breaks an implied treaty."
To us, this terse saying of Mr. Chesterton's seemed to
contain unintentionally the root of all cruelty to animals,
the quintessence of anthropocentric arrogance. The man
who breaks a cat's back, breaks a cat's back. Yes,
and the scientist who vivisects a dog, vivisects a dog ;
the sportsman who breaks up a hare, breaks up a hare.
That is all. The victims are not human. But it is a
distinction which has caused, in savage hands, the
immemorial ill-usage of the lower animals through the
length and breadth of the world.

Perhaps the strangest of Mr. Chesterton's charges
against humanitarians was one which he made in his
book *Orthodoxy*, that their trend is " to touch fewer
and fewer things," i.e. to abstain from one action after
another until they are left in a merely negative position.
He failed to see that while we certainly desire to touch
fewer and fewer things with whip, hob-nailed boot,
hunting-knife, scalpel, or pole-axe, we equally desire
to get into touch with more and more of our fellow-
beings by means of that sympathetic intelligence which
tells us that they are closely akin to ourselves Why,
ultimately, do we object to such practices as vivisection,
blood-sports, and butchery ? Because of the cruelty
inseparable from them, no doubt ; but also because of
the hateful narrowing of our own human pleasures
which these barbarous customs involve. A recognition
of the rights of animals implies no sort of disparagement
of human rights . this indeed was clearly indicated in
the sub-title of my book, *Animals' Rights* " considered
in relation to social progress."

During the winter of 1895-96, a course of lectures
on " Rights," as viewed from various standpoints—
Christian, ethical, secularist, scientific, theosophical, and
humanitarian—was organized by the Humanitarian
League ; and of these perhaps the most significant was
Mr. Frederic Harrison's address on the ethical view,
in which it was maintained that " man's morality

towards the lower animals is a vital and indeed
fundamental part of his morality towards his fellow-
men " At this same meeting some discussion arose
on the far from unimportant question of nomenclature,
objection being taken to Mr Harrison's use of the term
" brute," which he, on his part, defended as being
scientifically correct, and, in the sense of " inarticulate,"
wholly void of offence, even when applied to such highly
intelligent beings as the elephant, the horse, or the dog.
Humanitarians, however, have generally held that the
meaning of the word " brute," in this connection, is not
" inarticulate " but " irrational," and that for this
reason it should be discarded, on the ground that to
call an animal a brute, or irrational, is the first step
on the path to treating him accordingly. " Give a dog
a bad name," says the proverb ; and directly follows
the injunction : " and hang him."

For like reasons the Humanitarian League always
looked with disfavour on the expression " dumb
animals," because, to begin with, animals are not dumb,
and secondly, nothing more surely tends to their
depreciation than thus to attribute to them an unreal
deficiency or imperfection . such a term may be meant
to increase our pity, but in the long run it lessens what
is more important, our respect. In this matter the
League was glad to have the support of Mr. Theodore
Watts-Dunton, who, as long ago as 1877, had written
satirically in the *Athenæum* of what he called " the
great human fallacy " conveyed in the words " the
dumb animals," and had pointed out that animals
are no more dumb than men are. Years afterwards he
wrote to me to inquire about the authorship of an
article in the *Humanitarian* in which the same conclusion
was reached, and expressed his full sympathy with our
point of view.

But much more difficult to contend with than any
anti-humanitarian arguments is the dull dead weight of
that unreasoning prejudice which cannot see consan-

guinity except in the conventional forms, and simply
does not comprehend the statement that " the animals "
are our fellow-beings. There are numbers of good and
kindly folk with whom, on this question, one never
reaches the point of difference at all, but is involved
in impenetrable misapprehensions: there may be
talking on either side, but communication there is none.
Tell them, in Howard Moore's words, that the non-
human beings are " not conveniences but cousins," and
they will answer, assentingly, that they are all in favour
of " kindness to animals "; after which they will
continue to treat them not as cousins but as conveniences.
This impossibility of even making oneself intelligible
was brought home to me with great force, some years
ago, in connection with the death of a very dear friend,
a cat, whose long life of fifteen years had to be ended
in the chloroform-box owing to an incurable ailment.
The veterinary surgeon whose aid I invoked was an
extremely kind man, for whose skill I shall always
feel grateful; and from his patience and sympathetic
manner I thought he partly understood what the occasion
meant to me—that, like a human death-bed, it was a
scene that could never pass from the mind. It was,
therefore, with something of an amused shock that I
recollected, after he had gone, what I had hardly
noticed at the moment, that he had said to me, as he
left the door " You'll be wanting a new pussy-cat
soon."

Richard Jefferies has remarked that the belief that
animals are devoid of reason is rarely held by those
who themselves labour in the fields " It is the cabinet-
thinkers who construct a universe of automatons."
One is cheered now and then by hearing animals spoken
of, quite simply and naturally, as rational beings. I
once made the acquaintance, in the Lake District,
of an old lady living in a roadside cottage, who had for
her companion, sitting in an armchair by the fire, a
lame hen, named Tetty, whom she had saved and reared

from chicken-hood.   Some years later, as I passed that
way, I called and inquired after Tetty, but learnt that
she was dead.   "Ah, poor Tetty!" said the dame,
as tears fell from her eyes, "she passed away several
months ago, quite conscious to the end."   That to
attribute to a dying bird the self-consciousness which
is supposed to be the special prerogative of mankind,
should, to the great majority of persons, appear nothing
less than comical, is a measure of the width of that gulf
which religion has delved between "the beasts that
perish" and the Christian with his "soul" to save.

But it is not often that one hears of a case like that
of Tetty : as a rule, disappointment lurks in the hopes
that flatter the humanitarian mind.   We had a neighbour in Surrey, an old woman living in an adjoining
cottage, who professed full adherence to our doctrine
that cats should not be allowed to torture captured
birds.   "I always take them away from my cat : I
can't bear to see them suffering," she said.   We warmly
approved of this admirable sentiment   But then, as
she turned aside, she added quietly :   "Unless, of
course, they're sparrows."

A year or two ago the papers described a singular
accident at a railway station, where a cow got on the
line and was wedged between the platform and a
moving train   the cow, we were told, was killed, "but
fortunately there was no personal injury"—a view of
the occurrence which seemed, to a humanitarian, still
stranger than the accident itself.

Here, again, is an instance of unintended humour :
"Homeward Bound" as the title of a cheerful picture
in which a bronzed sailor is represented returning from
the tropics, carrying—a caged parrot.

It is this traditional habit of regarding the lower
animals not as persons and fellow-beings, but as
automata and "things," that lies behind the determined refusal to recognize that they have rights, and is
thus ultimately responsible for much of the callousness

with which they are treated. With this superstition
the League was in conflict from the first.

But perhaps some of my readers may still think that
time spent on the rights of animals is so much taken
away from the great human interests that are at stake.
Let us help men first, they may argue, and then, when
mankind is righted, we can help the animals after.
On the other hand, there are some zoophilists who take
the contrary view that men can help themselves, and
that it is the animals first and foremost who need aid
and protection   The League's opinion was that both
these arguments are mistaken, and, for the same reason,
viz. that, in our complex modern society, all great
issues of justice or injustice are crossed and inter-
mingled, so that no one cruelty can be singled out as
the source of all other cruelties, nor can any one reform
be fully realized apart from the rest. By "humanitarian"
we meant one who feels and acts humanely, not towards
mankind only, or the lower animals only, but towards
all sentient life—one who adopts the Humanitarian
League's principle that "it is iniquitous to inflict
avoidable suffering on any sentient being." We did
not regard as humanitarians, for example, those
"philanthropic" persons who, having made a fortune
by commercial competition, in which the depreciation
of wages was a recognized method, afterwards gave back
a portion of their wealth in "charity" This might,
perhaps, be philanthropy, but it did not seem to be
quite humanity   Nor did we think that the name
"humanitarian" should be given to those zoophilists
or animal lovers who keep useless and pampered animals
as pets and playthings, wasting on them time and money
which might be better spent elsewhere, and indeed
wasting the lives of the animals themselves, for animals
have their own lives to live as men have.

Perhaps the most able of all vindications of humane
principles is that contained in Mr Howard Moore's
The Universal Kinship, published by the League in

1906. It was through a notice which I wrote in the *Humanitarian* of an earlier book of his, *Better-World Philosophy*, that the League first came into association with him, and I remember with shame that when that "sociological synthesis," as its sub-title proclaimed it to be, first came into my hands, I nearly left it unread, suspecting it to be but the latest of the many wearisome ethical treatises that are a scourge to the reviewer, to whom the very word "sociology" or "synthesis" is a terror But fortunately I read the book, and quickly discovered its merits ; and from that time, till his death in 1916, Howard Moore was one of the truest and tenderest of our friends, himself prone to despondency and, as his books show, with a touch of pessimism, yet never failing in his support and encouragement of others and of all humanitarian effort. "What on earth would we Unusuals do, in this lonely dream of life," so he wrote in one of his letters, "if it were not for the sympathy and friendship of the Few ? "

Howard Moore died by his own hand (he had good reason for his action), and the timorous attitude which so many people adopt towards suicide was shown in the silence on this point which was maintained in most of the English zoophilist journals which mentioned his death : one editor hit upon the sagacious announcement that "he died very suddenly," which deserves, I think, to be noted as a consummate instance of how the truth may be truthfully obscured.

In *The Universal Kinship*, Howard Moore left to humanitarians a treasure which it will be their own fault if they do not value as it deserves. There is a tendency to forget that it is to modern evolutionary science that the ethic of humaneness owes its strongest corroboration. The physical basis of the humane philosophy rests on the biological fact that kinship is universal. Starting from this admitted truth, Moore showed, with much wealth of argument and epigram, that the supposed psychical gulf between human and non-human has no more existence, apart from the imagination of man, than the physical gulf which has now been bridged by science. The purpose of our movement was admirably stated by him : " to put science and humanitarianism in place of tradition and savagery." It was with that aim in view that our League of Humaneness had been formed.

X

TWENTIETH-CENTURY TORTURES

Why not bring back at once the boot, the stake, and the thumbscrew ?—PROFESSOR LAWSON TAIT.

IT is among the proudest boasts of this country that torture is not permitted within its borders "Torture," wrote Macaulay, " was inflicted for the last time in the month of May, 1640." But pleasant though it is to think that it was in the beautiful springtime that the barbarous practice came to an end, this is unfortunately one of the cases in which our people allow themselves to be beguiled and fooled by very transparent quibbles ; for a few minutes' thought would suffice to convince the most complacent of Britons that while some specialized forms of judicial torture have been abandoned, other tortures, some of them not less painful and fully as repulsive, are being inflicted to this day— nearly three hundred years after the glorious date of abolition For if " torture," as etymology and the dictionaries and common usage tell us, means nothing more or less than the forcible infliction of extreme pain, it is not a technicality but an absurdity to pretend that it finds no place among twentieth-century institutions.

Flogging is torture in a most literal sense, and in one of its grossest shapes : the " cat," as Mr. G K. Chesterton has well said, is " the rack without any of its intellectual reasons "[1] The horror of the old naval

[1] *Daily News*, June 6, 1908

and military lashings is within the memory of many officers who were compelled to witness them how is the punishment any less savage in its nature because it is now administered in a less severe degree, and on men convicted of robbery with violence or some breach of prison discipline ? In one of the Parliamentary debates of November, 1912, a Member who had been invited by the Home Secretary to examine the " cat," gave it as his opinion that " if *that* is not torture, then I do not know what torture is."

In the gloomiest but most impressive of his stories, *The Island of Dr. Moreau*, Mr. H. G. Wells has represented his savage " beast-folk " as monotonously chanting a certain " idiotic formula " about the infallibility of " the Law " With nothing more fitly than with this can be compared the undying legend, now over half a century old, that " garrotting was put down by the lash." It is not often that a popular fallacy, however erroneous it may be, can be actually disproved ; but in this particular case such refutation was possible, in the certified fact that the garrotting " epidemic " of 1862 had been suppressed by the ordinary law *before* flogging for that offence was legalized For many years the Humanitarian League issued a public challenge on the subject, and made the facts known in thousands of press letters ; the challenge was quietly ignored, and the false statement repeated, till it was plain that, as De Quincey remarked, " rarer than the phœnix is that virtuous man who will consent to lose a prosperous story on the consideration that it happens to be a lie." One such virtuous man, however, and one only, was found, namely, Mr. Montague Crackanthorpe, who actually recanted the statement which he could not substantiate [1] In view of his unique candour, it was suggested after his death that a statue should be erected to his memory.

Very different from the course taken by Mr.

[1] *The Times*, December 11 and 26, 1902

Crackanthorpe was the action of Sir Alexander Wood Renton, of the Supreme Court of Ceylon, who, in an article on " Corporal Punishment," introduced into the *Encyclopædia Britannica* of 1910 that very garrotting legend from which it had previously been kept free, and made the further mistake of giving the date of the Flogging Act of 1863 as 1861, thus lending to his blunder a misleading appearance of plausibility. When called to account, he was content to maintain a masterly silence—more eloquent than words—and to allow his misstatement, unacknowledged and uncorrected, to continue to keep alive a prevalent superstition. Can it be wondered that such fallacies persist, when a Chief Justice will thus lie low rather than admit himself at fault ?

It is an amusing fact, and far too little known, that the text which has long lent a sanctity to the use of corporal punishment, is not taken, as supposed, from the *Proverbs* of Solomon, but from a passage, and a rather unseemly one, in Butler's *Hudibras* (1663) [1] this, however, is as it should be, for it is fitting that an indecent practice should claim authority from an indecent source Thus encouraged, and with 'this divine precept in their thoughts, parents and school-masters, and magistrates, and judges, and all governors and rulers, have felt that in wielding the rod they were discharging a religious obligation, and not, as might otherwise have been suspected, gratifying some very primitive instincts of their own. For " the Wisdom of Solomon " has been quoted as our guide, in the correction of the old as well as of the young ; indeed, as a writer in the *People* sagely remarked, " the older the evil-doer, the more his need of the birch." On this principle, aged vagrants have on various occasions been sentenced to be corrected with the rod ; but it

[1] Then spare the rod and spoil the child.
          Hudibras, Part II, canto 1, 844.

is to the young that the blessings of the birch more
properly belong.

> Our British boys, from shore to shore,
>   Two priceless boons may find :
> The Flag that's ever waved before,
>   The Birch that's waved behind

In its campaign against flogging in the Royal Navy,
the Humanitarian League gained not only a considerable
success, but an amount of entertainment which of
itself would have more than repaid the labour expended
on the work.   To begin with, there was the technical
quibble, very characteristic of officialdom, that though
the backs of boys, or rather of young men, might be
cut into ribbons with the birch, there was no " flogging "
in the Navy, for " flogging " meant the infliction not
of the birch but of the " cat."   With Mr. Swift MacNeill
conducting the attack in the House of Commons, it
may be imagined that such prevarications—and there
were many similar instances—fared but badly ; and it
was no surprise when " these degrading practices," as
Sir Henry Campbell-Bannerman described them, were
brought to an end in 1906, though the use of the cane,
to the discredit of the Admiralty, is still permitted and
defended.

In this long controversy the League was brought into
conflict with all sorts of opponents, among them several
Admirals, of whom the " breeziest " were the Hon V. A.
Montagu and Sir William Kennedy.   With the latter
especially we had great fun, as we found in him an
antagonist of the utmost heartiness and good humour.
" Of what use is it," he wrote to me, " sending me all
this rubbish, except to fill the waste-paper basket ?
I don't care a damn for Admiral ——'s opinion."   On
another occasion he sent me a formal challenge to meet
him " at any time and place, when pistols and coffee
will be provided."   At a later date we had his support,

equally emphatic, in our protest against the practice of feeding snakes on live prey at the " Zoo."

Other friends, too, helped to lend gaiety to a rather dismal subject. Among those who actively co-operated with the League was a commercial traveller, who was deeply versed in the various laws relating to corporal punishment, and who, as he once confided to me, had been in the habit of working locally as a sort of free-lance and Bashi-Bazouk He had made a practice, for example, of writing " How about the Birch ? " on the Admiralty's printed notices in which boys were invited to reap the benefits of joining the Navy ; and this had touched so sore a point that the advertisements in question had at length been put within glass frames. Another of his little jokes was to write to private school-masters, saying that he had a son whom he was about to send to school (which was true), and asking whether they could guarantee that there would be no corporal punishment. Several masters responded favourably, but as the boy could not be sent to more than one place of education, these worthy folk were deprived of their *quid pro quo* ; in the end, however, a nemesis fell upon their betrayer, for once, when he had just returned home after a .long journey, tired, and wanting above everything his tea, who should be announced but one of those very pedagogues with whom he had been in communication. He too had travelled some distance, rather than miss the chance of a pupil, and, having "ideas " on the subject of corporal punishment, had come, as he said, for " a good talk " " I could have eaten him," was our friend's remark.

In the 'nineties of last century, the state of the Criminal Law, as Mr. Justice Mathew pointed out, was a hundred years behind the times, and a special depart-ment of the Humanitarian League was established in order to advocate certain much-needed reforms. It was felt that in view of the severity of the penal laws, the inequality of sentences, and the hard and indiscrimi-

nating character of prison discipline, an organized
attempt ought to be made to humanize both the spirit
of the law and the conditions of prison life, and to show
that the true purpose of imprisonment was the
reformation, not the mere punishment, of the offender.
In this campaign the League was able to avail itself of
a mass of expert information. It published, in 1893,
a very effective pamphlet, " I was in Prison," written
by Mr Robert Johnson, director of the Colonial College
at Hollesley Bay ; and this was followed, a year later,
by " A Plea for Mercy to Offenders," an address given
before the League by Mr. C. H. Hopwood, the Recorder
of Liverpool, who, with his friend Mr. Johnson, did
great service in showing the futility of long sentences
of imprisonment. I had several talks about that time
with Mr Johnson and Mr. Hopwood ; and they would
have thrown in their lot altogether with the Humanitarian League but for their fear that the inclusion within
its programme of many other questions, such as sport
and vivisection, would alienate sympathy in some
quarters from their special subject of prison reform ·
it was for this reason that Mr. Hopwood afterwards
founded the Romilly Society.

Two other names stood out conspicuously in the
same sphere of work—that of Dr. W Douglas Morrison,
the well-known criminologist, now Rector of Maryle-
bone, under whose guidance the League took a prominent part in the agitation which led to the Prisons
Act of 1898, and that of " Lex," one of the keenest
intellects of his time, whose pen was placed unreservedly
at the League's disposal Mr. W H S Monck—for
it was he who adopted that *nom de plume*—was Chief
Registrar in Bankruptcy in the King's Bench Division,
Dublin, a post which he filled with distinction, while
his extraordinarily active and versatile mind found
interest in many other studies · he was a mathematician,
an astronomer, a writer on logic, political economy,
and moral philosophy, and withal a chess-player of

note, among which pursuits he never failed to find time to help the humanitarian cause. His official position made it desirable that his name should not appear; but many were the press letters that he wrote, and many the resolutions, memorials, and letters to governmental departments that he drafted on the League's behalf. To "ask 'Lex' to draft it" was often the course taken by the Committee when dealing with some technical matter that needed exceptional care. The two subjects in which Mr. Monck was specially concerned, besides that of flogging, were the establishment of a Court of Criminal Appeal and a revision of the law relating to Imprisonment for Debt; and it was largely his unacknowledged labours that brought about the one reform and prepared the way for the other. In his press letters on corporal punishment he would sometimes adopt the ironic manner; that is, he would write as one who in part believed in the value of flogging, yet in such a way as to suggest rather the flaws and failures of the practice, and so to impair any faith in it which might linger in the minds of his readers.

Among other friends to whom this department of the League was much indebted were Mr. George Ives, author of *A History of Penal Methods*; Mrs. H. Bradlaugh Bonner; Mr. Carl Heath; Mr H B. Montgomery; Mrs. L. T. Mallet; Dr. T. Baty, the distinguished authority on International Law; and Mr. Joseph Collinson, who for some years acted as its honorary secretary. Mr. Collinson was a young north-countryman, self-taught, and full of native readiness and ingenuity, who at an early age had developed a passion for humanitarian journalism, and whose press letters became as well known as those of Mr Algernon Ashton, while he had a marked advantage over that gentleman in having an ethical purpose and something definite to write about. Any one who should glance over the files of the chief London and provincial journals, between the years 1895 and 1910, could not fail to see a number of letters

signed " Joseph Collinson," or to admire the pertinacity
with which the humanitarian view of a host of
controversial subjects, in particular those relating to
criminal law and prisons, was brought to the notice of
the public. Especially in regard to the flogging question
Mr. Collinson's services were of great value.

Thus supported, the Humanitarian League had no
cause to fear any reasoned opposition . our difficulty,
rather, was to meet with any ; for our antagonists were
mostly anonymous and often abusive correspondents of
newspapers, and the real obstacle with which we had to
cope was the crass weight of prejudice and the immense
stability of old institutions. Two of our adversaries,
however, must not go without mention. One was
Mr. William Tallack, then Secretary of the Howard
Association, whose hostility was dangerous because it
lurked under the guise of philanthropy. He was an old
gentleman of benevolent demeanour, whose method it
was to sit astutely " on the fence," making oracular
utterances, now on that side, now on this, so that, like
the writer of an astrological almanack, he might be
able in any event to run in and cry : " I told you so."
In his *Penological Principles*, a work much advertised
in those days, there was plenty of penology. but very
little principle, much more of the Tallack than of the
Howard : it was, in fact, a farrago of platitudes and
pieties, which said many things without ultimately
meaning anything at all. Yet, in spite of his much
verbiage and many estimable sentiments, Mr Tallack
was a reactionist ; he belonged to an antiquated school
of thought, quite out of sympathy with the new style
of prison reform ; and as he lost no opportunity of
disparaging the work of the League, we showed him
somewhat emphatically that that was a game at which
two parties could play. This he did not relish, especially
as we were strongly backed up by Mr Passmore Edwards
in his paper, the *Echo*. A conference was accordingly
proposed by Mr. Tallack, where it was agreed that in

future there should be a friendly arrangement of " hands
off " on either side.   I remember how, at that meeting,
he told me in his paternal manner, as an instance of
the advantages of not advocating " extreme " measures
of reform, that he enjoyed the privilege of being
able, now and then, to have a personal talk with the
Home Secretary.   " What would humanitarians think of
that ? "   The old gentleman was evidently unaware that
if he was a *persona grata* at the Home Office, it was
precisely because he was known to be a " tame "
reformer, a parasite of the old system, not a champion
of the new, and therefore useful to those who wished
to let matters go on as before.

In a prison-play " The Home Secretary's Holiday,"
which was acted before the Humanitarian League at
one of its social gatherings, Mr. Tallack was glanced at
in the character of Mr. Prim, a Visiting Justice, who
dwells on the value of " segregation," " introspection,"
" self-questioning," and " remorse," as heaven-sent
means by which the convicted sinner may be awakened
to a sense of his guilt.

Our other critic, of whom I must say a brief word,
was Sir Robert Anderson, then an ex-Assistant
Commissioner of Police , who, being of a choleric and
over-bearing nature, was consumed with wrathful
indignation at the activities of the Humanitarian
League.   In his book on *Criminals and Crime*, vengeful
tirades against the professional criminal were accompanied with scarcely less violent abuse of " professional
humanitarians "—a strange term this, to be applied to
honorary workers in an unpopular cause, and by one
who had himself been for many years a salaried official
at Scotland Yard !   In the same work we figured
variously   as   " humanity-mongers,"   " agitators,"
" fools," " hysterical faddists," " doctrinaire philanthropists," " spurious philosophers," " maudlin sentimentalists," and so on.   Authors sometimes describe
their books as " a labour of love."   Sir Robert's was

certainly a labour of hate, and among the punishments
which he indicated as suitable for an impenitent thief
were the gallows, crucifixion, thumb-screws, and the
rack, he added that it was consideration for the community, not for the thief, that prevented the use of
them. It is not pleasant to have to speak of such a
man; one would rather forget him. But in estimating
the savagery of the age, the fact that his most vindictive
proposals met with a good deal of public support is
one which cannot be left out of account.

A thorough-going condemnation of flogging is without
doubt a very unpopular policy, the Humanitarian
League lost many members and much pecuniary support
by its steadfastness on this point, especially, strange to
say, among zoophilists and anti-vivisectionists, many
of whom were firm believers in the propriety of vivisecting the backs of criminals, and would have gone
any distance, as I have heard said, " to see a vivisector
flogged " Not the least valuable part of the League's
duties was to put a check on foolish talk of that sort;
and in this we had the satisfaction of being warmly
supported by so distinguished an opponent of vivisection
as Professor Lawson Tait. It came about in a rather
strange way

The League held a meeting in Birmingham; and a
local member, who had the arrangements in hand, got
Mr. Tait to preside, but by some oversight did not
sufficiently apprise him beforehand of our aims and
objects. When he entered the room—a formidable-
looking figure, with slow gait, massive build, and heavy
brows—he was seen to be in a towering rage. The
storm broke at once Instead of the usual compli-
mentary remarks from the chair, he told us in wrathful
tones that he knew nothing of the Humanitarian League,
and that it was most improper that he should have been
left thus uninformed. This was true, and we wished
the earth would swallow us up; but there was nothing
for it but to go on with the business of the meeting,

and while the speeches were being made Mr. Tait sat and studied the League's printed manifesto. As he read it, the gloom gradually left him ; he began to mutter approval of point after point, then to chuckle with satisfaction, and presently he turned to me (I happened to be sitting next to him) and told me that he was in complete agreement with our programme. A great good humour now took the place of his former resentment, and presently he spoke at some length, and himself moved a resolution that the objects of the League were "worthy the support of all good citizens." He declared that he felt almost as strongly on the question of prison punishments as on that of vivisection, and severely censured the clamour for the lash that had been raised by some woman-suffragists of Edinburgh. It was then that he used the words prefixed to this chapter "Why not bring back at once the boot, the stake, and the thumbscrew ? "

That there are numbers of persons who would be quite willing to bring back, if it were possible, the medieval forms of torture cannot for a moment be doubted by any one who, like myself, has had the experience of working for over twenty-five years for the discontinuance of flogging. There are, of course, many reasonable advocates of corporal punishment in one or another of its forms ; but there are many more to whom the cry for flogging, and for more and yet more flogging, has become a veritable craze, as was seen when, in the agitation for the lashing of "white slavers " in 1912, a frenzied shriek of passion went up from a large section of the people. "We know," said a Member of Parliament at the time, " the extraordinary hysterical emotion which this Bill has aroused throughout England We get letters from all sorts of people, chiefly women, 'flog them,'' crucify them,' and anything else you like. It is a cry we have had all down the ages." [1]

[1] Mr J. F P. Rawlinson, in the House of Commons, November 1, 1912.

That there has been such a cry all down the ages is likely enough , but the age which tolerates it can hardly claim to be a civilized one.

In *The Flogging Craze, a Statement of the Case against Corporal Punishment,*[1] a book published for the Humanitarian League in 1916, with a preface by my friend Sir George Greenwood, I availed myself of the large amount of material amassed by the League during its long campaign against flogging, in the hope that such a work—the first of its kind, if pamphlets be excepted—might prove useful to many social reformers, who, though instinctively opposed to the use of the lash, are often silenced by confident assertions of its efficacy, and are unaware that in this, as in similar discussions, humanity and reason go hand in hand.

Let me now turn to another and still more gruesome form of torture. It is fitting, perhaps, that the twin tyrannies of Flogging and Vivisection should be linked together as Lawson Tait saw them, for they are indeed kindred expressions of one barbarous spirit. I use, for the sake of brevity and convenience, the customary term " vivisection," though there is force in the objection raised against it by certain humanitarian writers, that the Latin word somewhat conceals the vileness of the practice, and though the phrase suggested by Mr. Howard Williams, " experimental torture," is more strictly appropriate to the nameless thing for which a name has to be found. Here, at any rate, in the twentieth century of our barbarism, is torture in its most naked form—the rack, not indeed " without any of its intellectual reasons," as was said of the lash, but torture as surely as the boot and the thumbscrew were torture. As for the intellectual reasons alleged in excuse of the practice, it was pointed out in *Animals' Rights* that before holding vivisection justified on the strength of its utility, a wise man will take into consideration the other, the *moral* side of the

[1] London : George Allen & Unwin, Ltd.

question, " the hideous injustice of torturing a sentient animal, and the wrong thereby done to the humane sense of the community. This contention was quoted and corroborated in an unexpected quarter, viz. in a book published in 1901 by a Russian doctor, V. Veresaeff,[1] who, though himself justifying vivisection, did not conceal his misgivings as to the ethical aspect of the practice. " The question," he said, in reference to the passage in *Animals' Rights*, " is plainly put, and there can be no room for any equivocation. I repeat that we ought not to ridicule the pretensions of the anti-vivisectionists—the sufferings of animals are truly horrible ; and sympathy with them is not sentimentality." In view of that admission, I will waste no words in discussing the pretence that anæsthetics have relieved the vivisected animals of their " truly horrible " sufferings It is not so, even in this country, where the legal restrictions are a farce ; and if it were so here, the rest of the world would be open to experimentation unlicensed and unlimited.

The special application of the word " vivisection " to physiological experiments has led to a belief, in many minds, that the vivisecting scientist is the sole torturer of animals. This is unjust both to the laboratory and to its victims. The crusade against vivisection would be much strengthened if those who take part in it would remember that the cruelties of science are only part of the great sum of cruelty that in various forms disgraces the dealings of mankind with the lower animals. Granted that the worst barbarities of the vivisector exceed those of the sportsman or the slaughterman, both in duration and intensity, it is still a fact, as scientists have often pointed out, that there are other tortures than those of the laboratory, and that to some of these the name " vivisection " might as accurately be applied. For example, clumsy castration of domestic

[1] *The Confessions of a Physician*, translated by Simeon Linden, pp. 158, 159.

animals, as the law is beginning to recognize, is nothing less than "farmyard vivisection"; the "docking" of horses' tails is vivisection in a very revolting form; in the seal-fishery the wretched victims of "fashion" have often been skinned alive; nor can it be pretended that the torture of the egrets, flung aside to die when their nuptial plumes have been torn off, demands a milder name than vivisection; yet some zoophilists, who look upon a vivisecting physiologist as a fiend, do not hesitate to wear an aigrette or a sealskin cloak, or to be the owners of docked horses or cropped dogs. It is impossible to draw a strict line of division between those barbarities which amount to torture and those which fall short of it, and it is convenient that the cruelties of sport and fashion should be dealt with under a separate head; nevertheless there is one other practice on which a few words must be spoken before this chapter is closed

Under the antiquated methods of transport and butchery still permitted in England, it is impossible to doubt that something not far removed from torture is often practised in the cattle trade; for which reason, while aware that in vegetarianism lies the only full solution of the diet-question, humanitarians have long pressed for an amelioration of the worst features of cattle-ship and shambles, and, as a minimum, for the establishment of public abattoirs in place of private slaughterhouses. Even in this respect, owing to the supineness of the County Council, London has been left at the mercy of "the trade," though in some other districts there has been a gratifying improvement. The Humanitarian League, enjoying the advantage of being advised by such experts as Sir Benjamin Richardson, Mr H. F Lester (whose *Behind the Scenes in Slaughterhouses* we published in 1892), Mr. Charles W Forward, Mr. C. Cash, and Mr R. S. Ayling, lost no opportunity of making known the need of this long postponed reform; but the subject being so repulsive it was always difficult to enlist the sympathies of the public, that is, of the very persons whose conscience ought to have been touched ; or, if any interest *was* awakened, it might be among those who were traditionally or professionally opposed to the changes desired.

This danger was once curiously illustrated at a meeting held by the League in the rooms of the Royal Society for the Prevention of Cruelty to Animals, when Mr. John Colam, the Secretary of that Society, took the chair, and Mr. C. W. Forward gave an address on the Jewish method of slaughtering. A mere handful of our friends attended, but the hall was packed from end to end with Jewish visitors, who had seen the announcement of the meeting in the papers, and rallied to the defence of their ritual   We had intended to move a resolution, strongly condemning the Jewish system, but we decided, after a hurried consultation with Mr. Colam, that an academic discussion would better suit the circumstances ; and fortunately it did not occur to our Hebrew friends to propose and pass a resolution of the contrary kind · they talked long and volubly, and we were glad they did nothing worse. The meeting, however, was not without result, for it led, a couple of months later, to the reception by the Jewish Board of Shecheta of a deputation from the Humanitarian League, at which the Chief Rabbi, Dr. Adler, was present, and gave us a very courteous reply. The Jewish system of "casting," he said, which had especially been criticized as barbarous, was a good deal misunderstood owing to the word by which it was described in reality the animals were not " cast," but " let down gently with ropes." Mr. Forward, however, who had often witnessed the process, remained unconvinced on this point . it seemed to him that it was the public that was being let down gently with words.

The League had the satisfaction of seeing the Jewish system strongly condemned in the official report (1904)

of the Committee appointed to consider the Humane
Slaughtering of Animals; but nothing has yet been
done to carry the recommendations of that Committee
into effect, the supposed sanctity of a "religious"
usage having been allowed, as usual, to outweigh the
clearest dictates of humaneness.

There are not a few other current and strongly-
rooted practices to which the title of this chapter might
justly be applied; but enough has now been said to
show that the merry month of May, in the year of
grace 1640, did not witness, as has been supposed,
quite the last instance of the infliction of Torture in
this favoured land of the free.

XI

HUNNISH SPORTS AND FASHIONS

Half ignorant, they turn'd an easy wheel,
That set sharp racks at work, to pinch and peel
                                        KEATS.

FROM the subject of torture we pass naturally to that
of sport; indeed, it is difficult to separate them, for
they are psychologically and actually akin   There is
undoubtedly an element of sport in the gloating over
savage punishments, and some of the sufferings which
sportsmen inflict, such as the hunting to death of a
timid deer or hare, cannot fairly be distinguished from
torture.   But when I speak of " sport " in this connection, I mean of course *blood-sport ;* not the manly
games of playing-field or river, but the quest for personal
recreation at the expense of pain to others.   The term
" blood-sports " was first used, as far as I am aware,
by Mr. John Macdonald, who, under the name of
" Meliorist," was the author of some suggestive articles
that appeared in the *Echo* ; anyhow, the Humanitarian
League borrowed the word from him, and finding that
it " went home," made a point of using it on every
possible occasion.   It is the right and proper expression
for the practices which it connotes.

The League published in 1914 a volume of essays on
Killing for Sport, with Preface by Mr. Bernard Shaw,
in which the various aspects of blood-sports were for
the first time fully set forth and examined from the
standpoint of ethics and economics : the book, in
fact, formed a summary of the League's arraignment of

certain bloody and barbarous pastimes, just as *The Flogging Craze* was a record of its protests against the continued use of the lash I will here mention only a few of the more salient features of a long campaign.

For ten years, from 1891 to 1901, the League made the Royal Buckhounds serve as a " peg "—and a very useful peg it was—on which to hang an exposure of the cruelty of stag-hunting [1] The doings of the Buckhounds were watched from season to season ; detailed accounts of the " runs " were published, in contradiction of the shuffling reports sent to the papers by patrons of the Hunt, and a number of horrible cases of mutilation were dragged into light. Questions were put in Parliament ; leaflets, articles, and press letters printed in hundreds, and many lectures given at various clubs and institutions.

In this work we had the sympathy of many distinguished public men and the support of a section of the press (notably of the *Star*, which was then edited by Mr Ernest Parke) , but every possible difficulty was put in our way by officials, whether of the Court, the Government, or the Hunt, who in this case, as in all, desired nothing more than to save themselves trouble by letting things go on as before. Red tape cared little whether carted stags continued to be disembowelled on iron palings and worried by hounds. For example, when, in 1898, we wished to lay before Queen Victoria the case *against* the Royal Hunt, in answer to Lord Ribblesdale's book, *The Queen's Hounds*, her private secretary, Sir A Bigge, refused to bring the League's publications to her notice ; the Home Secretary also declined to do so, and so did the Prime Minister, each and all of them cordially advising us to apply elsewhere. Thus thwarted, we hit on the expedient of *petitioning* the Queen to allow the counter-case to be sent to her,

[1] A Member of Parliament who had charge of a Sports Bill once begged us not to get the Buckhounds abolished, because, as he said, they were the great incentive to vote for the Bill.

and in this way the Home Office was finally forced to
do what it had declared to be " contrary to practice."
The Queen, as we had known since 1891, from a private
letter addressed to Mr. Stratton by Sir Henry Ponsonby,
had been " strongly opposed to stag-hunting for many
years past " ; and when this fact was published after
her death it settled the fate of the Buckhounds.

Looking back twenty years and more, it is comical to
find the followers of the Royal Hunt trying to exploit
the visit of the German Emperor, in 1899, in order to
bolster up the failing reputation of their sport.   They
were very anxious that a " meet " of the Buckhounds
should be one of the entertainments provided for the
Kaiser, and on November 24th, in expectation of his
being present, an unusually large company assembled ;
but the Humanitarian League had been beforehand in
the matter, a letter of protest which it had addressed
to the Prince of Wales had the desired effect, and the
Kaiser had an engagement elsewhere.   Had he been
present, he would, as it happened, have seen a deer
staked and done to death in the manner which was
far from uncommon, and he would have learnt (if he
had any doubt on the subject) that " Huns " are not
entirely confined to Germany.

This rascally " sport," though no longer a State
institution, is still carried on by private packs in several
parts of the country, and nothing but fresh legislation
can prevent its continuance.   A " Spurious Sports Bill "
drafted by the Humanitarian League, with the purpose
of prohibiting the hunting of carted stags, the coursing
of bagged rabbits, and the shooting of birds released
from traps, has been introduced at various times in the
House of Commons by Mr. A. C. Morton, Mr. H. F.
Luttrell, Sir William Byles, Sir George Greenwood, and
other Members, and in the House of Lords by the
Bishop of Hereford (Dr. Percival) ; but its opponents
have always succeeded in preventing its becoming law.
On one occasion (1893) it was " talked out " by Sir

Frederick Banbury, who is renowned in the House as an anti-vivisectionist and friend of animals. It is not only human beings who have to pray, at times, to be delivered from their friends.

The Eton Beagles were another of the League's most cherished " pegs," and displayed as useful an illustration of the hare-hunt as the Royal Buckhounds of the deer-worry. Had humanitarians talked of the cruelty of hare-hunting in general, little attention would have been paid to them ; but with concrete instances drawn from the leading public school, and quoted in the words of the boys themselves as printed in the *Eton College Chronicle*—a disgusting record of " blooded " hounds and of the hare " broken up," or crawling " dead-beat," " absolutely stiff," " so done that she could not stand "—a great impression was made, and the memorials presented to the headmaster or the Governing Body, asking for the substitution of a drag-hunt (a form of sport which was formerly popular at Eton and led to very good runs), received a large number of very influential signatures, including that of the Visitor of Eton, the late Bishop of Lincoln, Dr. E. L. Hicks. But public opinion counts for very little at the school where ignorance is bliss ; a far more important consideration for Governing Bodies and headmasters is the opinion of Old Etonians ; indeed, it is doubtful whether a headmaster of Eton could even retain his position if he were to decree the discontinuance of what Dr. Warre described, with all due solemnity, as " an old Eton institution." So obvious was this that we were inspired to borrow the title of Gray's famous poem in an enlarged form, and to indite an " Ode on the Exceedingly Distant Prospect of Humane Reform at Eton College."

Dr. E. C. Selwyn, headmaster of Uppingham, wrote to me if he were made headmaster of Eton, he would abolish the Beagles " at the earliest opportunity." Unfortunately he was not the successful candidate for the post when Dr. Warre gave it up, or we might have seen some rare sport at Eton, and a hue and cry more exciting than any hare-hunt. Dislike of blood-sport as a school recreation is by no means confined to humanitarians, as may be seen from the following sentence which I quote from an interesting unpublished letter on the ethics of sport, addressed to Mr. Stratton in 1905 by Mr F. C. Selous, the great lion-hunter : " After reading your pamphlet, I certainly think it would be better to substitute drag-hunting for the pursuit and killing of a hare. To see one of these animals worried and torn by a pack of dogs is not an edifying sight for a young boy."

All hunting, whether of the hare, fox, stag, or otter, has many horrible features · perhaps the very nastiest is the custom of " blooding," i.e. baptizing with the blood of the mangled victim any children or young folk who partake in the sport for the first time. The practice has been described, but too modestly, it would seem, as " a hunting tradition which goes back to the Middle Ages " ; one would suppose it went back to still more primitive times. Yet to this day this savage ritual is patronized by our nobility and by royalty. " Prince Henry was blooded," was the conclusion of a newspaper report of a " kill " with a pack of fox-hounds, January 9, 1920. There is a double significance, it seems, in the expression " a prince of the blood."

" You can't eliminate cruelty from sport," says a distinguished sportsman, the Earl of Warwick, in his *Memories of Sixty Years.* In no form of blood-sport do we more clearly see what a veritable mania this amateur butchery may become than in one of Lord Warwick's hobbies, " big game hunting," the difficult and costly pursuit of wild animals in distant lands, for no better reason than the craze for killing. Tiger-shooting is doubtless an exciting pastime, and there are savage beasts that at times have to be destroyed ; but what of that other tiger that lurks in the heart of each of us ? and how is *he* going to be eliminated, so long as a savage lust for killing is a recognized form of amusement ?   For in spite of all the barriers and divisions that prejudice and superstition have heaped up between the human and the non-human, we may take it as certain that, in the long run, as we treat our fellow-beings, "the animals," so shall we treat our fellow-men

Every one knows how the possessors of such "trophies" as the heads and horns of "big game" love to decorate their halls with these mementoes of the chase.   I was once a visitor at a house which was not only adorned in this way, but contained also a human head that had been sent home by a member of a certain African expedition and "preserved" by the skill of the taxidermist.   When I was invited by the owner of the head—the *second* owner—to see that particular trophy, it was with some misgivings that I acquiesced ; but when, after passing up a staircase between walls plastered with portions of the carcases of elephant, rhinoceros, antelope, etc., I came to a landing where, under a glass case, was the head of a pleasant-looking young negro, I felt no special repugnance at the sight. It was simply a part—and, as it seemed, not a peculiarly dreadful or loathsome part—of the surrounding dead-house , and I understood how mankind itself may be nothing more than "big game" to our soldier-sportsmen abroad.   The absolute distinction between human and non-human is a fiction which will not bear the test either of searching thought in the study or of rough experience in the wilds.

Iniquitous as the Game Laws are, I have often thought it strange that Kingsley, even when regarding them, quite justly, from the poacher's standpoint, should have hurled at the game-preserver that eloquent denunciation :

There's blood on the game you sell, squire,
And there's blood on the game you eat,

without in the least realizing the full truth of the statement.   For there, literally, is blood on the "game"
which the squire (or the poacher) disposes of, viz.
the blood of the "game" itself ; and that Kingsley
should have forgotten this, is a singular proof of the
way in which the lower animals are regarded as mere
goods and chattels, and not as creatures of flesh and
blood at all—except to cook and eat.   The very use
of the word "game," in this sense, is most significant.

As mention has been made of the fall of the Royal
Buckhounds, a few words must be said of the man who
chiefly brought it about.   The Rev J Stratton was
Master of Lucas's Hospital, Wokingham, a charitable
institution founded in 1663, where a number of aged
labourers live as pensioners ;   and as Wokingham lay
in the centre of the hunting district, he was well placed
for observing what went on, and for obtaining exact
information .   he had, moreover, a first-hand knowledge
of "sport," and his detestation of it was based on his
own earlier experiences, as well as on a keen sense of
fair play.   Of all the active workers with whom I have
been privileged to be associated, Mr. Stratton was the
finest ;   I have known nothing more courageous than
the way in which, almost single-handed at first, and
with the whole hunting fraternity against him, he
gradually "pulled down" (to use a pleasant sporting
term) the cruel and stupid institution which was carried
on in the Sovereign's name and at the expense of the
public.

In character, as in appearance, Mr. Stratton was a
Roman ;   his stern and unswerving rectitude made him
respected even by his most active opponents.   His
outspokenness, where matters of real import were at
stake, was quite undaunted, and to an extent which
sometimes caused consternation among the weaker
brethren.   I was once asked by a sympathetic bishop
whether it would be possible "to keep Mr. Stratton
quiet."   More than one dignitary of the Church must

have mused on that problem ; for if Mr. Stratton had
a weakness, it was for a bishop. I do not mean that
he viewed bishops with undue reverence, somewhat the
reverse, for he loved to take a bishop to task ; and
some of his letters to bishops, in reference to their
sanction of vivisection or blood-sports, were of a nature
to cause a mild surprise in episcopal circles. But if
bishops did not always appreciate Mr. Stratton, other
persons did So well did the birds in his garden at
Wokingham understand him, that they would let him
talk to them and stroke them as they sat on their
nests. Could there be a more convincing proof of a
man's goodness ?

Another active champion of the reform of blood-sports
was Colonel W. L. B. Coulson, a well-known Northumber-
land country gentleman and J.P., who was one of the
first men of influence to join the Humanitarian League.
He possessed a fine military presence, and a voice
which, even at its whisper, had a volume and resonance
which could not fail to make it heard to the uttermost
corner of a room , his appearance, in brief, had so
little of the pale cast of thought that on the occasion
when he first met us we were the victims of an odd
misapprehension. It had been arranged that he would
preside at a public meeting in London, the first we
held, on the subject of deer-hunting ; and when the
members of our Committee arrived, some time before
the discussion began, we were troubled to find thus
early upon the scene a very large and powerfully built
man, whom, as he did not introduce himself, we imagined
to be a master of staghounds, or at least an opponent
of formidable calibre, come to intimidate us at the
start We were relieved when we discovered him to be
our missing chairman

Colonel Coulson was very popular with his audiences,
for there was a frankness about him which went straight
to the heart, and his speeches, though not cultured,
were full of raciness and humanity. Himself brought up

as a sportsman, he felt keenly about the sufferings of
animals, and after his retirement from the army devoted
much time to lecturing-tours, in which he visited many
parts of the country and especially addressed himself
to schools. Eton would not receive him, doubtless
fearing some reference to her hare-hunt ; but at several
of the other big public schools he was asked to speak
more than once Brave, simple, and courteous, he
was loved by all who knew him, and by none more than
by his colleagues in the humanitarian cause.

Nothing was more remarkable in the history of the
Humanitarian League than the diversity of character
in the persons whom its principles attracted. Lady
Florence Dixie, who joined the League at its start in
1891, had a strange and adventurous career, and has
been described, not inaptly, as " a sort of ' Admirable
Crichton ' among women, a poet, a novelist, an explorer,
a war correspondent, a splendid horse-woman, a convincing platform-speaker, a swimmer of great endurance,
and as keen a humanitarian as ever lived." It was as
humanitarian that I knew her , and she was certainly
one of the most faithful supporters of the League, ever
ready to help with pen or purse, and prompt, sincere,
and unwavering in her friendship Her poems, of which
she sent me more than one volume, had little worth ;
but her essay on " The Horrors of Sport " was one of
the most vivid and moving appeals that have been
written on the subject ; none of the League's pamphlets
had so wide a circulation, for it has been read and quoted
in every part of the English-speaking world. She here
wrote with full knowledge of the facts, and with a
sympathetic insight, which, together with a swift and
picturesque style, made her, at her best, a powerful
and fascinating writer. Of her personal eccentricities
many reports were rife , and I remembered that when
I lived at Eton she used to be seen in the garden
of her villa, on the Windsor bank of the Thames,
walking, like a modern Circe, with a number of wild

beasts in her train. On one occasion a jaguar made his escape from her control, and there was a mild panic in Windsor and Eton till he was recaptured. it might have indeed been serious if the bold youths who hunted the terror-stricken hare had started a quarry that showed fight

Another unfailing friend of the League's Sports Committee was the Hon. FitzRoy Stewart. When I first knew him he was Secretary of the Central Conservative Office, and we were rather surprised at finding an ally in that direction ; in fact, we had some suspicions, entirely unjust, as the result proved, that Mr. Stewart might be desirous of learning our plan of campaign against the Royal Buckhounds in the interest of his sporting friends. The first time I visited him at the Conservative headquarters I was introduced to Sir Howard Vincent, M.P., who, though a patron of the Royal Society for the Prevention of Cruelty to Animals, had not scrupled to throw in his lot with those who were fighting for the continuance of rabbit-coursing, pigeon-shooting and stag-hunting. He seemed to be a good-natured, vacuous-minded person, and one of his remarks, I remember, was that England is " a paradise for animals." This was hardly the opinion of FitzRoy Stewart, who was indefatigable with his schemes for the prohibition of the more cruel forms of sport. He had great hopes of young Mr. Winston Churchill, then beginning to be known as a rising star of the Tory party, and at his earnest request a letter was sent to Mr. Churchill from the office of the League, reminding him of Lord Randolph Churchill's strong denunciation of stag-hunting, and asking his aid against the Buckhounds. Mr. Churchill, however, unmoved by this appeal to his filial piety, sagely opined that the crusade against the Royal Hunt was too democratic.

Mr FitzRoy Stewart worked closely with the Humanitarian League till his death in 1914 ; and many were his press letters which he and I jointly composed at the office in Chancery Lane. He liked to come there armed with some sheets of his Carlton Club notepaper, on which the letters, when worded to his satisfaction, were duly copied and signed—" Old Harrovian," or " A Member of the Carlton Club," was his favourite signature—and then he sent them off to some influential editors of his acquaintance, whose disgust would have been unmeasured had they known what company their esteemed contributor had been keeping Mr. Stewart, I must in fairness add, though a strong opponent of blood-sport, was a firm believer in the beneficence of flogging ; but he was willing to sink this one point of difference in his general approval of the League's work So good-natured was he, that when the subject of corporal punishment was going to crop up at a Committee meeting, he used to ask me to put it first on the agenda, so that he might wait outside until that burning question was disposed of : then he would join us—coming in to dessert, as we expressed it—and take his share in the discussion Oh, if all colleagues were as reasonable ! As *The Times* truly said of him, " his sweetness of temper and social tact made him the most companionable of human beings."

Mr. John Colam, for many years Secretary of the Royal Society for the Prevention of Cruelty to Animals, was a well-known figure in the zoophilist movement at the time of which I am speaking, and had a great reputation for astuteness. Wily he certainly was, with the vast experience he had acquired in evading the double pressure of those who cried " forward " and of those who cried " back ", and he was a veritable Proteus in the skill with which he gave the slip to any one who tried to commit him to any course but the safest. He used privately to allege the backwardness of his Committee as a cause for this seeming timidity , thus he told me in 1901, when the fate of the Royal Buckhounds was hanging in the balance, that the R.S P.C.A. was unable to take any public action, not

from any remissness on his part, but because certain
members of the Committee were afraid of alienating
subscribers, including King Edward himself   Personally
I liked Mr Colam ; he was humane so far as his interests
permitted, and when one had realized, once for all,
the uselessness of attempting to bind him to any fixed
purpose, it was instructive to have an occasional talk
with him at Jermyn Street, and to observe the great
adroitness with which he conducted the affairs of the
Society ; and he, on his part, when he saw that one
had no longer any ethical designs on him, but approached
him rather as a fellow-student, albeit a mere amateur,
in the art of dealing with unreasonable people, would
become chatty and confidential and tell amusing stories
of a Secretary's adventures.   He would have made a
successful Prime Minister, for his " wizardry " was
of the highest order ; as a humanitarian he left something to be desired.

With the Sporting League, which professed to discountenance " malpractices " in sport, yet opposed the
Bill which would have prohibited rabbit-coursing and
kindred pastimes, we were of course involved in controversy. We sought to bring this to a point by
proposing a public discussion of the question . " What
are malpractices in Sport ? "   But this challenge was
declined, the *Sportsman* expressing the opinion that
" such piffling folly is best treated with contempt,"
and the *Evening News* that " cackling is the strong
point of the faddists."   We were more successful in
bringing to book some champions of aristocratic blood-
sports, among them Sir Herbert Maxwell and Sir Edward
Grey, who on one or two occasions appeared on neutral
platforms, and seized the opportunity to eulogize their
own favourite recreations, but showed little relish for
the discussion which they themselves had provoked.
Mr. F. G Aflalo was another of our many antagonists
in the magazines and the press ; and I have a pleasant
recollection of friendly encounters with him in the

Fortnightly Review and elsewhere. Many other apologists of blood-sports there were, of a more sentimental and unreasoning kind, and with these, too, we much enjoyed the argument, which was quite as good sport to us as their hunting or coursing was to them.

Before passing from Sports to Fashions, I will speak briefly of those popular places of recreation, known euphemistically as " Zoological Gardens," which in a civilized age would surely be execrated as among the saddest and dullest spots on the earth, being, in fact, nothing cheerier than big convict-stations, to which the ill-fated life-prisoners—" stuff," as the keepers call them—are conveyed from many distant lands. How any rational person can find pleasure in seeing, for example, " the lions fed " (the modern version of *Christianos ad leones*) is a mystery that baffles thought. I have not been to the London " Zoo " for a good many years ; but when I knew it, the incongruities of the place were so ludicrous as almost to obscure one's sense of its barbarity the Tiger's den, for instance, was labelled · " Beware of pickpockets," and the Eagle's cage bore the inscription . " To the Refreshment Rooms " ; and there, sure enough, within sight of the captive Bird of Jove moping disconsolate on his perch, was a waiter, serving out coffees or lemon-squashes, regardless of the great Raptor by whom his predecessor, Ganymede, had been carried off to be the god's cup-bearer. Could bathos have gone further ?

A friend of mine who, as an Eton boy, used to go to the " Zoo " in the holidays and amuse himself by teasing the captives, was converted to humanitarian principles in a rather curious way. An elk, or some large animal of the ruminant order, whose wrath he had deservedly incurred, *coughed* on him with such vehemence that he retired from the elk-house covered with a sort of moist bran, and with his top-hat irrevocably damaged. Though at the time this touched his hat rather than his heart, he afterwards came to regard the incident as what is called a " means of grace." It caused *him*, too, to " ruminate," and so brought home to him the fact that an elk is " a person."

A pamphlet of mine, issued by the Humanitarian League in 1895, entitled " A Zoophilist at the Zoo," was the beginning of an agitation which gradually led to a considerable improvement in the housing of the animals, in which discussion the most noteworthy feature was a series of articles contributed to the *Saturday Review* by Mr. Edmund Selous, and afterwards reprinted by the League. Another subject, debated with much liveliness, was the practice of feeding pythons and other large serpents on living prey—ducks, fowls, rabbits, and even goats being given to the reptiles, to be devoured in a manner which was sickening to witness and almost too loathsome to describe.[1] These exhibitions were open till 1881 ; then for publicity extreme secrecy was substituted, and all inquiries were met by the stereotyped statement that the use of live prey was confined to cases " where such food was a necessity."

Who feeds slim serpents must himself be slim.

The League found the reptile-feeders at Regent's Park exceedingly slippery to deal with, and it needed long time, and much patience, to bring them to book. In this task, however, I was encouraged by the recollection of a scene which I once witnessed in a crowded railway-carriage, when a large eel had made its escape from a basket which one of my fellow-travellers was holding, and created a mild panic among the company by its convolutions under the seat. An old lady sharply upbraided the owner of the eel, and I was struck by the reasonableness of his reply in rather difficult circumstances, when the eel had repeatedly slipped from his grasp. " Wait a little, mum," he said,

[1] See Dickens's description, Forster's *Life of Dickens*, iii. 146.

" until he gets a bit dusty " ; and the result proved
the man to be right. In like manner we waited till
the excuses given by the Zoological Society had become
very dusty indeed.

Some of the reasons offered for the old system of
snake-feeding were themselves truly reptilian. " We
follow God's ordinances, and they must be right," was
the reverent remark of a keeper ; and humanitarians
were told that " to declare the use of live food to be
cruel is to bring that charge against the Designer of
Nature Himself " So deep and fervent was the piety
of the Reptile House ! Nevertheless, we continued to
urge our point, and the subject was hotly debated at
more than one of the Zoological Society's annual
meetings, where, as a result of the protests raised by
Captain Alfred Carpenter, R N., Mr Stephen Coleridge,
Mr. Rowland Hunt, and other F Z S 's, it was made
evident that the majority of the Fellows, who regarded
the Society as a sort of private club, were indignant at
public opinion being brought to bear upon their con-
cerns It was a situation not devoid of humour. I
happen to know that in the course of an excited meeting
held in November, 1907, when the Duke of Bedford,
as President of the Zoological Society, was in the chair,
the following telegram was despatched to his Grace .

Beg you to stand firm for live food and maintain the
ordinances of the Creator.

From ANNA CONDA

This artless prayer of an unknown lady was fully in
accord with the spirit of the meeting Nevertheless,
things moved, even in Regent's Park ; and, when we
had shown that the snakes in the New York Zoological
Park were successfully fed on freshly-killed animals,
we had the satisfaction of seeing the same less barbarous
method adopted at the London " Zoo."

I once had the advantage of hearing some of the
inner history of a large menagerie from the wife of one

of the keepers, a charwoman in the house where I was
staying, who was of a somewhat loquacious and com-
municative disposition, the staple of her talk being
the adventures of her husband, Johnnie. "Johnnie
came home dead-tired last night, sir," she said on one
occasion. "Why was that, Mrs. Smith?" I asked.
"Why, sir, he had had to beat the elephant;
and after that he was too stiff and tired to take his
supper." My natural inquiry whether the elephant
had been able to take *his* supper was set aside as
frivolous.

Knowing something of the profound piety of the
keepers at the (London) "Zoo" in relation to snake-
feeding, I was pained to learn from this good woman
that her husband, who, unfortunately, was not employed
in a reptile-department, had "lost his faith," and for
a reason which I think has not before been recorded
among the many modern causes of unbelief. "You
see, sir, Johnny can never again hold with the Church,
after the way he's seen clergymen going on with girls
in the elephant house."

When speaking of cruel pastimes, I referred to the
value of the term "blood-sports" in the many controversies which we waged. Just as the fortunes of a
book may be affected by its title, so in ethical and
political discussions there is often what may be called
a winning word; and where none such is found ready
to hand, it is advisable to invent one. Thus the
League made good play with "flagellomania," as used
by Mr. Bernard Shaw in one of his lectures; and "brutalitarian" (an invention of our own, I think) did us
yeoman service, as will be seen in a later chapter.
"Murderous Millinery," another term which has gained
a wide circulation, was first used as a chapter-heading
in my *Animals' Rights*; and though it rather shocked
some zoophilists of the older school, who presumably
thought that only a human being can be "murdered,"
it served a useful purpose, perhaps, in drawing attention

to the revolting cruelty that underlies the plumage trade.
In its condemnation of these barbarities, as in other
matters, the Humanitarian League was a pioneer; its
pamphlet on " The Extermination of Birds," written
by Miss Edith Carrington, and published nearly thirty
years ago, played a marked part in the creation of a
better public opinion; and a Bill drafted by the League
in 1901, to prohibit the use of the plumage of certain
rare and beautiful birds, attracted very wide public
attention, and was the basis of subsequent attempts
at legislation.   But here it must be added that the
man who has done more than all the Societies together
to insure the passage of a Plumage Bill is Mr. James
Buckland.   Nothing in the humanitarian movement has
been finer than the way in which Mr. Buckland forced
this question to the front and made it peculiarly his
own.

Every whit as savage as the feather-trade is the
fur-trade, responsible as it is for some most horrible
methods of torture—the steel-trap, which inflicts
shocking injuries on its victim; the spring-pole, which
jerks both trap and captive high in air, there to hang till
the trapper next comes on his rounds; the terrible
" dead-fall " used for bears and other large animals;
the poisoning of wolves with strychnine; and the
abominations in the butchery of seals   Even the fashionable people who wear furs (in a climate where there is
not the least need of such clothing) would hardly be
able to continue the habit if they knew how their
" comforts " were provided; as it is, the Feather-
Headed Woman is not a commoner sight in our streets
than the Ass in the skin of the (Sea) Lion.   It would
seem that fur-wearers are almost unconscious that their
sables and sealskins are the relics of previous possessors,
and, like the heroines of modern drama, have very
decidedly had " a past "; or, if they do not wholly
forget this fact, they think it quite natural that *they*
should now have their turn with the skin, as the

animal had before.   Thus Pope, in a well-known couplet :

> Know, Nature's children all divide her care ;
> The fur that warms a monarch warmed a bear.

One would have thought that the bear who grew the skin had somewhat more right to it than the monarch ! Politicians may talk of " one man, one vote ", but really, if there is ever to be a civilized state, a programme of " one man, one skin " seems fairer and more democratic.

XII

A FADDIST'S DIVERSIONS

No greyhound loves to cote a hare, as I to turn and course a
  fool —Scott's *Kenilworth*.

I wonder how many times, during the past thirty
years, we humanitarians were told that we were
" faddists," or " cranks," or " sentimentalists," that
our hearts were " better than our heads," and that
we were totally lacking in a sense of humour. I feel
sure that if I had kept all the letters and press-cuttings
in which we found ourselves thus described, they
would amount not to hundreds but to thousands;
for it seemed to be a common belief among the genial
folk whose unpleasant practices were arraigned by us
that the Committee of the Humanitarian League must
be a set of sour Puritans, sitting in joyless conclave,
and making solemn lamentation over the wickedness
of the world. Our opponents little knew how much
we were indebted to them for providing a light and
comic side in a controversy which might otherwise
have been just a trifle dull

It was said by Gibbon, that it was the privilege of
the medieval church " to defend nonsense by cruelties."
Nowadays we see the patrons of sport, vivisection,
butchery, and other time-honoured institutions, adopt-
ing the contrary process, and defending cruelties by
nonsense. And by *what* nonsense ! I do not know
where else one can find such grotesque absurdities,
such utter topsy-turvydom of argument, as in the

quibbling modern brutality which gives sophisticated reasons for perpetuating savage customs.

Of some of the fallacies of the cannibalistic conscience I have already spoken : a volume could easily be filled with not less diverting utterances culled from kindred fields of thought. The apologists of the Royal Buckhounds, for instance, were comedians of the first rank, a troupe of entertainers who long ago anticipated " The Follies." Did they not themselves assure us that, in hunting the carted stag, they " rode to save the deer for another day " ? Such devotion needed another Lovelace .

> Did'st wonder, since my love was such,
>   I hunted thee so sore ?
> I could not love thee, Deer, so much,
>   Loved I not Hunting more.

The stag, so a noble lord pointed out at a meeting of the Sporting League, was " a most pampered animal." " When he was going to be hunted, he was carried to the meet in a comfortable cart. When set down, the first thing he did was to crop the grass. When the hounds got too near, they were stopped. By and by he lay down, and was wheeled back to his comfortable home. It was a life many would like to live." Thus it was shown to be a deprivation, to humans and non-humans alike, not to be hunted by a pack of staghounds over a country of barbed wire and broken bottles. Life seemed poor and mean without it.

Fox-hunting, too, has always been refreshingly rich in sophistries The farmer is adjured to be grateful to the Hunt, because the fox is killed, and the fox because his species (not himself) is " preserved " : thus the sportsman takes credit either way—on the one hand, for the destruction of a pest ; on the other, for saving similar pests from extermination. It is a scene for a Gilbertian opera or a " Bab Ballad " ;

it makes one feel that this British blood-sport must
be deleterious not only to the victims of the chase,
but to the mental capacity of the gentlemen who
indulge in it.

The climax of absurdity was reached, perhaps, in
the dedication by the Archbishop of York (Dr. Cosmo
Lang) of a stained window—a *very* stained window,
as was remarked at the time—in the church of Moor
Monkton, to the memory of the Rev. Charles Slingsby,
an aged blood-sportsman who broke his neck in the
hunting-field. That a minister should have been
"launched into eternity," as the phrase is, while
chasing a fox, might have been expected to cause a
sense of deep pain, if not shame, to his co-religionists:
what happened was that an Archbishop was found
willing to eulogize, in a consecrated place of worship,
not only the old gentleman whose life was thus thrown
away, but the sport of fox-hunting itself: Dr. Lang
pronounced, in fact, what may be called the Foxology.
Of the stained window, with its representation, on
one part, of St. Hubert and the stag, and on the
other of St Francis—yes, St. Francis—giving his
blessing to the birds, one can only think with a smile.
A few months later, an Izaak Walton memorial window
was placed in Winchester Cathedral in honour of " the
quaint old cruel coxcomb " whom Byron satirized.
Whether, in this work of religious art, the pious angler
is portrayed in the act of impaling the live frog on
the hook " as if he loved him," the newspapers did
not state.

Many instances might be quoted of the deep god-
liness, at times even religious rapture, felt by the
votaries of blood-sports ; perhaps one from the German
Crown Prince's *Leaves from my Hunting Diary* is most
impressive · " To speak of religious feelings is a difficult
matter. I only know one thing—I have never felt
so near my God as when I, with my rifle on my knee,
sat in the golden loneliness of high mountains, or in

the moving silence of the evening forest." This sort of sentiment is by no means exclusively of German make. Listen to the piety of a big game-hunter, Mr H W. Seton-Karr: "Why did Almighty God create lions to prey on harmless animals? And should we not, even at the expense of a donkey as bait, be justified in reducing their number?" Here, again, is what the Rev Walter Crick had to say in defence of the fur-trade "If it is wrong to carry a sealskin muff, the camel's-hair raiment of St. John Baptist, to say nothing of the garments worn by our first parents in the Garden of Eden, stands equally condemned."

Strictly ecclesiastical was the tone of a pamphlet which hailed from New York State, entitled "The Dog Question, discussed in the Interest of Humanity," and concluded in these terms· "Now, my boy or girl, whichever you are, drop this nonsense about dogs They are demanding valuable time that should be employed in teaching such as you. A dog cannot love you. You cannot love a dog. Naught beside a divine soul can love or be loved. Chloroform your dog, and take to reading your Testament"

I once overheard a clergyman, who had taken his seat at a tea-table in a Surrey garden, sharply call to order some boys of his party who were striking wildly at wasps and mashing them with any instrument that was handy. I listened, thinking that at last I was going to hear some wise words on that silly and disgusting practice in which many excitable persons indulge; but it turned out that the cause of the reverend gentleman's displeasure was merely that he had not yet "said grace": that done, the wasp-mashing was resumed without interruption.

Space would fail me, were I to attempt to cite one-hundredth part of the amazing Book of Fallacies written in defence of Brutality. "Methinks," said Sir Herbert Maxwell, "were it possible to apply the referendum to our flocks and herds, the reply would come in a fashion on which vegetarians scarcely calculate." There would be a universal roar of remonstrance, it seems, from oxen, sheep, and swine, at the proposal to sever their grateful association with the drover and the slaughterman. Even more delightful was Mr. W. T Stead, when he received from the spirit world a message to the effect that vegetarianism was good for some persons but not good for *him*. That message, I think, smacked less of the starry spheres than of the *Review of Reviews* office: if it was not pure spirit, it was pure Stead.

The " mystics " were often a great joy to us ; for example, Mr J. W Lloyd, author of an occult work called *Dawn-Thought*, expressed himself as follows : " When I go afield with my gun, and kill my little brother, the Rabbit, I do not therefore cease to love him, or deny my relationship, or do him any real wrong. I simply set him free to come one step nearer to me." Here was Brer Fox again, only funnier. We suggested to Mr. Lloyd that " Brawn-Thought " might be a more appropriate title for his book.

Thus, like pedagogues, we faddists, too, had our diversions ; cheered as we were in the weary work of propaganda by such mental harlequinades as those of which I have quoted a few specimens almost at random.

Perhaps the most laughable thing about the poor spavined Fallacies was the entire confidence with which they were trotted out. They were very old and very silly ; they had again and again been refuted , yet they were always advanced in a manner which seemed to say " Surely *this* is an argument you have never heard before ? Surely you will give up your humanitarian sentiment *now* ? " As the frequent oral exposure of such inveterate sophisms was a tedious task, we found it convenient to print them, tabulated and numbered, each with its proper refutation, under some such title as " Familiar Fallacies," or, borrowing from Sydney Smith, "The Noodle's Oration"; and then, when some opponent came along exultingly with one or other of them, all we had to do was to send him the list, with a mark against his own delusion. Trust one who has tried the plan: it is more effective than any amount of personal talk. The man who will bore you to death with his pertinacious twaddle, in the belief that he is saying something new, will soon tire of it when he finds the whole story already in print, with a " See number —" written large in blue pencil against his most original argument.

But the League did not stop at that point: we felt ourselves competent, after years of experience, to carry the war into the enemies' camp—to hoist them with their own petard by means of the *reductio ad absurdum*, a pretended defence of the very practices which we were attacking. The publication of the first and only number of *The Brutalitarian, a Journal for the Sane and Strong*, went far towards achieving our aims. The printers were inundated with requests for copies, and the editor (as I happen to know) received many letters of warm congratulation on his efforts " to combat the sickly sentiments of modern times." The press, as a whole, regarded the new paper with amusement tempered with caution: some suspecting in it the hand of Mr. G. K. Chesterton, some of Mr. Bernard Shaw, while one venturesome editor hinted that the humanitarians themselves might have been concerned in it, but prudently added that " perhaps that would be attributing too much cleverness to the Humanitarian League." So the authorship of the *Brutalitarian*, like that of the letters of Junius, remained a secret; but the laughter caused by its preposterous eulogies of Flogging put a stop for the time to the cry that had been raised in *Blackwood* by Mr. G. W. Steevens and others, that " we have let Brutality die out too much." They did not relish their own panacea, when it was served to them in an undiluted form, and with imbecility no less than brutality as its principal ingredient.

The Eton Beagles, of course, offered a tempting mark for satire, as it was easy to hit upon a strain of balderdash, in mock defence of hare-hunting, the absurdity of which would be apparent to the ordinary reader, yet would escape the limited intelligence of schoolboys and sporting papers. Accordingly, there appeared in 1907, two numbers of *The Beagler Boy*, conducted by two Old Etonians with the professed purpose of " saving a gallant school sport from extinction," and with the ulterior design of showing that there is nothing too fatuous to be seriously accepted as argument by the upholders of blood-sports.

The success of the *Beagler Boy* in this adventure was not for a moment in doubt. The Etonians were enthusiastic over it. The *Sportsman* found it " a publication after our own heart," and " far more interesting and invigorating than anything we are capable of "; and the hoax was welcomed in like manner by *Sporting Life, Horse and Hound*, and the *Illustrated Sporting and Dramatic News*, a periodical described (by itself) as " bright, entertaining, and original." One of the most solemnly comic notices was that in *Countryside*, Mr. E Kay Robinson's paper, which found the *Beagler Boy* " clever and strenuous, but of course *ex parte* ", but the gem of the collection was a long and serious dissertation on " Boys and Beagles " in the *British Medical Journal*, which thought that its readers would be glad to have their attention directed to the new sporting organ. There was a *sauve qui peut* among these worthy people when, from the general laughter in the press, they learnt that they had been imposed upon ; but the shock was borne most good-humouredly " Even the beagler boys," as was remarked by the *Evening Standard*, " those of them, at least, who know how rare and precious an instrument satire is, may forgive, after

they have read : perhaps some will even be converted."
Their disillusionment must certainly have been rather
keenly felt at the time ; like that of the lion who,
as related in *The Man-Eaters of Tsavo*, had carried
off what he thought was a coolie from the tent, only
to find, when he had gone some distance, that it was
a sack of sawdust.

The *Beagler Boy* was added, by request, to Lord
Harcourt's collection of books, pamphlets, and other
matter relating to Eton, which at a later date he
presented to the School It must, I feel sure, be
gratifying to Sir George Greenwood, and to the other
Old Etonian who collaborated with him in the editor-
ship, to know that the fruits of their toil are thus
enshrined in the archives of Eton College.

Some twelve months after the meteoric career of
the *Beagler Boy* it happened that there was a good
deal of talk about an Eton Mission to China, which
was to give the Chinese " an opportunity of the best
education and of learning Christianity " Then a very
curious thing happened. A Chinese gentleman, Mr.
Ching Ping, who was in England at the time, wrote
to Dr Lyttelton, the headmaster, and offered to conduct
a Chinese Mission to Eton, in order to bring " a message
of humanity and civilization to your young barbarians
of the West " The proposal was not accepted, and
it was even hinted in the press that Mr. Ching Ping
came from this side of Suez ; but however that may
have been, his letter to Dr. Lyttelton had a wide
circulation, both in England and in the Far East.

Such were some of a faddist's diversions ; others
too we had, of a different kind, for the every-day work
that goes on behind the scenes in an office is by no
means devoid of entertainment to one who is interested
in the eccentricities of human nature, and is prepared
to risk some wasted hours in studying them. There
was a time when I went to the headquarters of the
Humanitarian League in Chancery Lane almost daily

for some years, and there had experience of many strange visitors and correspondents of every complexion —voluble cranks and genial impostors; swindlers begging for the cost of a railway-ticket to their distant and long-lamented homes; ex-convicts proposing to write their prison-story at the League's expense; needy journalists anxious to pick up a paragraph; litigants who wanted gratuitous legal advice; and, worst of all, the confidential Bores who were determined to talk to one for hours together about what Mr. Stead used to call " the progress of the world."

Nor did the post often fail to bring me some queer tidings—a letter perhaps, from some zealot who sent his latest pamphlet about " God's Dumb Animals " (himself, alas! not one of them), with a request that it should be at once forwarded to the Pope; a volu- minous work in manuscript, propounding, as its author assured me, " opinions of an extraordinary and un- dreamt of kind "; an anthology of Bible-texts in praise of some disputed practice; a suggestion that a notorious murderer should be flogged before being hanged; a grave remonstrance from a friend who feared that public abattoirs " would pave the way for Socialism ", a request from a very troublesome correspondent that the League would award a medal to a man who had saved her from drowning; two twenty-page epistles from an American lady, who, in the first, complimented me on my " markedly intelligent view of the universe," and in the second told me frankly that I was a fool; a note inviting me to call at a certain address, to fetch a cat whom the writer wished me to destroy; and an urgent inquiry whether sea-sand was a healthy bedding for pigs. Such communications were the daily reward of those who sat in offices to promote humanitarian principles. It was remarkable how few persons volunteered for the work.

Even arbitration, of a most delicate and thankless

12

sort, was thrust upon us. My opinion was once asked on a point of manners, by a young man who was a member of the Humanitarian League. He had never been in the habit of doffing his hat to ladies ; he hardly knew how to do so ; yet having come to London from Arcadia he found himself upbraided for not making the customary obeisance to the wife of his employer. What was he to do ? I gave him what I thought was the tactful advice, that he should so far make compromise as to raise his hat slightly, eschewing flourishes. A fortnight later he returned in reproachful mood, with the news that my too slender regard for principle had had a disastrous result. He had met the lady on the steps of some underground station, and in his attempt to bow to her, had dropped his hat in the stream of outgoing passengers, where it had been trampled underfoot.

All this was well enough for an amateur like myself who could withdraw when it became unbearable ; but it made me understand why the official secretaries of propagandist societies often acquire a sort of defensive astuteness which is wrongly ascribed to some inborn cunning in their character. To do reform work in an office open at certain hours, is like being exposed as a live-bait where one may be nibbled at by every prowling denizen of the deep, or, to speak more accurately, of the shallows ; and it is no exaggeration to say that the secretarial work of a cause is hindered much less by its avowed enemies than by its professed friends. Among zoophilists, especially, there are a number of good people, ladies, who go about talking of their " mercy-work," yet show a merciless indifference to the value of other persons' time. Here, incidentally, I may say that one of the most considerate visitors whom I ever saw at the office of the Humanitarian League was Mr. G. K. Chesterton, who repeatedly expressed his fears that, if he occupied much of my time, our friends the animals might be the sufferers.

"Can you assure me," he said, "that, if I stay a few minutes longer, no elephant will be the worse for it?"

By far the most deadly consumer of humanitarian energies is the benevolent Bore. There was a very good and worthy old gentleman who used to pay me frequent visits, the reason of which I did not discover till many years later; on several occasions he brought with him a written list of questions to be put to me, twelve or more perhaps in number, the only one of which I still remember was the not very thrilling inquiry: "Now, Sir, do you read the *Echo*?" In particular he pressed on my attention, as demanding most earnest study, a book called *The Alpha*, written by a friend of his, and differing, as he explained to me, from all other printed works in this—that whereas *they* expressed merely the opinions of their respective writers, *The Alpha* conveyed the actual and absolute truth. In my liking and respect for a sincere friend of our cause, I not only replied as well as I could to his string of questions, but even made an attempt to read *The Alpha* itself: here, however (as with *The Works of Henry Heavisides* mentioned in a previous chapter), I failed so utterly that all I could do was to agree with the donor of the book that it was certainly unique. This was too ambiguous to satisfy him; he was disappointed in me, and from that time his visits were fewer, till they altogether ceased: thus *The Alpha* became in a manner the Omega or the end of our intercourse. After his death I learnt that he had left money to found a Society; and then only did I comprehend why he had "sampled" the Humanitarian League with such assiduous care. Without knowing it, we had been weighed in the balance and found wanting: we were not capable of so great and sacred a trust.

Sometimes the visitation came from oversea; in one case we unwittingly brought it on ourselves, by sending to the Madrid papers an account of a scandalous scene that had taken place with the Royal Buckhounds, our object being to show that British deer-hunting and Spanish bull-baiting came of the same stock. We did not know with what zest the Spanish papers had taken to the subject, till one day there arrived in Chancery Lane an infuriated American, who told us that his work in the Canary Islands had been blasted and ruined by our action. For years, he said, he had preached kindness to animals, making England his exemplar, and now at one fell swoop all his labours had been demolished, for the story of the British stag-bait had gone like wild-fire through the Spanish papers, and thence to the Canaries. We expressed our sincere regret to him for this mishap, but tried to make him see that it was no fault of ours if he had based his propaganda on a false principle, viz. the superiority of Anglo-Saxon ethics, instead of on the universal obligation of humaneness. It was useless. He consumed much time in excited talk, and went away unappeased. This incident should be classed, I feel, not with our diversions, but with our tribulations; but having no chapter on the latter theme, I must let it remain where it stands.

But here some of my readers may be wondering why the office of the Humanitarian League should have been so open to attack: they imagine it perhaps as a luxurious suite of apartments, one within the other, with a hall-porter in the outer premises, skilled in the art of the sending the undesirable visitor into space. In reality, the circumstances of the League were very humble, and its housing was in accord with its income; some of our friends, in fact, used to be pleased to chaff us by quoting that well-known verse in Lowell's stanzas to Lloyd Garrison:

In a small chamber, friendless and unseen,
  Toiled o'er his types one poor unlearn'd young man;
The place was dark, unfurnitured and mean;
  Yet there the freedom of a race began.

Thus it was that, with an ante-room of very diminu-
tive size, we were almost at the mercy of any one who
opened the outer door ; for though the secretary of
the League, Miss Whitaker, would rush forward most
devotedly to bear the brunt of the charge, not a
few of our assailants were through the front lines,
and well in our midst, before we were aware of it.
To this I owe my not inconsiderable knowledge of
the time-devouring Bore.

Among the ex-prisoners who visited us were occa-
sionally some very good fellows, with a real wish to
do something to improve the penal system, which
they all described as thoroughly bad ; but as a rule
they lacked the power of expressing what they knew,
or were hampered by some personal ailment. There
was one, a quiet civil man, who was anxious to give
a lecture before the League, and assured us that,
though he was prone to drink, he would take care
that none of his lapses should coincide with the date
of his appearance on our platform. That was a risk
which we were not disposed to take ; but strange to
say, the very disaster which we shunned in this case
actually befell us, a year or two afterwards, at a most
respectable meeting which we organized jointly with
another Society On the very stroke of the clock,
when the audience was all seated in expectation, and
the chairman was ready to ascend the platform,
supported by the members of our Committee, the
news reached us that the lecturer himself could not
be present : it was *he* in fact, who was having to be
" supported," in another and more literal sense.

Ex-warders did not often favour us with a visit ;
but one there was who had been employed in Reading
Gaol at the time when Oscar Wilde was imprisoned
there such was his story, and I had no reason to
disbelieve it. He told me several edifying anecdotes,
among them the following It used to be a great hard-
ship to Wilde that the glazed window of his cell allowed

him no skyward view (one recalls his allusion, in *The Ballad of Reading Gaol*, to " that little tent of blue, which prisoners call the sky "); and once, when the prison chaplain was visiting him, he spoke sorrowfully of this grievance. But the chaplain only offered him spiritual comfort, and urged him to lift up his thoughts " to Him who is above the sky "; whereat Wilde, suddenly losing his patience, exclaimed, " Get out, you d——d fool ! " and pushed him to the door. For this he was reported to the Governor.

The League had not often the honour of finding itself in agreement with the Prison Commissioners; but we did think that they were wise to decline the too generous offer of a body calling itself the Poetry Recital Society to read poetry to prisoners. The words, " I was in prison, and ye came unto me," would receive a new and fearful significance, if a number of versifiers and reciters were to be let loose on the helpless inmates of our gaols. It seemed barbarous on the part of these minstrels to try to secure an audience which had no choice in the matter, and which had not got even an open window to jump through if the strain should have become too acute.

Of beggars and swindlers we had no lack in Chancery Lane; it suited their purpose to regard a Humanitarian League as primarily designed for the relief of the impecunious; its very name, they felt, could imply nothing less. They were mostly young men who seemed to act in concert; for they usually came, as if on circuit, at certain times of the year. Their mentality was of a low order (or they thought that ours was), for though they showed a certain ingenuity in collecting previous information about the parties on whom they tried to impose, they often presented their case so badly as to make it palpably absurd. Sometimes, however, a really clever and humorous rogue would make his appearance. There was one such who began a wordy statement that if I would

but grant him twenty minutes, he could convince me
that he was deserving of half a crown ; but when I
hinted that if the interview was going to cost me half
a crown, I would rather be spared the twenty minutes,
his solemnity fell from him like a cloud, and with a
twinkling eye he said that he would be only too pleased
to cut his story as short as I liked.

When I was a master at Eton I used to subscribe
to the Charity Organization Society, and I was presented
by that austere body with a number of tickets, one
of which was to be given to every beggar who called ;
but the trouble was that the tramps declined to regard
the "scrap of paper" seriously, and informed us, in
effect, that when they asked for bread we were offering
them a stone. It certainly did not seem quite a human
way of treating a fellow-being ; unless one could hold
the comfortable belief, confidently expressed to me
by one of my Eton colleagues, a very religious man,
that every mendicant one meets has had a good chance
in life, and has deliberately thrown it away. The
logic of that view was to say "no" to everybody.

I once had an opportunity of seeing the exactly
opposite theory put into practice. When I was living
in Surrey, I had a visit from Prince Kropotkin, who
was looking for a house in the district, and we spent
a day in walking about on that quest. We met a
troop of beggars whose appearance was decidedly
professional ; and I noticed that Kropotkin at once
responded to their appeal. Later in the day we fell
in with the same party, and again, when they told
their tale of woe, Kropotkin put his hand in his pocket.
At this I ventured to ask him whether he had observed
that they were the same lot, to which he replied :
"Oh, yes. I know they are probably impostors
and will drink the money at the public house ; but
we are going back to our comfortable tea, and I cannot
run the risk of refusing help where it may possibly
be needed." If in this matter one sympathizes with

Kropotkin rather than with the Charity Organization folk, I suppose it is on Shelley's principle—that he would "rather be damned with Plato and Lord Bacon than be saved with Paley and Malthus."

I will conclude this chapter on our diversions with a rather diverting passage from Mr. George Moore's *Confessions* :

> "Self, and after self, a friend ; the rest may go to the devil ; and be sure that when any man is more stupidly vain and outrageously egotistic than his fellows, he will hide his hideousness in humanitarianism. . . . Humanitarianism is a pigsty where liars, hypocrites, and the obscene in spirit congregate ; it has been so since the great Jew conceived it, and it will be so till the end. Far better the blithe modern pagan in his white tie and evening clothes, and his facile philosophy. He says : ' I don't care how the poor live ; my only regret is that they live at all ' ; and he gives the beggar a shilling."

Many years ago, at a meeting of the Shelley Society, I had the pleasure of a talk with Mr. George Moore ; and I remember that when he asked me what work I was doing, and I said it was mostly humanitarian, there came over his expressive face a look of half-incredulous surprise and disgust—the sort of look a bishop might give to one who coolly remarked that he had just committed the sin against the Holy Ghost. I was rather puzzled at the moment ; and it was not till long after, when I read Mr. Moore's *Confessions*, that I realized of what crimes I had convicted myself in his eyes by my too careless avowal. But as for " the blithe modern pagan," I suspect he would be a little less blithe if his wish were fulfilled, and the poor did not live at all ; for how then would he obtain his evening clothes and his white tie ? He would have to live entirely, one fears, upon his " facile philosophy," as snails were once reputed to subsist on their own succulence.

XIII

HOOF-MARKS OF THE VANDAL

The barbarian gives to the earth he lives on an aspect of rough brutality —ELISÉE RECLUS.

HUMANITARIANISM is not merely an expression of sympathy with pain : it is a protest against all tyranny and desecration, whether such wrong be done by the infliction of suffering on sentient beings, or by the Vandalism which can ruthlessly destroy the natural grace of the earth. It is in man's dealings with the mountains, where, owing to the untameable wildness of the scenery, any injury is certain to be irreparable, that the marks of the modern Vandal are most clearly seen.

It so happens that as I have known the mountains of Carnarvonshire and Cumberland rather intimately for many years, the process of spoliation which, as Elisée Reclus has remarked, is a characteristic of barbarism, has been there forced on my attention. It is close on half a century since I was introduced to some of the wildest mountains of North Wales by that muscular bishop, Dr G. A. Selwyn, of whom I have spoken in an earlier chapter, when, as tutor to his nephew, I was one of an episcopal party that went on a summer holiday from Lichfield to Penmaenmawr. There the bishop relaxed very genially from the austere dignities of his Palace : and having procured an Ordnance map, was not only taken with a desire to find his way across the heights to Llyn-an-Afon, a tarn which nestles under the front of the great range

of Carnedd Llewelyn, but insisted on being accompanied
by his nephew and his nephew's tutor.   Mountaineering,
as I afterwards saw, could not have been one of Dr.
Selwyn's many accomplishments ; for we had to make
more than one expedition before we set eyes on the
lake, and in the course of our first walk he slipped on
a steep ridge and put his thumb out of joint, to the
secret amusement, I had reason to fear, of my pupil,
who, greatly disliking these forced marches into the
wilderness, regarded the accident as a nemesis on an
uncle's despotism   But to me the experience of those
bleak uplands was invaluable, for it was the beginning
of a love of mountains, both Cambrian and Cumbrian,
which led me to return to them again and again, until
I had paid over a hundred visits to their chief summits.
Thus I could not fail to note, now in the one district,
now in the other, how the hand of the desecrator had
been busy

Recent discussions in the press on the subject of
the proposed Sty Head motor-road have been useful
in two ways : first, they called forth so strong and
general an expression of opinion against that ill-advised
project, as to render its realization extremely unlikely
for a long time to come ; and secondly, they drew
attention to the wider and deeper under-lying question
of the preservation of British mountain scenery against
Vandalism of various kinds   The attempt on the
Sty Head was in itself a significant object-lesson in
the dangers by which our mountain "sanctuaries"
are beset. A hundred and fifty years ago the poet
Gray could write thus of the hamlet of Seathwaite,
where the famous Pass has its entrance on the Borrow-
dale side

"All further access is here barred to prying mortals, only
there is a little path winding over the fells, and for some weeks
in the year passable to the dalesmen , but the mountains know
well that these innocent people will not reveal the mysteries
of their ancient kingdom."

If the mountains held that belief, it was *they*, not the dalesmen, who were the innocents, for the little path has been found passable at every season of the year ; and Mr. G D. Abraham, himself a distinguished climber, and a native of the district, was so willing to reveal the mountain mysteries as to plead in his book on *Motor Ways in Lakeland* for the construction of a highroad from the very point where all farther access used to be barred " The quaint little old-world hamlet," he said, " will doubtless recover its glory of former days when the highway over Sty Head Pass becomes an accomplished fact "

The love of mountains, itself a growth of modern times, has in fact brought with it a peril which did not exist before ; it has opened the gateway and pointed the path to the shrine ; but where the worshipper enters, what if the destroyer enters too ? What if the pilgrim is close followed by the prospector ?

Some years ago Mr. C P Trevelyan, M.P , introduced an " Access to Mountains Bill," which while safeguarding the interests of land-owners, would have permitted pedestrians to indulge their love of highland scenery by making their way to the summits of uncultivated mountain or moorland. All nature-lovers must desire that such a measure may become law , and it might be hoped that landlords themselves would not persist in opposing it, for consideration should show them that it is impossible permanently to exclude the people from the hilltops of their native land Even now, since it is the difficult and the forbidden which attract, there is a certain relish in the attempted ascent of those heights which in the landlord's sense (not the climber's) are still " inaccessible "—just as the cragsmen find a pleasure in striving to surmount the obstacles of rock-face or gully. Who has not longed to cross the lofty frontier into some deer-stalking or grouse-shooting Thibet, where, beyond the familiar lying

sign-post stating that " trespassers will be prosecuted,"
all is vagueness and mystery ? What mountain-lover
has not at times sought to snatch an " access to
mountains " where access was denied ?

I still recall the zest of a raid, albeit unsuccessful,
on one of the summits of the Grampians, when our
small party of climbers, starting from Aviemore, and
passing the heathery shores of Loch-an-Eilan, fell in
near " the Argyle Stone " with a number of deer-
stalkers, who groaned aloud in their fury when they
heard by what route we had ascended, and insisted
on our going down to Kincraig. We had spoiled
their day's sport, they told us ; and we, while regretting
to have done so, could not refrain from saying that
they had equally spoiled ours. We were consoled,
however, in some measure, during that inglorious
descent, by the sight of an osprey, or fishing-eagle,
hovering over the river Spey : doubtless the bird
was one of a pair that for years haunted Loch-an-
Eilan, until the cursed cupidity of egg-collectors drove
them from almost their last breeding-place.

One of the most inaccessible heights in England at
the present day is Kinderscout, the " Peak " of Derbyshire, a triangular plateau of heathery moorland, with
rocky " edges " broken into fantastic turrets and
" castles." Here only do the Derbyshire hills show
some true mountain characteristics ; and the central
position of the " Peak," which is about twenty miles
equidistant from Sheffield, Manchester, and Hudders-
field, would seem to mark it as a unique playground
for the dwellers in our great manufacturing towns.
In reality, it is a *terra incognita* to all but a very few,
a place not for workers to find health in, but for sportsmen to shoot grouse ; and there is no spot in England
which is guarded against intruders with more jealous
care. I speak advisedly, for I once tried, with some
friends, to " rush " the summit-ridge from the public
path which crosses its western shoulders, only to be

overtaken and turned back by some skilfully posted
gamekeeper [1] The loss to the public of a right of
way over these moors, as over many similar places,
is deplorable , and here, as elsewhere, the compromise
that has been arrived at has been greatly to the landlord's advantage, for while the grouse-shooter excludes
the public from a vast area of moorland, the wayfarer
finds himself limited to the narrowest of roundabout
routes, and is insulted, as at Ashop Head, by a perfect
plague of notice-boards threatening all the imaginary
pains and penalties of the law for any divergence on
to the hillside   Certainly an Access to Mountains Bill
is urgently required.

But there is one thing which is even worse than too
little access to mountains, and that is the concession
of too much. It were heartily to be wished that such
districts as those of the Lakes, Snowdonia, and others
which might be named, had long ago been made
inaccessible, in this sense, to the railway-lord, the
company-promoter, and all the other Vandals who
for commercial purposes would destroy the sanctitude
of the hills. We have, in fact, to consider what *sort*
of access we propose, for just as there is all the difference
in the world between the admission of the public to
see a grand piece of statuary, and the admission of
the man who has a design to chip the statue's nose,
so we have to distinguish between those who come
to the mountains to speculate on the beauties of
Nature and those who come there to speculate in a
baser sense. Access to mountains is in itself most
desirable, but what if we end by having no mountains
to approach ? In this respect the Bill might be
strengthened, by making it withhold from the

[1] Some years later I was enabled, by the courtesy of the
owner, to visit the top of Kinderscout on a frosty afternoon
in December, when it had the appearance of a great snow-clad
table-land, intersected by deep ruts, and punctuated here and
there by the black masonry of the tors

Vandal the access which it would bestow on the mountaineer.

Already much that was of inestimable value has been lost. The Lake District has in this respect been more fortunate than some other localities, because, owing to the powerful sentiment aroused by the Lake poets, there is a considerable public opinion opposed to any act of desecration. For this we have to thank, in the first place, the great name of Wordsworth, and, next, the faithful band of defenders which has stood between the enterprising contractor and his prey, as in the case of the once threatened railway to Ambleside and Grasmere. But even in Lakeland no little damage has been done, as by the mining which has ruined the scenery of Coniston, and by the permission granted to Manchester to turn the once sylvan and secluded Thirlmere into a suburban tank—Thirlmere first, and now the ruin of Haweswater is to follow.

Mention has been made in an earlier part of this book of a visit which I paid to Coniston in the winter of 1878-79. It so happened that a spell of severe frost and cloudless skies had then turned the Lakeland mountains into a strange realm of enchantment, the rocks being fantastically coated with fronds and feathers of snow, and the streams and waterfalls frozen into glittering masses of ice. I was the only visitor in the place (it was before Mr. Harrison Riley's arrival), and for several days I had been scrambling over the range of the Old Man mountain without meeting a human being, when one afternoon, on the shore of Levers Water, a solitary figure came suddenly round a buttress of the hill and stalked silently past me as if wrapped in thought. I knew at once that it was Ruskin, for what other inhabitant of Coniston would be on the fells at such a season?

A few days later, when I went to Brantwood with Harrison Riley, as I have described, Ruskin talked

a good deal of his favourite mountain haunts, as he
showed us his wild strawberry beds, and terraces on
the hillside made like Swiss roads, also a small beck
running through his grounds to the lake, which he
said was never dry, and was as precious to him as a
stream of pure gold   The Lake scenery, he said, almost
compensated him for the loss of Switzerland, which
he could not hope to see again ; his feeling for it was
one less of affection than of " veneration "   But the
sunsets had been a disappointment to him, for the
sky above the Old Man was often sullen and overclouded,
and this he attributed to the poisonous influence of
the copper mines.

At present the chief danger to the quietude and
beauty of the Lake district seems to be the motor-
craze, especially that form of it which has been called
" the fascinating sport of hill-hunting," a game which
has turned the Kirkstone Pass into a place of terror,
where noisy machines pant and snort up one side
and scorch furiously down the other, and which is
now craving new heights to conquer. If not on the
Sty Head, why not make a motor-way of the old track
from Langdale to Eskdale over the passes of Wrynose
and Hardknott ? Such was the " compromise " which
some mountain-lovers unwisely suggested, forgetting,
first, that even this surrender, though less deadly than
that of the Sty Head, would involve the destruction
of a wild and primitive tract, and secondly that, as
there is no finality in such dealings, it would only
whet the motorists' appetite for more. It is generally
overlooked, too, though the point is a very important
one, that the invaders have already got much more
than their due share of the district, for the making
of many of the roads now in existence would have
been strongly opposed years ago, if it had been possible
to foresee the riotous use to which they would be put.

But it is when we turn to the mountains of Snowdonia
that we see what inexcusable injury has been done

by the rapacity of private enterprise, connived at by the indifference of the public. It is a somewhat strange fact that, while there is an English branch of the League for the Preservation of Swiss Scenery, no organized attempt is made to preserve our own mountain scenery, not from desecration merely, but from destruction.[1]

Take, for example, the case of the River Glaslyn, which flows from the heart of Snowdon through Cwm Dyli and Nant Gwynant, till it finds its way by the Pass of Aberglaslyn to the sea. Visitors are often invited to admire the "power works," erected some years ago at the head of Nant Gwynant, and other signs of enterprise; but from the nature-lover's point of view there is a different tale to tell. The once shapely peak of Snowdon has been blunted into a formless cone by the Summit Hotel, which has since added to its premises a battlemented wall built of red brick; both Glaslyn and Llyn Llydaw, two tarns of flawless natural beauty, have long been befouled with copper mines; and more recently the glorious waterfall, through which the stream dashed headlong from Cwm Dyli to Nant Gwynant, has been replaced by a line of hideous metal pipes, by which the whole hillside is scarred. As for the far-famed Pass of Aberglaslyn, defaced as it is by railway works and tunnellings, remorselessly begun and then temporarily abandoned, its state can only be described as one of stagnant devastation.

Yet all this mountain scenery, which has been foolishly sacrificed for private purposes, might have been a public possession of inestimable value had it been tended as it deserved; and much yet remains in Snowdonia that might be saved for the enjoyment and refreshment of future generations, if the apathy of public feeling, and of the Welsh people, could be

[1] I have here incorporated the substance of a letter on " The Preservation of Mountain Scenery " published in *The Times*, April 28, 1908.

dispelled. But it is useless to look for local resistance to this vandalism, for one is always met by the assertion, true but irrelevant, that such enterprises " give work " ; which, indeed, would equally justify the pulling down of Westminster Abbey to "give work" to the un-employed of London. Nothing but an enlightened public opinion, unmistakably expressed, can now avert the destruction (for such it is) of the noblest of Welsh, perhaps of all British mountains.

It is strange that the incongruity—the lack of humour—in these outrages on the sanctitude of a great mountain does not make itself felt. What could be more ridiculous, apart from the gross vandalism of the act, than to put a railway-station on Snowdon ? A friend who knows the Welsh mountains intimately told me that on his first visit to the peak, after the building of the Summit Hotel, he remarked to a companion : " We shall be expected to have a green chartreuse after lunch here " A waiter, overhearing him, said : " We ain't got no green chartreuse, sir ; but we have cherry brandy and curaçoa, if you like."

In a little book entitled *On Cambrian and Cumbrian Hills*, published in 1908, I commented strongly on these outrages, and the justice of my criticisms with regard to the ruin of Welsh mountain scenery was not seriously disputed in the local press, though one editor did accuse me of being guilty of " a wicked libel upon the people of Wales," and expressed himself as having been caused " real pain " by my remarks. When, however, I asked him to consider what real pain the disfigurement of Snowdon had caused to mountain-lovers, and suggested that, instead of taking me to task, he should try to arouse his readers to put an end to the vandalism which, for the sake of a temporary profit, is ruining some of the finest portions of Carnarvonshire, he made a reply which was, in fact, a most signal corroboration of my complaint ; for he stated that I had evidently " no conception of

the difficulties which residents in North Wales have
to encounter when they oppose any commercial enterprise, backed up by English speculators, which threatens
to spoil our beauty-spots."[1]   There we have the fatal
truth in a sentence !   What is spoiling Snowdonia is
the commercial cupidity of the Welsh themselves,
utilized by English capitalists.   The editor naïvely
added that, were I myself living in North Wales, I
should be "more sympathetic."   More sympathetic,
that is, with the Welsh residents, who know that their
country is being spoiled, but dare not say so ; less
sympathetic with the mountain-lovers who deplore this
crime !

In the excuses put forward for the invasion of the
mountains with funicular railways, motor high-roads,
and the like, there is a comic element which would
be vastly entertaining if the very existence of mountain
scenery were not at stake.   Thus I have been met
with the argument that a mountain railway, such
as that on Snowdon, "takes into a purer atmosphere
and into an ennobling environment those who have
no other way of learning the lesson that grand mountains
can teach," to wit, "the enfeebled toilers of the towns."
I was reminded, as one convicted of "a little selfishness," that "the weak and the feeble have to be
considered, as well as the athletic and the hardy."
But, in the first place, those who travel by so expensive
a route as this mountain railway are rarely the toilers
of the towns, nor, so far as I have observed them,
are they "the weak and the feeble."   They seem
to be mostly able-bodied well-to-do tourists, who are
too lazy to use their legs.   I once overheard a passenger
in a train, describing a recent Swiss trip, make the
remark: "Oh, no, I didn't *walk* a step.   Funicular
railways up nearly all the mountains—Pilatus, Rigi,
and the rest.   I wouldn't give a fig to *walk*."

It is amusing, too, to find "imperial" reasons

[1] *North Wales Weekly News*, May 15, 1908.

advanced in defence of the Snowdon railroad, in what is called the " Official Guide," a pamphlet published by the London and North-Western Railway at Llanber 1 England, we are proudly told, " does not usually care to be behind other countries in matters of progress, but, with regard to the application of mechanical means for reaching the peaks of mountains, until now it has certainly been so " The inference is obvious. Patriotic climbers should ascend Snowdon by train.

Then there is the clever appeal to the sense of peril and romance. We are informed in the same disinterested treatise that the owner of Snowdon (yes, reader, Snowdon is *owned!*), " having regard to the exigencies of the modern tourist, the increasing eagerness of people to ' do ' Snowdon, and the dangers which beset the ordinary ways available for that purpose, felt that the solitude and sanctity of Snowdon ought, to a certain extent, to give way before the progressive advance of the age." And again · " Hitherto none but the most daring or the most sanguine would venture to ascend during a storm. . . . None the less, however, Snowdon during a storm presents a scene of impressive grandeur, and the new railway will make it possible to see it under this aspect without risk " Henceforth poets will know how to view the grandeur of the gathering storm. " I climbed the dark brow of the mighty Helvellyn," sang Scott. The modern singer will take a ticket on the Snowdon Mountain Tramroad.

The true objection to mountain railways is not that they bring more people to the mountain, but that they spoil the very thing that the people come to see, viz. the mountain itself. The environment, in fact, is no longer " ennobling " when a mountain-top is vulgarized, as Snowdon has been, by a railway and hotel ; it is then not a mountain scene at all. There are numberless points of view in North Wales, and in every highland district, to which the weak and feeble can be easily conveyed, and from which they can see the mountains at their best; but to construct a railway to the chief summit is "to kill the goose that laid the golden eggs," because, when that is done, there is no mountain (in the true sense) any longer for the enjoyment of either feeble or strong.

And surely the feeble can seek their enjoyment in fitter ways than in being hauled up mountains by steam. I have heard of a blind man who walked, with a friend to guide him, to the top of Goatfell, in the Isle of Arran, because he wished to feel the mountain air and to hear the thunder of the sea waves far away below. Was not that better than spoiling Goatfell with a rail? Not, of course, that such railways are really made for the benefit of the feeble-bodied; they are built for commercial purposes, to put money into private pockets at the expense of scenery which should belong to the community as a whole.

But it is not only the nature-lover and the rock-climber who are interested in the preservation of mountains; the naturalist also, and the botanist, are very deeply concerned, for the extermination of the rarer fauna and flora is practically assured unless the onroad of this vandalism is checked. The golden eagle, the kite, and the osprey are gone. Do we desire such birds as the raven, the chough, the buzzard, and the peregrine falcon to survive in their few remaining strongholds? If so, we must take measures to stop the depredations not only of the egg-collecting tourist, but of the death-dealing gamekeeper.

The flight of the buzzard is one of the greatest glories of the hills of Cumberland and Carnarvonshire, and it is deeply to be regretted that so beautiful and harmless a bird should be wantonly destroyed. The worst—or should we say the best?—that can be said of the buzzard is that in very rare instances he has been known to "stoop" at persons who approach his eyrie. In a letter which appeared in the *Lakes Chronicle* some years ago a tourist absurdly complained that he had been attacked on a mountain near Windermere by a " huge bird "—evidently a buzzard—and urged that " it would be to the advantage of the public if some good shot were to free the mountain of this foul-fiend usurper." The buzzard defending his nest is a " foul-fiend usurper " ! Such is the amount of sympathy which the average tourist has with the wild mountain bird ! And as for the ornithological knowledge, this may be judged from the fact that a similar incident on the same mountain was actually described in the papers under the head, " *Bustard* attacks a clergyman."

Of the wild upland flora there is the same tale to tell. The craze for collecting, and what is worse, uprooting, the rarer Alpine plants has almost brought about the extinction of several species, such as the *saxifraga nivalis*, which used to be fairly frequent on Snowdon, Helvellyn, and other British hills , and this in spite of the many appeals that have been made to the better feeling of tourists Public spirit in these matters seems to be wellnigh dead.

What, then, is being done, in the face of these destructive agencies, to preserve our wild mountain districts, and the wild life that is native to them, from the ruin with which they are threatened ? As far as I am aware, apart from occasional protests in newspapers, this only—that appeals are made to the public from time to time by the National Trust and kindred societies to save, by private purchase, certain " beauty spots " from spoliation. These appeals cannot but meet with the entire approval of nature-lovers, and the rescuing of such estates as Catbells, Gowbarrow, Grange Fell, and others that might be mentioned, represents a real measure of success. Still the question has to be faced—what is to be done in the future if, as is certain to happen, the menace to our mountains is maintained ? It is too much to hope that large sums can always be raised by private subscription ; also, while one favoured place is being safeguarded,

others, less fortunate, are being destroyed. We cannot
save our mountains generally by these piecemeal
purchases ; for even if the money were always procurable, the rate of destruction exceeds that of purchase,
and the power of the many syndicates that would
exploit the mountains must necessarily be greater
than that of the few Societies that would preserve
them. In a word, private action is quite inadequate,
in the long run, to repel so extensive an attack.

What is needed is public action on a scale com-
mensurate with the evil, in the direction of the " reser-
vation " of certain districts as sanctuaries for all wild
life. We need, in fact, highland parks, in which the
hills themselves, with the wild animals and plants
whose life is of the hills, shall be preserved in their
wildness as the property of the people ; an arrangement
which would be equally gratifying to the nature-lover,
the naturalist, and the mountaineer, and of vastly
more " profit " to the nation as a whole than the
disfigurement of its beautiful places.

Without at all suggesting that the National Trust
should relax its efforts for the rescue by purchase of
particular tracts, I think that it would be doing a
still greater service if it could see its way to organizing
a movement for pressing on the Government the urgent
need of taking some active steps to counteract the
injury which is being done by commercial interests
to the true interests of the people. Otherwise the
result will be that while a few spots are saved, whole
districts will be lost, and eventually all that the nation
will possess will be some oases of beauty in a desert
of ugliness.

As I have elsewhere pointed out,[1] there is only one
thorough solution of the problem, and that is, to
nationalize such districts as Snowdonia, Lakeland,
the Peak of Derbyshire, and other public holiday-
haunts, and so to preserve them for the use and enjoy-

[1] *On Cambrian and Cumbrian Hills.*

ment of the people for all time. " If parks, open spaces, railways, tramways, water, and other public needs can be nationalized, why not mountains? It is impossible to over-estimate the value of mountains as a recreation-ground for soul and body; yet, while we are awaking to the need of maintaining public rights in other directions, we are allowing our mountains —in North Wales and elsewhere—to be sacrificed to commercial selfishness   If Snowdon, for instance, had been purchased by the public twenty years ago, the investment would have been a great deal more profitable than those in which we usually engage , but while we are willing to spend vast sums on grabbing other people's territory, we have not, of course, a penny to spare for the preservation of our own."

XIV

THE FORLORN HOPE

At least we witness of thee, ere we die,
That these things are not otherwise, but thus.
                                        SWINBURNE.

TWENTY-FOUR years' work with the Humanitarian
League had left many problems unsolved, many practical
matters undecided ; but on one point some of us were
now in no sort of uncertainty—that a race which still
clung tenaciously to the practices at which I have
glanced in the foregoing chapters was essentially
barbaric, not in its diet only, though the butchery
of animals for food had first arrested our attention,
but also, and not less glaringly, in its penal system,
its sports, its fashions, and its general way of regarding
that great body of our fellow-beings whom we call
" the animals " It did not need Mr Howard Moore's
very suggestive book, *Savage Survivals*,[1] to convince
us of this ; but we found in the conclusions reached
by him an ample corroboration of those we had long had
in mind, and which alone could explain the stubborn
adherence of educated as well as uneducated classes
to a number of primitive and quite uncivilized habits.
" It is not possible," he says, " to understand the
things higher men do, nor to account for the things
that you find in their natures, unless you recognize
the fact that higher men are merely savages made
over and only partially changed."

[1] Charles H Kerr & Co , Chicago, 1916 ; Watts & Co.,
London, 1918.

Professor F. W. Newman's warning, that the time was not ripe for a Humanitarian League, had to this extent been verified · if we had thought that we were going to effect any great visible changes, we should have been justly disappointed. But those who work with no expectation of seeing results cannot be disappointed; they are beyond the scope of failure, and may even meet, as we did, with some small and unforeseen success The League was thus, in the true sense of the term, a Forlorn Hope; that is, a troop of venturesome pioneers, who were quite untrammelled by "prospects," and whose whim it was to open out a path by which others might eventually follow.

Perhaps the success of the League lay less in what it did than in what it *demanded*—less, that is, in the defeat of a flogging Bill, or in the abolition of a cruel sport, than in the fearless, logical, and unwavering assertion of a clear principle of humaneness, which applies to the case of human and non-human alike. After all, it does not so greatly matter whether this or that particular form of cruelty is prohibited; what matters is that *all* forms of cruelty should be shown to be incompatible with progress Here, I venture to think, the intellectual and controversial side of the League's work was of some value; for before a new system could be built up, the ground had to be cleared, and the main obstacle to humanitarianism had long been the very widespread contempt for what is known as "sentiment," and the idea that humanitarians were a poor weakly folk who might be ridiculed with impunity. The Humanitarian League changed all that; and a good many pompous persons, who had come into collision with its principles, emerged with modified views and a considerably enlarged experience.

I have already spoken of some of the protagonists of the League: at this point it may be fitting to recount, in epic fashion, the names and services of a

few of the influential allies who from time to time
lent us their aid.

Mr. Herbert Spencer's philosophical writings were
fully imbued with the humane spirit. An opponent
of militarism, of vindictive penal laws, of corporal
punishment for the young, of cruel sports, and indeed
of every form of brutality, he had done as much as
any man of his generation to humanize public
opinion   He willingly signed the Humanitarian
League's memorials against the Royal Buckhounds
and the Eton Beagles.

Dr. Alfred R. Wallace was also in full accord with
us, and he was especially interested in our protest
against the Game Laws, "those abominable engines
of oppression and selfishness," as he described them
in one of several letters which I received from him.
He was anxious that some Member of Parliament
should be found who would move an annual resolution
for the abolition of these laws, and he considered that
such a motion " would serve as a very good test of
Liberalism and Radicalism."   In reference to flogging
under the old Vagrancy Act, he wrote : " There are
scores or hundreds of these old laws which are a disgrace
to civilization   Many years ago I advocated enacting
a law for the automatic termination of *all* laws after,
say, fifty years, on the ground that one generation
cannot properly legislate for a later one under totally
different conditions."

" The Truth about the Game Laws," a pamphlet
of which Dr. Wallace expressed much approval, was
written by Mr. J. Connell, author of " The Red Flag,"
whose democratic instincts had led him to acquire
first-hand knowledge of the nocturnal habits of game-
keepers, and was prefaced with some spirited remarks
by Mr Robert Buchanan, who, as having been for
many years a devotee of sport, here occupied, as he
himself expressed it, " the position of the converted
clown who denounces topsy-turvydom."   Buchanan's

humane sympathies were shown in many of his poems, as in his " Song of the Fur Seal," inspired by one of the League's pamphlets ; he wrote also a powerful article on " The Law of Infanticide," in reference to one of those cruel cases in which the death-sentence is passed on some poor distracted girl, and which clearly demonstrate, as Buchanan pointed out, that " we are still a savage and uncivilized people, able and willing to mow down with artillery such subject races as are not of our way of thinking, but utterly blind and indifferent to the sorrows of the weak and the sufferings of the martyred poor."

George Meredith, for the last ten or twelve years of his life, was a friend and supporter of the League. " On a point or two of your advocacy," he wrote to me," I am not in accord with you, but fully upon most." He declared the steel trap to be " among the most villainous offences against humanity " ; and he more than once signed the League's memorials against such spurious sports as rabbit-coursing and stag-hunting. When the Royal Buckhounds were abolished in 1891, he wrote to us " Your efforts have gained their reward, and it will encourage you to pursue them in all fields where the good cause of sport, or any good cause, has to be cleansed of blood and cruelty. So you make steps in our civilization."

Mr. Thomas Hardy more than once lent his name to the League's petitions, and recognized that in its handling of the problem of animals' rights it was grappling with the question " of equal justice all round." In an extremely interesting letter, read at the annual meeting in 1910, he expressed his opinion that " few people seem to perceive fully, as yet, that the most far-reaching consequence of the establishment of the common origin of all species is ethical , that it logically involved a readjustment of altruistic morals, by enlarging, as a necessity of rightness, the application of what has been called the Golden Rule from the area of mere mankind to that of the whole animal kingdom." This was, of course, the main contention of the Humanitarian League.

In 1896 the League addressed an appeal to a number of leading artists, asking them to make it plain that their sympathies were on the humanitarian side, and that they would at least not be abettors of that spirit of cruelty which is the ally and companion of ugliness. Very few replies were received, but among them was one from Mr. G. F. Watts, who, in becoming a member, wrote us a letter on the cruelty of docking horses' tails ("barbarous in those who practise it, infinitely degrading in those who encourage it from so mean a motive as fashion—only not contemptible because so much worse"), which was very widely published in the press, and did great service in bringing an odious fashion into disrepute. Mr. Walter Crane was another artist who gave support on many occasions to humanitarian principles; so, too, was Mr. Martin Anderson ("Cynicus"), who employed on the League's behalf his great powers as a satirist in a cartoon which castigated the tame deer hunt.

Count Tolstoy, it goes without saying, was in full sympathy with us; and so was that many-sided man of genius, M. Elisée Reclus. Famed as geographer, philosopher, and revolutionist, one is tempted to sum him up in the word "poet"; for though he did not write in verse, he was a great master of language, unsurpassed in lucidity of thought and serene beauty of style. He was a vegetarian, and the grounds of his faith are set forth in a luminous essay on that subject which he wrote for the Humanitarian League. Very beautiful, too, is his article on "The Great Kinship," worthily translated by Edward Carpenter, in which he portrayed the primeval friendly relations of mankind with the lower races, and glanced at the still more wonderful possibilities of the future. His anarchist views prevented him from formally joining an association which aimed at legislative action, but his help was always freely given. "I send you my small subscription," he wrote, "without any engagement for the future, not knowing beforehand if next year I will be penniless or not." I only once saw Elisée Reclus, it was on the occasion of an anarchist meeting in which he took part, and he then impressed me as being the Grand Old Man without rival or peer, never elsewhere have I seen such magnificent energy and enthusiasm combined with such lofty intellectual gifts.

Ernest Crosby, another philosophic anarchist, was perhaps as little known, in proportion to his great merits, as any writer of our time. Elected as a Republican to the Assembly of New York State, he had been appointed in 1889 to be a Judge of the International Court in Egypt; but after serving there five years, his whole life was suddenly changed, owing largely to a book of Tolstoy's which fell into his hands: he resigned his post, and thenceforward passed judgment on no man but himself. A poet and thinker of high order, he stood up with unfailing courage against the brute force of "imperialism" in its every form—the exploitation of one race by another race, of one class by another class, of the lower animals by mankind. It is strange that his writings, especially the volume entitled *Swords and Plowshares*, should be almost unknown to English democrats, for they include many poems which touch a very high standard of artistic excellence, and a few that are gems of verse. "The Tyrant's Song," for instance, expresses in a few lines the strength of the Non-Resistant, and of the conscientious objector to military service (" the man with folded arms "), yet during all the long controversy on that subject I never once saw it quoted or mentioned. A superficial likeness between Crosby's unrhymed poetry and that of Edward Carpenter led in one case to an odd error on the part of an American friend to whom I had vainly commended Carpenter's writings ; for in his joy over *Swords and Plowshares* he rashly jumped to the conclusion that " Ernest Crosby " was a *nom de plume* for the other E.C. " I owe you a confession," he wrote. " Hitherto I have not been able to find in Carpenter anything that substantiated your admiration for him ; but *now* a flood of light is illuminating his *Towards Democracy.*" I communicated this discovery to the poets concerned, and they were both charmed by it.

Crosby was a tall handsome man, of almost military appearance, and this, too, was a cause of misapprehension ; for an English friend whom he visited, and who knew him only through his writings, spent a long afternoon with him without even discovering that he was the Crosby whose poems he admired.

Clarence Darrow, brother-in-law of Howard Moore and friend of Crosby, was another of our American comrades. He arrived one afternoon unexpectedly at the League's office, with a letter of introduction from Crosby. It is often difficult to know what to do with such letters in the presence of their bearer—whether to keep him waiting till the message has been deciphered, or to greet him without knowing fully who he is—but on this occasion a glance at Crosby's first three words was enough, for I saw · " This is Darrow," and I knew that Darrow was the author of " Crime and Criminals," an entirely delightful lecture, brimming over with humour and humanity, which had been delivered to the prisoners of the Chicago County Gaol , and I had heard of him from Crosby as a brilliant and successful advocate, who had devoted his genius not to the quest of riches or fame, but to the cause of the poor and the accused. It *was* Darrow ; and as I looked into a face in which strength and tenderness were wonderfully mingled, the formalities of first acquaintance seemed to be mercifully dispensed with, and I felt as if I had known him for years. Since that time Darrow has become widely known in America by his pleadings in the Haywood and other Labour trials, and more recently through the McNamara case. He is the author of several very remarkable works His *Farmington* is a fascinating book of reminiscences, and *An Eye for an Eye* the most impressive story ever written on the subject of the death-penalty

Let me now pass to a very different champion of our cause. In connection with the *Humanitarian*, the *Humane Review*, and the League's publications in general, I received a number of letters from " Ouida," written mostly on that colossal notepaper which her handwriting required, some of them so big that the easiest way to read them was to pin them on the wall and then stand back as from a picture Her large vehement nature showed itself not only in the passionate wording of these protests against cruelties of various kinds, but in her queer errors in detail, and in the splendid carelessness with which the envelopes were often addressed. One much-travelled wrapper, directed wrongly, and criss-crossed with postmarks and annotations, I preserved as a specimen of the tremendous tests to which the acumen of the Post Office was subjected by her.

Ouida was often described as " fanatical ," but though her views were certainly announced in rather unmeasured terms, I found her reasonable when any error or exaggeration was pointed out. Her sincerity was beyond question ; again and again she lent us the aid of her pen, and as the press was eager to accept her letters, she was a valuable ally, though through all that she wrote there ran that pessimistic tone which marked her whole attitude to modern life. Whatever her place in literature, she was a friend of the oppressed and a hater of oppression, and her name deserves to be gratefully remembered for the burning words which she spoke on behalf of those who could not speak for themselves.

It was always a cause of pride to the Humanitarian League that its principles were broad enough to win the support of thoughtful and feeling men, without regard to differences of character or of opinion upon other subjects. A striking instance of this catholicity was seen on an occasion when the Rev. Hugh Price Hughes was lecturing before the League on the attitude of Nonconformists towards Humanitarianism, and Mr. G. W Foote, editor of the *Freethinker*, and President of the National Secular Society, was present in the audience; for Mr Price Hughes and Mr Foote had been engaged in a very bitter personal controversy concerning the alleged conversion of a certain " atheist shoemaker." When Mr. Foote rose to take part in the discussion, I noticed a sudden look of concern on the face of the lecturer, as he whispered to me : " Is that Mr. Foote ? " expecting doubtless a recrudescence of hostilities ; but on the neutral, or rather the universal ground of humanitarianism, hostilities could not be ; and questions bearing on the subject of the lecture were courteously asked and answered by antagonists who, however sharply at variance on other questions, were in their humanity at one.

Looking back over a large period of the League's work, I can think of no one who gave us more constant proofs of friendship than Mr. Foote , and his testimony was the more welcome because of the very high and rare intellectual powers which he wielded. Few men of his time combined in equal degree such gifts of brain and heart. I have heard no public speaker who had the faculty of going so straight to the core of a subject —of recapturing and restoring, as it were, to the attention of an audience that jewel called " the point," on which all are supposed to be intent, but which seems so fatally liable to be mislaid. It was always an intellectual treat to hear him speak ; and though, owing to religious prejudices, his public reputation as thinker and writer was absurdly below his deserts

he had the regard of George Meredith and others who
were qualified to judge, and the enthusiastic support
of his followers. All social reformers, whether they
acknowledge it or not, owe a debt of gratitude to
iconoclasts like Bradlaugh and Foote, who made free
speech possible where it was hardly possible before.

Mr. Passmore Edwards, renowned as a philanthropist,
was another of our supporters ; indeed, he once proposed
indirectly, through a friend, that he should be elected
President of the League ; but this suggestion we did not
entertain, because, though we valued his appreciation,
we were anxious to keep clear of all ceremonious titles
and " figure-heads " that might possibly compromise
our freedom of action. Perhaps, too, we were a little
piqued by an artless remark which Mr Edwards had
made to the Rev. J. Stratton, who was personally
intimate with him . " It is for the League to do the
small things, Mr. Stratton. Leave the great things
to me " None the less, Mr Edwards remained on
most friendly terms with the League ; and when the
Warden of the Passmore Edwards Settlement curtly
requested us not to send him any more of our " cir-
culars," Mr. Edwards expressed his surprise and regret,
and added these words " If the Passmore Edwards
Settlement does as much good [as the Humanitarian
League] in proportion to the means at its disposal, I
shall be abundantly satisfied "

Two other friends I must not leave unmentioned.
Mr. W. J Stillman's delightful story of his pet squirrels,
Billy and Hans, was the most notable of the many
charming things written by him in praise of that
humaneness which, to him, was identical with religion.
A copy of the book which he gave me, and which I
count among my treasures, bears marks of having
been nibbled on the cover " The signature of my
Squirrels," Mr. Stillman had written there. I value
no autograph more than that of Billy or Hans.

Mr R. W. Trine used often to visit the League when

he was in London. He had an extraordinary aptitude for re-stating unpopular truths in a form palatable to the public ; and his *Every Living Creature*, which was practically a Humanitarian League treatise in a new garb, has had a wide circulation. Mr. Trine, many years ago, asked me to recommend him to a London publisher with a view to an English edition of his *In Tune with the Infinite* ; and I have it as a joke against my friend Mr. Ernest Bell that when I mentioned the proposal to him he at first looked grave and doubtful. Eventually he arranged matters with Mr. Trine, and I do not think his firm has had reason to regret it, for the book has sold by hundreds of thousands.

Enough has been said to show that the humanitarian movement was not in want of able counsellors and allies ; and there were not a few others of whom further mention would have to be made if this book were a history of the League. The support of such friends as Mr. Edward Carpenter, Mr. Bernard Shaw, Mrs. Besant, Mr. W. H. Hudson, and Mr. Herbert Burrows, was taken for granted. Sir Sydney Olivier, distinguished alike as thinker and administrator, was at one time a member of the Committee ; a similar position was held for many years by Captain Alfred Carpenter, R.N. Even Old Etonians were not unknown in our ranks. Mr. Goldwin Smith paid tribute to the justice of our protests against both vivisection and the Eton hare-hunt, as may be seen in two letters which he wrote to me, now included in his published Correspondence. In Sir George Greenwood our Committee had for years a champion both in Parliament and in the press, whose wide scholarship, armed with a keen and rapier-like humour, made many a dogmatical opponent regret his entry into the fray. Readers of that subtly reasoned book, *The Faith of an Agnostic*, will not need to be told that its author's philosophy is no mere negative creed, but one that on the ethical side finds expression in very real humanitarian feeling.

Belonging to the younger generation, Mr. and Mrs. Douglas Deuchar were among the most valuable of the League's "discoveries" · rarely, I suppose, has a reform society had the aid of a more talented pair of writers. Mr. Deuchar has a genuine gift of verse which, if cultivated, should win him a high place among present-day poets : if anything finer and more discriminating has been written about Shelley than his sonnet, first printed in the *Humane Review*, I do not know it ; and in his small volume of poems, *The Fool Next Door*, published under a disguised name, there are other things not less good. Mrs. Deuchar, as Miss M. Little, earned distinction as a novelist of great power and insight : she, too, was a frequent contributor to the *Humane Review* and the *Humanitarian*.

The *Humane Review*, which has been mentioned more than once in the foregoing pages, was a quarterly magazine, published by Mr. Ernest Bell, and edited by myself, during the first decade of the century. It was independent of the Humanitarian League, but was very useful as an organ in which the various subjects with which the League dealt could be discussed more fully than was possible in the brief space of its journal. The list of contributors to the *Review* included the names of many well-known writers ; and if humanitarians had cared sufficiently for their literature, it would have had a longer life · that it survived for ten years was due to the fact that it was very generously supported by two excellent friends of our cause, Mr. and Mrs. Atherton Curtis.

The Humanitarian League itself resembled the *Humane Review* in this, that its ordinary income was never sufficient to meet the yearly expenditure, and had it not been for the special donations of a few of its members, notably Mr. Ernest Bell, and some welcome bequests, its career would have closed long before 1919. The League ended, as it began, in its character of Forlorn Hope. We had the goodwill

of the free-lances, not of the public or of the professions.
I have already mentioned how the artists, with one
or two important exceptions, stood aloof from what
they doubtless regarded as a meddlesome agitation ;
literary men, even those who agreed with us, were
often afraid of incurring the name " humanitarian " :
schoolmasters looked askance at a society which condemned the cane ; and religious folk were troubled
because we did not begin our meetings with prayers
(as was the fashion a quarter-century ago), and because
none of the usual pietistic phrases were read in our
journal   From the clergy we got little cheer ; though
there were a few of them who did not hesitate to say
personally with Dean Kitchin, that the League " was
carrying out the best side of our Saviour's life and
teaching." Mr. Price Hughes, in particular, was
most courageous in his endorsement of an ethic which
found little favour among his co-religionists. Archbishop Temple and some leaders of religious opinion
personally signed our memorials against cruel sport :
and the Bishop of Hereford (Dr Percival) introduced
our Spurious Sports Bill in the House of Lords ; yet
from Churchmen as a body our cause received no
sympathy, and many of them were ranged against it.

In the many protests against cruelty in its various
forms, whether of judicial torture, or vivisection, or
butchery, or blood-sport, the reproachful cry : " Where
are the clergy ? " has frequently been raised, but
raised by those who have forgotten, in each case,
that there was nothing new in the failure of organized
Religion to aid in the work of emancipation.

I wish to be just in this matter. I know well from
a long experience of work in an unpopular cause that
humaneness is not a perquisite of any one sect or
creed, whether affirmative or negative, religious or
secular ; it springs up in the heart of all sorts of persons
in all sorts of places, according to no law of which
at present we have cognisance. In every age there

have been men whose religion was identical with their humanity ; men like that true saint, John Woolman, whose gift, as has been well said, was love.   St. Francis is the favourite instance of this type ; but sweet and gracious as he was, with his appeals to " brother wolf " and " sister swallows," his example has perhaps suffered somewhat by too frequent quotation, which raises the suspicion that the Church makes such constant use of him because its choice is but a limited one.   Less known, and more impressive, is the story, related by Gibbon, of the Asiatic monk, Telemachus (A D. 404), who, having dared to interrupt the gladiatorial shows by stepping into the arena to separate the combatants, was overwhelmed under a shower of stones.   " But the madness of the people soon subsided ; they respected the memory of Telemachus, who had deserved the honour of martyrdom, and they submitted without a murmur to laws which abolished for ever the human sacrifices of the amphitheatre."   Gibbon's comment is as follows · " Yet no church has been dedicated, no altar has been erected, to the only monk who died a martyr in the cause of humanity."

Religion has never befriended the cause of humaneness.   Its monstrous doctrine of eternal punishment and the torture of the damned underlies much of the barbarity with which man has treated man ; and the deep division imagined by the Church between the human being, with his immortal soul, and the soulless " beasts," has been responsible for an incalculable sum of cruelty.

I knew a Catholic priest, of high repute, who excused the Spanish bull-fight on the plea that it forms a safety-valve for men's savage instincts ; their barbarity goes out on the bull, and leaves them gentle and kindly in their domestic relations.   It is, in fact, the story of the scape-goat repeated ; only the victim is not a goat, and he does not escape.   Everywhere among the religious, except in a few individuals, one meets the persistent disbelief in the kinship of all sentient life : it is the religious, not the heretics, who are the true infidels and unbelievers. A few years ago the Bishop of Oxford refused to sanction a prayer for the animals, because "it has never been the custom of the Church to pray for any other beings than those we think of as rational."

I was told by the Rev. G. Ouseley, an old man whose heart and soul were in the work of alleviating the wrongs of animals, that he once approached all the ministers of religion in a large town on the south coast, in the hope of inducing them to discountenance the cruel treatment of cats. He met with little encouragement ; and one of the parsons on whom he called, the most influential in the place, bluntly ridiculed the proposal. "One can't chuck a cat across the room," he said, "without some old woman making a fuss about it." Mr Ouseley's only comment, when he repeated this remark, was : "A Christian clergyman !"

The following is an extract from a letter written at Jerusalem by my friend Mr. Philip G. Peabody, who has travelled very widely, and has been a most careful observer of the treatment accorded to animals, especially to horses, in the various countries visited by him

"When I reflect that for centuries, and from all parts of the world, the most earnest Christians have been coming here, and are still coming, that often they remain here until they die, that scores of great churches here are crowded with pious thousands, and that not one human being of them, so far as I can see or can learn, has the slightest regard for the cruelties occurring hundreds of times daily, so atrocious that the most heartless ruffian in Boston would indignantly protest against them—what am I to think of the value of Christianity to make men good, tender, and kind ? "

This opinion would seem to be corroborated by that of Dean Inge, who has described Man as " a bloodthirsty savage, not much changed since the first Stone Age." Unfortunately, the Gloomy Dean, whose oracular utterances are so valued by journalists as providing excellent material for "copy," does not himself extend any sympathy to those who are endeavouring to mitigate the savageness which he deplores, and which his religion has failed to amend.

Perhaps no better test of a people's civilization could be found than in the manner of their religious festivals What of our Christmas—the season when peace and goodwill take the form of a general massacre followed by a general gormandizing, with results not much less fatal to the merry-makers than to their victims ? One would think that a decent cannibal would be sickened by the shows of live cattle, fattened for the knife, and thousands of ghastly carcases hung in the butchers' shops ; but, on the contrary, the spectacle is everywhere regarded as a genial and festive one. The protests which the Humanitarian League used to make, in letters to ministers of religion and other persons of influence, met with hardly any response , sometimes a press-writer would piously vindicate the sacred season, as " Dagonet " once did in the *Referee* : " We are, of course, from a certain point of view, barbarians in our butchery of beasts for the banquet. The spectacle of headless animals hanging on hooks and dripping with blood is not æsthetic. But Nature is barbarous in her methods, and it is a law of Nature that one set of live things should live upon another set of live things. To kill and eat is a natural instinct. To denounce it as inhuman is not only absurd, but in a sense impious." Piety and pole-axe, it will be seen, go together, in the celebration of the Christian Saturnalia.

> Christmas comes but once a year ·
>   Let this our anguish soften !
> For who could bide that season drear
> Of bogus mirth and gory cheer,
>   If it came more often ?

From Religion, then, as such, the League expected nothing and got nothing ; but it must be owned that its failure to obtain any substantial help from the Labour movement was something of a disappointment ; for though not a few leaders, men such as Keir Hardie, J. R. Clynes, J R Macdonald, Bruce Glasier, and George Lansbury, were good friends to our cause, the party, as a whole, showed little interest in the reforms which we advocated, even in matters which specially concerned the working classes, such as the Vagrancy Act, the Game Laws, and the use of the cane in Board Schools. As for the non-humans, it is a curious fact that while the National Secular Society includes among its immediate practical objects a more humane treatment of animals, and their legal protection against cruelty, the Labour movement, like the Churches, has not cared to widen its outlook even to the extent of demanding better conditions for the more highly organized domestic animals

I have often thought that Walter Crane's cartoon, " The Triumph of Labour," has a deep esoteric meaning, though perhaps not intended by its author. Every socialist knows the picture—a May-day procession, in which a number of working-folk are riding to the festival in a large wain, with a brave flutter of flags and banners, and supporting above them, with up-turned palms, a ponderous-looking globe on which is inscribed " The Solidarity of Labour "—the whole party being drawn by two sturdy Oxen, the true heroes of the scene, who must be wishing the solidarity of labour were a little less solid, for it would appear that those heedless merry-makers ought to be prosecuted for overloading their faithful friends. The Triumph of Labour seems a fit title for the scene, but in a sense which democrats would do well to lay to heart. Do not horses and other " beasts of burden " deserve their share of citizenship ? Centuries hence, perhaps, some learned antiquarian will reconstruct, from such anatomical data as may be procurable, the gaunt, misshapen, pitiable figure of our now vanishing cab-horse, and a more civilized posterity will shudder at the sight of what we still regard as a legitimate agent in locomotion.

Such, then, was the position of our Forlorn Hope in the years that saw the menace of Armageddon looming larger. Like every one else, humanitarians underrated the vastness of the catastrophe towards which the world was drifting ; but some at least saw the madness of the scaremongers who were persistently fostering in their respective nations the spirit of hatred ; and five years before the crash came it was pointed out in the *Humanitarian* that a terrible war was, consciously or unconsciously, the aim and end of the outcry that was being raised about the wicked designs of Germany, to the concealment of the more important fact that every nation's worst enemies are the quarrelsome or interested persons within its own borders, who would involve two naturally friendly peoples in a foolish and fratricidal strife

We knew too well, from the lessons of the Boer War, what sort of folk some of these were, who, themselves without the least intention of fighting, had stirred up such warlike passions in the Yellow Press I had been acquainted with some of them at that time, and had not forgotten how, meeting one such firebrand, I noticed with surprise that he had become facially, as well as journalistically, yellow, his cheeks having assumed an ochreous hue since I had seen him a day or two before. He confided his secret to me. He had once enlisted in the army ; and having, as he supposed, been discharged, was now stupefied by receiving a notice to rejoin his regiment And there he sat, wondering how he could meet his country's call, a yellow journalist indeed · I saw him in his true colours that day.

But even thus, though we suspected, with a great

eruption in prospect, that to pursue our humanitarian work was but to cultivate the slopes of a volcano, we did not at all guess the magnitude of the coming disaster. It might bring a return, we feared, to the ethics of, say, the Middle Ages ; our countrymen's innate savagery would be rather more openly and avowedly practised—that would be all. They would be like the troupe of monkeys who, having been trained to go through their performance with grave and sedate demeanour, were loosed suddenly, by the flinging of a handful of nuts, into all their native lawlessness. What we did *not* anticipate—the very thing that happened—was that the atavism aroused by such a conflict would bring to light much more aboriginal instincts than those of a few centuries back ; that it was not the medieval man who was being summoned from the vasty deep, but the prehistoric troglodyte, or Cave-Man, who, far from having become extinct, as was fondly supposed, still survived in each and all of us, awaiting his chance of resurrection.

XV

THE CAVE-MAN RE-EMERGES

I scan him now,
Beastlier than any phantom of his kind
That ever butted his rough brother-brute
For lust or lusty blood or provender.

TENNYSON.

IT is a subject of speculation among zoologists whether
the swamps and forests of Central Africa may still
harbour some surviving Dinosaur, or Brontosaur, a
gigantic dragon-like monster, half-elephant, half-reptile,
a relic of a far bygone age. The thought is thrilling,
though the hope is probably doomed to disappointment. What is more certain is that not less marvellous
prodigies may be studied, by those naturalists who
have the eyes to see them, much nearer home; for
though Africa has been truly called a wonderful museum,
it cannot compare in that respect with the human
mind, a repository that still teems with griffins and
gorgons, centaurs and chimæras, not less real because
they are not creatures of flesh and blood. Two thousand
years ago it was shown by the Roman poet Lucretius
that what mortals had to fear was not such fabled
pests as the Nemean lion, the Arcadian boar, or the
Cretan bull, but the much more terrible in-dwelling
monsters of the mind. In like manner, it was from
some hidden mental recesses that there emerged that
immemorial savage, the Cave-Man, who, released by
the great upheaval of the war, was sighted by many

eye-witnesses, on many occasions, during the five-years' carnival of Hatred.[1]

Some day, perhaps, a true history of the war will be written, and it will then be made plain how such conflict had been rendered all but inevitable by the ambitious schemes and machinations not of one Empire, but of several; by the piling up of huge armaments under the pretence of insuring peace; by the greed of commercialists; and by the spirit of jealousy and suspicion deliberately created by reckless speakers and writers on both sides; further, how, when the crisis arrived, the working-classes in all the nations concerned were bluffed and cajoled into a contest which to their interests was certain in any event to be ruinous. Then, the flame once lit, there followed in this country the clever engineering of enforced military service, rendered possible by the preceding Registration Act (disguised under the pretence of a quite different purpose), and by a number of illusory pledges and promises for the protection of conscientious objectors to warfare. The whole story, faithfully told, will be a long record of violence and trickery masquerading as " patriotism "; but what I am concerned with here is less the war itself than the brutal spirit of hatred and persecution which the war engendered.

As a single instance of Cave-Man's ferocity, take the ill-treatment of " enemy aliens " by non-combatants, who, themselves running no personal risks, turned their insensate malice against helpless foreigners who had every claim to a generous nation's protection. " They are an accursed race," said a typical speaker

---

[1] See the address on " War and Sublimation," given by Dr. E. Jones, in the subsection of Psychology, at the meetings of the British Association, September 11, 1915   In war, he pointed out, impulses were noticed which apparently did not exist in peace, except in the criminal classes   Primitive tendencies never disappeared from existence; they only vanished from view by being repressed and buried in the unconscious mind.

at one of the meetings held in London. " Intern them all, or rather leave out the *n*, and inter them all Let the name ' German ' be handed down to posterity, and be known to the historian as everything that was bestial, damnable, and abominable " These would be words of criminal lunacy—nothing less— in the mouth of civilized beings, yet they are merely examples of things said on innumerable occasions in every part of our land. Great masses of Englishmen were, for the time, in a mental state lower than that of remote tribes whom we regard as Bushmen and cannibals.

Perhaps the most curious feature of this orgie of patriotic Hatred was its artificial nature it was at home, not at the front, that it flourished ; and if those who indulged in it had been sane enough to read even the war-news with intelligence, they would there have found ample disproof of their denunciations Half a dozen lines from one of Mr Philip Gibbs's descriptions would have put their ravings to shame. " Some of them [English wounded] were helped down by German prisoners, and it was queer to see one of our men with his arms round the necks of two Germans. German wounded, helped down by our men less hurt than they, walked in the same way, with their arms round the necks of our men ; and sometimes an English soldier and a German soldier came along together very slowly, arm in arm, like old cronies." Not much patriotic Hatred *there*.

Nor, of course, was it only the wounded, companions in misfortune, who thus forgot their enmity ; for the practice of " fraternizing " sprang up to such an extent at the first Christmas of the war, that it was afterwards prohibited. " They gave us cigars and cigarettes and toffee," wrote an English soldier who took part in this parley with the accursed race, " and they told us that they didn't want to fight, but they had to. We were with them about an hour, and the officers couldn't make head or tail of it " To this a military correspondent adds : " There is more bitterness against the Germans among the French soldiers than among the British, who as a rule show no bitterness at all, but the general spirit of the French army is much less bitter than that of many civilians." It is an interesting psychological fact that it was the civilians, the do-nothings, who made Hatred into a cult.

And what a beggarly, despicable sort of virulence it was ! For a genuine hatred there is at least something to be said ; but this spurious manufactured malevolence, invented by yellow journalists, and fostered by Government placards, was a mere poison-gas of words, a thing without substance, yet with power to corrupt and vitiate the minds of all who succumbed to it. Men wrangled, as in Æsop's fable, not over the ass, but over the shadow of the ass. Theirs was, in Coleridge's words ·

> A wild and dreamlike trade of blood and guile,
> Too foolish for a tear, too wicked for a smile.

Yet it was difficult not to smile at it. The Niagara of nonsense that the war let loose—the war that was supposed to be " making people think "—was almost as laughable as the war itself was tragic ; and satirists [1] there were who, like Juvenal, found it impossible to keep a grave countenance under such provocation. Hereafter, no doubt, smiles and tears will be freely mingled, when posterity realizes, for example, what tragi-comic part was played by " the scrap of paper," that emblem of national adherence to obligations of honour ; by the concern felt among the greater nations for the interests of the smaller , or by the justification of the latest war as " the war to end war." [2] What

[1] *Cf.* Mr Edward Garnett's *Papa's War, and Other Satires,* George Allen & Unwin, Ld , 1918.

[2] " We were told that the war was to end war, but it was not : it did not and it could not " So said Field-Marshal Sir Henry Wilson, May 18, 1920 ; at which date it was no longer necessary to keep up the illusion.

a vast amount of material, too, will be available for
an illustrated book of humour, when some wag of the
future shall collect and reprint the series of official
war-posters, including, of course, those printed as
advertisements of the war-loans (the melancholy
lady, reminded that " Old Age must Come," and
the rest of them), and when it shall be recollected
that these amazing absurdities could really influence
the public ! As if militarism in itself were not comical
enough, its eulogists succeeded in making it still
more ridiculous by their cartoons. As for the blind
credulity which the war-fever inspired, the legend of
the Angels of Mons will stand for age-long remembrance.

Parturiunt mures, nascetur ridiculus Mons.

This credulity begins, like charity, at home. Whenever a war breaks out, there is much talk of the dis-
ingenuousness of " enemy " writers ; but the sophisms
which are really perilous to each country are those
of native growth—those which lurk deep in the minds
of its own people, ready, when the season summons
them, to spring up to what Sydney Smith called " the
full bloom of their imbecility." That egregious maxim,
si vis pacem para bellum, " If you wish for peace, prepare
for war," is now somewhat discredited ; but it did
its " bit " in causing the war, and after a temporary
retirement will doubtless be brought forward again
when circumstances are more favourable. It is perhaps
as silly a saying as any invented by the folly of man
Imagine a ward of lunatics, who, having got their
keepers under lock and key by a reversal of position
such as that described in one of Poe's fantastic stories,
should proceed to safeguard peace by arming themselves
with pokers and legs of tables. For a time this
adoption of the *para bellum* principle might postpone
hostilities ; but even lunatics would be wasting time
and temper in thus standing idly arrayed, and it is

certain that sooner or later that madhouse would realize its Armageddon. For opportunity in the long run begets action ; and whether you put a poker into a lunatic's hand, or a sword into a soldier's, the result will eventually be the same.

Or perhaps we are told that war is " a great natural outburst," mysterious in its origin, beyond human control : the creed expressed in Wordsworth's famous assertion that carnage is " God's daughter." Could any superstition be grosser ? There is nothing mysterious or cataclysmic in the outbreak of modern wars. Antipathies and rivalries of nations there are, as of individuals, and of course if these are cherished they will burst into flame ; but it is equally true that if they are wisely discountenanced and repressed they will finally subside. We do not excuse an individual who pleads his jealousy, his passion, his thirst for revenge as a reason for committing an assault, though personal crime is just as much an " outbreak " as war is. There seems to be an idea that when such passions exist it is better for them to " come out." On the contrary, the only hope for mankind is that such savage survivals should *not* come out, but that " the ape and tiger " should be steadily repressed until they die.

But "*this* war was justifiable." In every nation the belief prevails that, though war in general is to be deprecated, any particular contest in which they may be engaged is righteous, inevitable, one of pure self-defence, in their own words, " forced on us." Even if this were true, in some instances, in bygone years when international relations were less complex, and when it was possible for two countries to quarrel and " fight it out," like schoolboys, without inflicting any widespread injury upon others, it is wholly different now ; for the calamity caused by a modern war is so great that it hardly matters, to the world at large, who, in schoolboy phrase, " began it." It takes two

to make a quarrel ; and the two are jointly responsible for the disaster that their quarrel entails upon
mankind.

The more one looks into these fallacies about fighting
—and their number is legion—one is compelled to
believe that the spirit which chiefly underlies the
tendencies to war, apart from the direct incentive
of commercial greed, is one of Fear. Hatred is more
obvious, but it is fear which is at the bottom of the
hatred This alone can account for the extraordinary
shortsightedness with which all freedom, both of speech
and of action, is trampled on, when a war is once commenced. In such circumstances, society at once reverts,
in its panic alarm for its own safety, to what may
be called the Ethics of the Pack Of all the absurd
charges levelled against those objectors to military
service who refused to sacrifice their own principles
to other persons' ideas of patriotism, the quaintest
was that of " cowardice " , for, with all respect to
the very real physical bravery of those who fought,
it must be said that the highest courage shown during
the war was that of the persons who were denounced
and ridiculed as cravens. It was a moment when it
required much more boldness to object than to consent ,
one of those crises to which the famous lines of
Marvell are applicable :

> When the sword glitters o'er the judge's head,
> And fear has coward churchmen silencéd,
> Then is the poet's time , 'tis then he draws,
> And single fights forsaken virtue's cause.

The despised " Conchie " was, in truth, the hero and
poet of the occasion.

Again, it must be owing to fear, above all other
impulses, that when a war is over, the conquerors,
instead of offering generous terms—a course which
would be at least as much to their own advantage
as to that of the vanquished—enforce hard and ruinous

conditions which rob them of a permanent peace. This they do from what Leigh Hunt calls

> The consciousness of strength in enemies,
> Who must be strain'd upon, or else they rise.

It was this that caused the Germans, fifty years ago, to dictate at Paris those shameful terms which have now been their own undoing ; and it was this which caused the French, in their hour of victory, to imitate the worst blunders of their enemies.

We are but a world of savages, or we should see that in international as in personal affairs generosity is much more mighty than vengeance. Some years before the war there appeared in the *Daily News* an article by its Paris correspondent, the late Mr. J. F. Macdonald, which even at the time was very impressive, and which now, as one looks back over the horrors of the war, has still greater and more melancholy significance. He called it " A Dream." He pointed out that the sole obstacle to a friendly relationship between France and Germany, and the chief peril to European peace, was the lost provinces of Alsace-Lorraine.

" During my fifteen years' residence in France I have often dreamt a dream—so audacious, so quixotic, so startling, that I can hardly put it down on paper. It was that the German Emperor restored the provinces of Alsace-Lorraine to France. . . . What a thrill throughout the world, what a heroic and imperishable place in history for the German Emperor, were the centenary of Waterloo to be commemorated by the generous, the magnificent release of Alsace-Lorraine "

A dream, indeed, and of a kind which at present flits through the ivory gate , but a true dream in the sense that it conveyed a great psychological fact, and of the sort which will yet have to be fulfilled, if ever the world is to become a fit place for civilized beings —not to mention " heroes "—to dwell in.

But let us return to realities and to the Cave-Man.

However irrational the Hatred which surged up in
so many hearts, it nevertheless had power to trample
every humane principle under foot. That gorilla-
like visage which looked out at us from numbers of
human faces meant that our humanitarian cause, if
not killed or mortally injured by the war-spirit, was
at least, in military parlance, "interned" What we
were advocating was a more sympathetic conduct of
life with regard to both our human and our non-human
fellow-beings, and what we mainly relied on, and aimed
at developing by the aid of reason, was the compassionate instinct which cannot view any suffering
unmoved. We had advanced to a point where some
sort of reprobation, however inadequate, was beginning
to be felt for certain barbarous practices ; and though
we could not claim to have done more than curb the
ferocious spirit of cruelty that had come down to us
from the past, it was at least some satisfaction that
limits were beginning to be imposed on it. What
result, then, was inevitable, when, in a considerable
area of the world, all such ethical restrictions were
suddenly and completely withdrawn, and mankind
was exhorted to take a deep draught of aboriginal
savagery ?

Terrible as are the wrongs that countless human
beings have to suffer, when great military despotisms
are adjusting by the sword their " balance of power,"
and exhibiting their entire lack of balance of mind,
still more terrible are the cruelties inflicted on the
innocent non-human races whose fate it is to be involved
in the internecine battles of men. In a message
addressed to the German people, the Kaiser was
reported to have said " We shall resist to the last
breath of man and of horse." As if the horse could
enjoy the comforts of " patriotism," and were not
ruthlessly sacrificed, like a mere machine, for a quarrel
in which he had neither lot nor part ! More suffering
is caused to animals in a day of war than in a year

of peace ; and so long as wars last it is idle to suppose
that a humane treatment of animals can be secured.
Do the opponents of blood-sports, of butchery, of vivisection, wonder at the obstinate continuance of those
evils ? Let them consider what goes on (blessed by
bishops) in warfare, and they need not wonder any
more.

"Do men gather figs from thistles ? " It seemed
as if some of our sages expected men to do so, if one
might judge from the anticipations of a regenerated
Europe that was to arise after the close of the war !
Already we see the vanity of such prophesyings—of
making a sanguinary struggle the foundation of idealistic
hopes. Not all the wisdom of all the prophets can
alter the fact that like breeds like, that savage methods
perpetuate savage methods, that evil cannot be suppressed by evil, nor one kind of militarism extinguished
by another kind of militarism. Hell, we say, is paved
with good intentions ; but those who assumed that
the converse was true, and that the pathway of their
good intentions could be paved with hell, have been
woefully disillusioned by the event.

There is a too easy and sanguine expectation of
" good coming out of evil." People talked as if
Armageddon would naturally be followed by the
millennium. But history shows that modern wars
leave periods of exhaustion and repression. " Reconstruction " is a phrase now much in vogue, but
reconstruction is not progress. If two neighbouring
families, or several families, quarrel and pull down
each others' houses, there will certainly have to be
" reconstruction ", but it will be a long time before
they are even as well off as they were before. So it
is with nations. The question is : Does war quicken
men's sympathies or deaden them ? To some extent,
both, according to the difference in their temperaments ;
but it is to be feared that those who are quickened
by experience of war to hatred of war are but a small

minority, compared with those who are rendered more callous.

One great obstacle to the discontinuance of bloodshed is the incorrigible sentimentality with which war has always been regarded by mankind. "Who was it," exclaimed the poet Tibullus, "that first invented the dreadful sword? How savage, how truly steel-hearted was he!" But surely the reproach is less deserved by the early barbarian who had the ingenuity to discover an improved method of destruction than by the so-called civilized persons who, for the sake of lucre, prolong such inventions long after the date when they should have been abandoned. "War is hell," men say, and continue to accept it as inevitable But if war is hell, who but men themselves are the fiends that people it?

In like manner the outbreak of war is often called "a relapse into barbarism," but rather it is a proof that we have never emerged from barbarism at all, and the knowledge of that fact is the only rational solace that can be found, when we see the chief nations of Europe flying at each other's throats For if this were a civilized age, the prospect would be without hope; but seeing that we are not civilized—that as yet we have only distant glimpses of civilization— we can still have faith in the future For the present, looking at the hideous lessons of the war, we must admit that the growth of a humaner sentiment has been indefinitely retarded. We cannot advance at the same time on the path of militarism and of humaneness we shall have to make up our minds, when the fit of savagery has spent itself, which of the two diverging paths we are to follow. And the moral of the war for social reformers will perhaps be this · that it is not sufficient to condemn the barbarities of warfare alone, as our pacifists have too often done. The civilized spirit can only be developed by a consistent protest against all forms of cruelty and oppression;

it is only by cultivating a whole-minded reverence for the rights of all our fellow-beings that we shall rid ourselves of that inheritance of selfish callousness of which the militarist and imperialist mania is a part.[1]

Is it not time that we sent the Cave-Man back to his den—henceforth to be his sepulchre—and buried for ever that infernal spirit of Hatred which he brought with him from the pit?

[1] If any doubt existed as to the national insensibility caused by the war, it must have been dispelled by the comparative indifference with which the news of the Amritsar massacre— a more terrible atrocity than any for which German commanders were responsible—was received in this country.

XVI

POETRY OF DEATH AND LOVE

And Death and Love are yet contending for their prey.
                                        SHELLEY.

To look back over a long stretch of years, or to re-read the annals of a Society with which one has been closely associated, is to be reminded of the loss of many cherished comrades and friends. During the past decade, especially, there are few households that have not become more intimately associated with Death ; but even in this matter, it would seem, the war, far from "making men think," has thrown them back more and more on the ancient substitutes for thought, and on consolations which only console when they are quite uncritically accepted.

For though the ceaseless conflict between death and love has brought to the aid of mankind in this age, as in all ages, a host of comforters who, whether by religion or by philosophy, have made light of the terrors of the grave, they have as yet failed to supply the solace for which mankind has long looked and is still looking. They profess to remove " the sting of death," but leave its real bitterness—the sundering of lover from lover, friend from friend—unmitigated and untouched

Death is the eternal foe of love ; and it is just because it is the foe of love, not only because it is the foe of life, that it is properly and naturally dreaded. Its sting lies not in the mortality, but in the separation.

A lover, a friend, a relative, grieves, not because the loved one is mortal, still less because he himself is mortal, but because they two will meet no more in the relation in which they have stood to each other.

They told me, Heraclitus, they told me you were dead.
They brought me bitter news to hear, and bitter tears to shed.
I wept as I remembered how often you and I
Had tired the sun with talking, and sent him down the sky.

It is useless to surmise, or to assert, that the spirit passes, after death, into other spheres of activity or of happiness; for, even if there were proof of this, it would in no way lessen the grief of those who are bereaved of the actual. It was long ago pointed out by Lucretius that even a renewed physical life would in any case be so different from the present life that it could not be justly regarded as in any true sense a continuance of it:

> Nor yet, if time our scattered dust re-blend,
> And after death upbuild the flesh again—
> Yea, and our light of life arise re-lit—
> Can such new birth concern the Self one whit,
> When once dark death has severed memory's chain? [1]

In like manner a future spiritual life could never compensate for the severance of love in *this* life; for it is of the very essence of love to desire, not similar things, nor as good things, nor even better things, but the same things. As Richard Jefferies wrote: "I do not want change; I want the same old and loved things, the same wild flowers, the same trees and soft ash-green: the turtle-doves, the blackbirds, . . . and I want them in the same place."

And what is true of the nature-lover is not less true of the human-lover, be he parent, or brother, or husband, or friend. It is not a solace but a mockery of such

[1] *De Rerum Naturâ*, iii, 847–850, as translated in *Treasures of Lucretius*.

passionate affection to assert that it can be compensated for its disruption in the present by a new but changed condition in the future. A recognition of this truth may be seen in Thomas Hardy's poem, " He Prefers Her Earthly ":

> . . . Well, shall I say it plain ?
> I would not have you thus and there,
> But still would grieve on, missing you, still feature
> You as the one you were.

But this, it may be said, is to set love in rebellion against not death only, but the very laws of life. There is truth in such censure ; and wisest is he who can so reconcile his longings with his destiny as to know enough of the sweetness of love without too much of the bitterness of regret. Perhaps, in some fairer society of a future age, when love is more generally shared, the sting of death will be less acute ; but what centuries have yet to pass before that " Golden City " of which John Barlas sang can be realized ?

> There gorgeous Plato's spirit
>   Hangs brooding like a dove,
> And all men born inherit
>   Love free as gods above ;
> There each one is to other
> A sister or a brother,
> A father or a mother,
>   A lover or a love

Meantime it would almost seem that to the religious folk who assume a perpetuity of individual life, the thought of death sometimes becomes less solemn, less sacred, than it is to those who have no supernatural beliefs. The easy assurance of immortality to which friends who are writing letters of condolence to a mourner too often have recourse, is usually a sign less of sympathy than of the lack of it ; for it is not sympathetic to repeat ancient formulas in face of a present and very real grief ; indeed, it is in many cases

an impertinence, when it is done without any regard
to the views of the person to whom such solace is
addressed Among the professional ghouls who watch
the death-notices in the papers, none, perhaps, are
more callous—not even the would-be buyers of old
clothes or artificial teeth—than the pious busybodies
who intrude on homes of sorrow with their vacant
tracts and booklets Nay, worse : nowadays mourners
are lucky if some spiritist acquaintance does not have
a beatific vision of the lost one , for the dead seem
to be regarded as a lawful prey by any one who sees
visions and dreams dreams, and who is determined
to call them as witnesses that there is no reality in
the most stringent ordinances of nature :

> Stern law of every mortal lot ;
>   Which man, proud man, finds hard to bear,
> And builds himself I know not what
> Of second life I know not where.

With much appropriateness did Matthew Arnold
introduce his trenchant rebuke of human arrogance
into a poem on the grave of a dog ; for mankind has
neither right nor reason to presume for itself an hereafter which it denies to humbler fellow-beings who
share at least the ability to suffer and to love. Can
any one, not a mere barbarian, who has watched the
death of an animal whom he loved, and by whom he
was himself loved with that faithful affection which
is never withheld when it is merited, dare to doubt
that the conditions of life and death are essentially the
same for human and for non-human ? Is an animal's
death one whit less poignant in remembrance than
that of one's dearest human friend ? Must it not
remain with us as ineffaceably ?

That individual love should resent the thraldom of
death may be unreasonable ; but it is useless to ignore
the fact of such resentment, or to proffer consolations
which can neither convince nor console. From the

earliest times the poets, above all others, have borne
witness to love's protest.   Perhaps the most moving
lyric in Roman literature is that short elegy written
by Catullus at his brother's grave, full of a deep passion
which can hardly be conveyed in another tongue.

> Borne far o'er many lands, o'er many seas,
>   On this sad service, brother, have I sped,
> To proffer thee death's last solemnities,
>   And greet, though words be vain, the silent dead :
> For thou art lost, so cruel fate decrees ,
>   Ah, brother, from my sight untimely fled !
> Yet take these gifts, ordained in bygone years
>   For mournful dues when funeral rites befell ,
> Take them, all streaming with a brother's tears :
>   And thus, for evermore—hail and farewell !

A similar cry is heard in that famous passage of Virgil,
where the bereaved Orpheus refuses to be comforted
for the loss of his Eurydice   And nearly two thousand
years later we find Wordsworth, a Christian poet,
echoing the same lamentation ·

> . . When I stood forlorn,
> Knowing my heart's best treasure was no more ;
> That neither present time, nor years unborn,
> Could to my sight that heavenly face restore.

Mark the reference to " years unborn "   Wordsworth
was a believer in immortality ; but immortality itself
cannot restore what is past and gone.   All the sages
and seers and prophets, that have given mankind the
benefit of their wisdom since the world began, have
so far failed to provide the least crumb of comfort
for the ravages of death, or to explain why love should
be for ever built up to be for ever overthrown, and why
union should always be followed by disseverance.

There may, of course, be a solution of this tragedy
hereafter to be discovered by mankind ; all that we
know is that, as yet, no human being has found the
clue to the mystery, or, if he has found it, has vouch-

safed the knowledge to his fellow-mortals. For we must dismiss as idle the assertion that such things cannot be communicated in words. Anything that is apprehended by the mind can be expressed by the mouth—not adequately, perhaps, yet still, in some measure, expressed—and the reason why this greatest of secrets has never been conveyed is that, as yet, it has never been apprehended.

It is, doubtless, this lack of any real knowledge, of any genuine consolation, that drives mankind to seek refuge in the more primitive superstitions. Something more definite, more tangible, is not unnaturally desired ; and therefore men turn to the assurances of what is called spiritualism—the refusal to believe that death, in the accepted sense, has taken place at all This creed is at least free from the vagueness of the ordinary religious view of death. It is small comfort to be told that a lost friend is sitting transfigured, harp in hand, in some skiey mansion of the blest ; but it might mitigate the bereavement of some mourners (not all) to converse with their lost one, and to learn that he exists in much the same manner, and with the same affections as before. Some who " prefer him earthly " are less likely to be disappointed in spiritualism than in any other philosophy ; the danger is rather that they should find him *too* earthly—enjoying a cigarette, perhaps, as in a case mentioned in recent revelations of the spirit-life. This is literalness with a vengeance , but however ludicrous and incredible it may be, it is not—from the comforter's point of view —meaningless , whereas it *is* unmeaning to tell a mourner that the loved one is not lost, to him, when the whole environment and fabric of their love are shattered and destroyed.

Is there, then—pending such fuller knowledge as mankind may hereafter gain—no present comfort for death's tyranny ? I have spoken of the poets as the champions of love against death ; and it is perhaps

in poetry, the poetry of love and death, that the
best solace will be found—in that open-eyed and quite
rational view of the struggle, which does not deny
the reality of death, but asserts the reality of love.
It is amusing to hear those who do not accept the
orthodox creed as regards an after-life described as
cold "materialists" and "sceptics" For who have
written most loftily, most spiritually, about death and
the great emotions that are implied in the word—
the religionists and "spiritualists," who pretend to
a mystic knowledge, or the great free-thinking poets,
from the time of Lucretius to the time of Shelley and
James Thomson? Can any "spiritualist" poetry
match the great sublime passages of the *De Rerum
Naturâ*, or, to come to our own age, of *The City of
Dreadful Night*?

It is to the poets, then, not to the dogmatists, that
we must look for solace ; for, where knowledge is
still unattainable, an aspiration is wiser than an assertion, and the theme of death is one which can be far
better treated idealistically than as a matter of doctrine.
In poetry, as nowhere else, can be expressed those
manifold moods, and half-moods, in which the noblest
human minds have sought relief when confronted by
this mighty problem , and far more soothing than any
unsubstantial promises of futurity is the charm that
is felt in the magic of beautiful verse. In Milton's
words .

> . . . I was all ear,
> And took in strains that might create a soul
> Under the ribs of death.

At the present time, when a great war has brought
bereavement into so many homes, and when superstition is reaping its harvest among the sad and broken
lives that are everywhere around us, how can rational
men do better than recall as many minds as possible
from the false teachers to the true, from the priests,
who claim a knowledge which they do not possess, to

the poets, in whom, as Shelley said, there is " the power of communicating and receiving intense and impassioned conceptions respecting man and nature " ? And the testimony of the poets cannot be mistaken ; their first word and their last word is Love. Whether it be Cowper, gazing on his mother's portrait ; or Burns, lamenting his Highland Mary , or Wordsworth, in his elegies for Lucy , or Shelley, in the raptures of his " Adonais " ; or pessimists, such as Edgar Poe and James Thomson, to whom love was the " sole star of light in infinite black despair "—the lesson that we learn from them is the same For death there is no solace but in love , it is to love's name that the human heart must cling

> Ah ! let none other alien spell soe'er,
> But only the one Hope's one name be there,
> Not less, nor more, but even that word alone !

XVII

THE TALISMAN

Comprendre c'est Pardonner —MADAME DE STAEL.

ARE we, then, a civilized people? Has the Man of to-day, still living by bloodshed, still striving to grow rich at the expense of his neighbour, still using torture in punishment, still seeking sport in destruction, still waging fratricidal wars, and, while making a hell on earth, claiming for himself an eternal heaven hereafter—has this selfish, predatory being arrived at a state of " civilization "?

It may be said, perhaps, that as the ideal is always in advance of the actual, and it is easy to show that any present stage of society falls far short of what it might be and ought to be, the distinction between savagery and civilization is a matter of names. This, in one sense, is true; but it is also true that names are of great importance as reacting upon conduct, and that to use flattering titles as a veil for cruel practices gives permanence to evils that otherwise would not be permitted. Our present self-satisfaction in what we are pleased to call our civilization is a very serious obstacle to improvement

In this manner euphemism plays a great part in language; for just as the Greeks used gracious terms to denote malignant powers, and so, as they thought, to disarm their hostility, the modern mind seeks, consciously or unconsciously, to disguise iniquities by misnaming them. Thus a blind tribal hatred can be masked as " patriotism "; living idly on the work

of others is termed " an independence "; vivisection
cloaks itself as "research"; and the massacre of wild
animals for man's wanton amusement is dignified as
" sport " There is undoubtedly much virtue in names.

But here another objection may be raised, to wit,
that in view of the vast advance that has been made
by mankind from primeval savagery to the present
complex social state, it is impossible to apply to
the higher man the same name as to the lower man ;
for if *we* are savages, what are the Bushmen or the
Esquimaux ?

Better fifty years of Europe than a cycle of Cathay.

It may be doubted whether of late years Europe
has been pleasanter as a residential district than
Cathay, but, letting that pass, must we not admit
that a real culture implies something more than material
and mental opulence? " Civilization," as a French
writer has lately said, " is not in this terrible trumpery :
if it is not in the heart of man, then it exists nowhere "[1]
It is easy to frame " ethnical periods," as is done in
Morgan's *Ancient Society*, in which are postulated the
three phases—Savagery, Barbarism, and Civilization—
the last-named commencing with the invention of a
Phonetic Alphabet ; but such a definition, when put
to practical test, seems a somewhat fanciful one. The
brute who tortures or butchers a sentient fellow-being
remains a brute, whether a Phonetic Alphabet has
been invented or not. He has not learnt the ABC
of civilization What is needed, for the measurement
of human progress, is a standard of ethical, not ethnical
refinement.

That mankind has already advanced so far is a
sign, not that it has now reached its zenith, but that
it has yet further to advance ; and this advance will
be delayed, not promoted, by the refusal to recognize

[1] *Civilization*, by George Duhamel. Translated by T. P.
Conwil-Evans.

that the physical and mental sciences have far outrun the moral—that, despite our multifarious discoveries and accomplishments, we are still barbarians at heart.

In this sense, then, we are savages; and the knowledge of that fact is the first step toward civilization. There is a line which pious zoophilists are fond of quoting to sportsmen or other thoughtless persons who ill-use their humbler fellow-creatures:

Remember, He who made thee made the brute.

The reminder is wholesome, for kinship is too apt to be forgotten; but I would venture to interpret that significant verse in a much more literal sense; for it must be confessed that many a human being, if judged by his actions, is not only *related* to the brute, but is *himself* the brute. The old Greek maxim, "Know thyself," is the starting-point of all reformation.

Through this knowledge, and only through it, can come the patience which forgives because it fully understands: "Comprendre c'est pardonner" is assuredly one of the world's greatest sayings.

He pardons all, who all can understand

There is no need to search for extenuating circumstances, because, as Ernest Crosby has remarked: "Is not the fact of being born a man or a woman an all-sufficient extenuating circumstance?" All is explained, when once we are content to look upon our fellow-beings, and upon ourselves, as what we verily are—a race of rough but not unkindly barbarians, emerging with infinite slowness to a more humanized condition, and to recognize that if mankind, even as it is, has been evolved from a still more savage ancestry, that fact is in itself a proof that progress is not wholly chimerical.

Considered from the point of view of personal happiness and peace of mind, the question is the same.

To what sort of comfort can a person of sensibility hope to attain, in sight of the immense sum of wretchedness and suffering that is everywhere visible, and audible, around us ? I know not a few humanitarians whose lives are permanently saddened by the thought of the awful destitution that afflicts large masses of mankind, and of the not less awful cruelties inflicted on the lower animals in the name of sport and science and fashion. How can sensitive and sympathetic minds forget the loss of other persons' happiness in the culture of their own, especially if they have realized that not a little of their well-being is derived from the toil of their fellows ?

Here, again, some measure of consolation may be found, if we look at the problem in a less sanguine and therefore less exacting spirit. People often indignantly ask, with reference to some cruel action or custom, whether we are living " in an age of civilization or of savagery," the implication being that in an era of the highest and noblest civilization, such as ours is assumed to be, some unaccountably barbarous persons are stooping to an unworthy practice. Is it not wiser, and more conducive to one's personal peace of mind, to reverse this assumption, and to start with the frank avowal that the present age, in spite of its vast mechanical cleverness, is, from an ethical point of view, one of positive barbarism, not so savage, of course, as some that have preceded it, but still undeniably savage as compared with what we foresee of a civilized future ?

Viewed in this more modest light, many usages which, if prevalent in a civilized country, might well make one despair of humankind, are seen to be, like the crimes of children, symptoms of the thoughtless infancy of our race. We are not civilized folk who have degenerated into monsters, but untamed savages who, on the whole, make a rather creditable display, and may in future centuries become civilized.

For example, when one meets a number of " sportsmen " going forth, with horses and with hounds, to
do to death with every circumstance of barbarity
some wretched little animal whom they have actually
bred, or " preserved," or imported for the purpose,
such a sight—if one regards them as rational and
civilized beings—might well spoil one's happiness for
a fortnight. But if we take a lower stand, and see
in them nothing more than fine strapping barbarians,
engaged in one of the national recreations of those
" dark ages " in which we live, 'the outlook becomes
immediately a more cheerful one ; and instead of
being surprised that ladies and gentlemen in the
twentieth century should desire to " break up " a fox,
we are able to recognize the moderation and civility
with which in other respects they conduct themselves.

One advantage, at least, can be drawn by humanitarians from the present state of affairs—a more
accurate apprehension of the obstacles by which their
hopes are beset Much has been said and written
about the causes of the war ; and it is inevitable that
the *immediate* causes (for they alone are discussed)
should be thoroughly investigated But the deeper
underlying causes of the recent war, and of every
war, are not those upon which diplomatists and
politicians and journalists and historians are intent :
they must be sought in that callous and selfish habit
of mind—common to all races, and as such accepted
without thought, and transmitted from one generation
to another—which exhibits itself not in war only,
but in numerous other forms of barbarity observed
in so-called civilized life.

No League of Nations, or of individuals, can avail,
without a change of heart. Reformers of all classes
must recognize that it is useless to preach peace by
itself, or socialism by itself, or anti-vivisection by
itself, or vegetarianism by itself, or kindness to animals
by itself. The cause of each and all of the evils that

afflict the world is the same—the general lack of humanity, the lack of the knowledge that all sentient life is akin, and that he who injures a fellow-being is in fact doing injury to himself. The prospects of a happier society are wrapped up in this despised and neglected truth, the very statement of which, at the present time, must (I well know) appear ridiculous to the accepted instructors of the people.

The one and only talisman is Love. Active work has to be done, but if it is to attain its end, it is in the spirit of love that it must be undertaken. Perhaps the most significant symptom of the brutishness aroused by the war-fever was the blank inability which many Christians showed not only to practise such injunctions as " Love your enemies," but even to understand them.[1] Had it not been that humour, like humaneness, was sunk fathoms deep in an ocean of stupidity, one would have been tempted to quote Ernest Crosby's delightful lines on " Love the Oppressors " ·

> Love the oppressors and tyrants :
> It is the only way to get rid of them !

In these days, when the voice of hatred and malevolence is so dominant, it is a joy to turn to the pages of writers who proclaim a wiser faith. " This is a gray world," says Howard Moore " There is enough sorrow in it, even though we cease to scourge each other—the sorrow of floods, famines, fires, earthquakes, storms, diseases, and death. We should trust each other, and love each other, and sympathize with and help each other, and be patient and forgiving." Nor is it only the human that claims our sympathy ; for does not Pierre Loti, in his *Book of Pity and Death*,

[1] I heard a Derbyshire gamekeeper actually quote " Vengeance is mine ; I will repay, saith the Lord," as if it were an injunction to the righteous to follow the example of a vengeful Deity.

imagine even his stray Chinese cat, whom he had befriended on shipboard, addressing him in similar words: " In this autumn day, so sad to the heart of cats, since we are here together, both isolated beings . . . suppose we give, one to the other, a little of that kindness which softens trouble, which resembles the immaterial and defies death, which is called affection, and which expresses itself from time to time by a caress."

Has not this distracted world had enough, and more than enough, of jealousies and denunciations? Is it not time that we tried, in their stead, the effect, say, of a bombardment of blessings? If there are light-waves, heat-waves, sound-waves, may there not also be love-waves? How if we sent out a daily succession of these to earth's uttermost parts? A benediction is as easily uttered as a curse, and it needs no priest to pronounce it. At least it is pleasant to think (and men put faith in creeds that are much less believable) that gentle thoughts, the "wireless" of the heart, may penetrate and be picked up in regions that are beyond our ken, and so create a more favourable atmosphere for gentle deeds. "Why did none of them tell me," asks Crosby, "that my soul was a loving-machine?" It is strange, certainly, that we take so much more pains to kindle the fires of hate than the fires of love.

"Boundless compassion for all living beings," says Schopenhauer, "is the surest and most certain guarantee of pure moral conduct, and needs no casuistry. Whoever is filled with it will assuredly injure no one, do harm to no one, encroach on no man's rights; he will rather have regard for every one, forgive every one, help every one as far as he can, and all his actions will bear the stamp of justice and loving-kindness." [1] Incidentally it may be observed that, as Schopenhauer

[1] *The Basis of Morality.* Translated by Arthur Brodrick Bullock, 1903 (George Allen and Unwin, Ltd.).

246 SEVENTY YEARS AMONG SAVAGES

points out, the difficulties of what is called the sex question would in large measure be solved, if this rule of "injure no one" were more fully believed and acted on

The lesson of the past six years is this. It is useless to hope that warfare, which is but one of many savage survivals, can be abolished, until the mind of man is humanized in other respects also—until *all* savage survivals are at least seen in their true light. As long as man kills the lower races for food or sport, he will be ready to kill his own race for enmity. It is not *this* bloodshed, or *that* bloodshed, that must cease, but *all* needless bloodshed—all wanton infliction of pain or death upon our fellow-beings Only when the great sense of the universal kinship has been realized among us, will love cast out hatred, and will it become impossible for the world to witness anew the senseless horrors that disgrace Europe to-day

Humanitarians, then, must expect little, but claim much ; must know that they will see no present fruits of their labours, but that their labours are nevertheless of far-reaching importance Let those who have been horrified by the spectacle of an atrocious war resolve to support the peace movement more strongly than ever , but let them also support the still wider and deeper humanitarian movement of which pacifism is but a part, inasmuch as all humane causes, though seemingly separate, are ultimately and essentially one.

POSTSCRIPT

In the preparation of this book I have used the substance of several articles that first appeared in the *Humane Review, Humanitarian, Literary Guide, Rationalist Press Association's Annual, Vegetarian Messenger*, or elsewhere. Acknowledgment of certain other obligations is made in the footnotes.

INDEX

Printed in Great Britain by

UNWIN BROTHERS, LIMITED

WOKING AND LONDON

Works by Henry S. Salt

The Flogging Craze   A Statement of the Case against
Corporal Punishment
With FOREWORD by SIR GEORGE GREENWOOD.   3s. 6d. net.

Godwin's Political Justice   A reprint of the Essay
on Property
Edited by HENRY S. SALT.   3s. 6d. net.

GEORGE ALLEN & UNWIN LTD.

Treasures of Lucretius   (Translations)   1s. 6d. net.

The Life of James Thomson ("B.V.")
Revised Edition   2s. 6d. net.

WATTS & CO.

The Life of Henry David Thoreau   1s. 6d. net.
Second Edition

Songs of Freedom   1s. 6d. net.
Edited by HENRY S. SALT.

WALTER SCOTT PUBLISHING CO.

Richard Jefferies : His Life and his Ideals   1s. 6d. net.

Eton under Hornby   2s. 6d. and 1s. 4d.

Tennyson as a Thinker   6d.

A. C. FIFIELD

De Quincey
Bell's Great Writers. Short Monographs.   1s. 6d. net.

Animals' Rights
Revised Edition   1s. 6d.

The Logic of Vegetarianism   6d.

Killing for Sport   Essays by Various Writers   1s.
With PREFACE by G. BERNARD SHAW. Edited by HENRY S. SALT.

G. BELL & SONS LTD.

Ruskin the Prophet

And Other Centenary Studies

By JOHN MASEFIELD, DEAN INGE,
C. F. G. MASTERMAN, AND OTHERS

EDITED BY J. HOWARD WHITEHOUSE

Demy 8vo. 8s. 6d. net.

An important and authoritative book on Ruskin, containing critical appreciations and essays by John Masefield, Dean Inge, J. A. Hobson, Charles Masterman, H W Nevinson, Laurence Binyon, and the editor, Howard Whitehouse. Among the subjects dealt with are the Influence of Ruskin in Modern Life, his social and economic teaching, his relation to Plato, and many other aspects of his teaching and influence. The book will be a fitting complement to the remarkable exhibition of Ruskin's drawings recently held at the Royal Academy

The Harvest of Ruskin

By PRINCIPAL JOHN W. GRAHAM, M.A.

Cr 8vo 7s. 6d. net.

A critical but sympathetic estimate of the net result of Ruskin's teaching in the regions of economics and social reform, education and religion, examined in the light of the present situation between Capital and Labour, the advocacy of Guild Socialism, and the widespread unsettlement about religion

Pagan and Christian Creeds

Their Origin and Meaning

Demy 8vo. By EDWARD CARPENTER 10s 6d. net.

"A splendid theory, and Mr Carpenter's exposition of it is done with an infectious enthusiasm like all this veteran writer's work, a sincere contribution to the world's stock of knowledge."—*Daily Chronicle*

" . A genius which is both scientific and artistic, philosophic and poetic Such genius sees and gives the reader visions "—*Observer*.

The Making of Humanity

Demy 8vo. By ROBERT S. BRIFFAULT 12s. 6d. net.

"An astonishing book . . . a *tour de force* of rapid historical exposition. A masterly analysis of human progress. We hope Democracy will study this brave and brilliant book."—*English Review*.

The History of Social
Development   By Dr.
F. MÜLLER-LYER
Translated by
ELIZABETH COOTE LAKE & H. A. LAKE, B.Sc. (Econ.)
With an Introduction by
Professors L. T. HOBHOUSE & E. J. URWICK

Demy 8vo.   18s. net

This translation of Dr. F. Muller-Lyer's famous book, "Phasen der Kultur," will appeal to all who are interested in labour problems at the present time. It contains a series of studies of the different economic phenomena of to-day, describing the gradual evolution of each from the earliest times, with an indication of the probable trend of future developments. The inter-connection of the different conditions so described is well illustrated, and each chapter ends with a brief summary of its subject matter The accounts of the various stages of food production, of clothing, of housing and of the use of tools contain in a brief and readable form the results of the investigations of the past century, and Part III, "The History of the Evolution of Labour," will be read with especial interest

The Perils of Wealth and
Poverty   By CANON S. A. BARNETT,
M.A., D.C.L
Edited by the Rev. V. A BOYLE, M.A.
With an Introduction by Mrs S. A. BARNETT, C B.E.

Cr. 8vo.   2s 6d. net

Canon Barnett was so careful a student of social conditions, and so sane an idealist, that this little book (which he was engaged in writing just before his last illness) will be of interest to all who think, and who desire the common welfare.

The Sickness of an Acquisitive
Society   By R. H. TAWNEY

Cr. 8vo.   *Second Impression*   2s. net.

In this booklet the author analyses the causes of the present discontents which are troubling modern society, and traces their origin to the divorce of property rights from social duties.

Co-operation and the Future
of Industry   By LEONARD S. WOOLF

Cr. 8vo   *Second Edition*   5s. net

"A book of great immediate and practical importance Every one who desires industrial reconstruction would do well to master it."—*Herald*

Government and Industry

By C. DELISLE BURNS

Author of "Political Ideals"

Demy 8vo.   *About 16s. net.*

This is a description of the existing relations between British government and the industrial system. The present tendencies are shown to indicate the formation of an organized "economic" community, based upon the State organization but distinct from it. The dominant conception operating in this economic community is that of public service. The theory expressed in the book, however, is subordinated to a description of actual facts—the administrative treatment of labour conditions, unemployment, commerce and finance, which will be found valuable even by those who do not agree with the theory, since the description is the only one which covers contemporary post-war administration.

Problems of a New World

By J. A. HOBSON

Cr. 8vo.   *7s. 6d. net.*

Events of the last few years have shaken our political and economic systems to their foundations. The old guarantees of order and progress no longer suffice. The problems of 1920 are not those of 1914. Human Nature itself, as an operative force, has changed.

These chapters discuss the revelations and describe the new ideals that are struggling to get themselves realized in the new Industry, the new State, and the new World-Order.

What the Workers Want

A Study in British Labour

By ARTHUR GLEASON

Demy 8vo.   *About 16s. net.*

A record of the aims and achievements of British Labour, the result of five years' continuous study of Labour conditions. It deals with what the workers want, who the leaders are, what the strikes mean, what the workers have won, and what they seek. There are chapters by Messrs. Smillie, Frank Hodges, C. T. Cramp and others ; and the appendix contains all the important documents of the industrial revolution.

LONDON : GEORGE ALLEN & UNWIN LIMITED
RUSKIN HOUSE, 40 MUSEUM STREET, W.C. 1.

LaVergne, TN USA
25 October 2010

202109LV00003B/159/P